EVELYN ROSE
GOES MICROWAVE

IN THE JEWISH KITCHEN

Also by Evelyn Rose
and published by Robson Books

The Complete International Jewish Cookbook

The Entertaining Cookbook

The First-Time Cookbook (with Judi Rose)

The Israel Good Food Guide

The New Jewish Cuisine

EVELYN ROSE
GOES MICROWAVE
IN THE JEWISH KITCHEN

Evelyn Rose

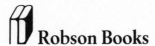

Robson Books

Photographs by Bob Wilkins

Design by Linda Wade
Food prepared by Evelyn Rose and styled by
Steven Kitchen, Head chef, Stanneylands Hotel,
Wilmslow, Cheshire

Dried flower arrangement (A Consommé of Forest
Mushrooms) by Derryl Fielden Designs, Knutsford,
Cheshire

Corian Board (three preserves) by Whitehall
Fabrications Ltd, Leeds, Yorkshire

Exotic fruit and vegetables (for many of the
photographs) loaned by Stanneylands Hotel,
Wilmslow, Cheshire

All other properties from the collection of Evelyn Rose

MICROWAVE OVENS USED IN DEVELOPING
AND TESTING THE RECIPES
Toshiba model ER 682ET
Sharp Carousel model R 8680 (B)
Panasonic Dimension 4 model NE 993

First published in Great Britain in 1989 by Robson
Books Ltd, Bolsover House, 5–6 Clipstone Street,
London W1P 7EB.

Copyright © 1989 Evelyn Rose

British Library Cataloguing in Publication Data

Rose, Evelyn
  Evelyn Rose goes microwave.
  1. Food: Dishes prepared using microwave
  ovens – Recipes
  I. Title
  641.5'89

ISBN 0 86051 472 2

Printed in Great Britain by St Edmundsbury Press Ltd,
Bury St Edmunds, Suffolk.

CONTENTS

To Myer
For the gift of his tireless
patience – and palate

I am particularly grateful to Sharp Electronics (UK) Ltd, Toshiba UK Ltd and Panasonic Consumer Electronics UK, who each loaned me one of their microwave ovens for my test work and so helped to ensure that the book would be of use to a wide spectrum of microwave users.

I would also like to acknowledge the advice of Dayan O.Y. Westheim of the Manchester Beth Din.

Finally, I must thank my patient publisher, Jeremy Robson, and my equally patient editor, Anthea Matthison, who managed to remain friends with me even as they saw successive deadlines disappearing down the nearest rabbit hole.

Evelyn Rose
Manchester
England
1989

ACKNOWLEDGEMENTS

In writing this book, I have had practical help as well as advice from many people.

Through the months of selection, testing, tasting and finally putting it all down on paper, my husband, Myer, gave me constant support and encouragement as well as much useful help in the preparation of the manuscript.

My secretary, Diane Ward, was tireless in producing an immaculate manuscript. Philippa Blank did the initial testing, while Christine Windeler helped me test the final selection of recipes.

I would like to pay tribute to the help and friendship of Sula Leon, my partner in 'Master Classes in Food and Wine' for which some of the recipes were first devised. I owe a debt of gratitude for his friendship and practical support to Gordon Beech, Managing Director of Stanneylands Hotel, Wilmslow, Cheshire. I would also like to acknowledge the help of his Head Chef, Steven Kitchen, who styled the photographs for the book.

My thanks for permission to quote from his book go to Chinese food expert, Deh-Ta Hsiung, author of *Microwave Chinese Cooking* (Macdonald Orbis). ■

INTRODUCTION

The aim of this book is to put the microwave in its rightful place as part of the total 'batterie de cuisine' alongside other labour-saving aids such as the food processor, the electric whisk, the blender and the freezer.

We now know from experience that each of these appliances does some jobs supremely well; others it can do if necessary but with only partial efficiency and success. And so it is with the microwave.

On the debit side, cooking by microwave does not bring the same aesthetic pleasure as conventional cookery. One is somehow distanced from the raw ingredients by the oven door, as well as being deprived of the satisfying tactile contact that processes such as frying, sautéeing, simmering and basting normally bring. But on the credit side, it does bring enormous benefits by way of the saving in time and labour, and a kind of satisfaction unique to this form of cookery that only develops as you explore all its functions. However, it should never be considered a 'maid of all work'.

In writing this book I have tried to be completely honest in choosing the recipes to include. In the first place each one has to 'pay its way' in terms of flavour and quality. But in addition each must have some advantage – be it speed, convenience, or quality of result – over a similar dish cooked by conventional means. The book would have been twice as long if I had simply included dishes that 'worked' in the microwave.

I have been using a microwave oven for the past fifteen years, starting with the early 'basic' models that had very little flexibility in power levels as well as very uneven distribution of microwave energy. Today one model in my kitchen is so sophisticated that I only have to punch in the type and weight of a joint of meat and the machine will select the correct combination of microwave power and convection oven temperature to produce a traditional roast.

However, this book has been written for the majority of people who have a 'middle of the road' machine, which incorporates what I consider are the two essential features – variable power and a stirrer fan or turntable to promote even cooking. If you have a more sophisticated machine you will have add-on benefits but the basic method for preparing the recipes remains the same.

In the last decade and a half my relationship with my microwave has changed. At first it was enough that it could do such jobs as baking apples and potatoes, heating up soup, defrosting bread or reheating a plate of dinner for a latecomer with what seemed like miraculous speed. Then I began to use it to do some of the more tedious or time-consuming jobs that are part of so many conventional recipes – melting chocolate, toasting nuts, sterilizing jam jars, plumping dried fruit, softening butter for sandwiches or cakes – all without the need for any forethought and with the minimum of washing up. My role as 'cook hostess' was also made much easier when I discovered that vegetables could be cooked earlier in the day then reheated between courses, in their serving dishes without any deterioration in colour, flavour or texture.

Then I began to experiment further and found that for certain food, such as fish and poultry, microwave cooking was in many respects superior to conventional methods, while for other dishes, such as soups and starters, though the flavour developed was not always so intense as with conventional cooking, the cooking period was so short that when time was of the essence the microwave gave me an extra option to serving a 'convenience' food.

A recent poll has suggested that by the turn of the century, there will be no home cooking. If this scenario is correct, most of the food we eat will be prepared in a factory rather than the home kitchen and cooking as we know it today will be just another leisure pursuit like gardening, painting or sport. Most of us would agree that some of the pieces of this daunting jigsaw are already in place. We accept, for example, that buying the occasional chilled 'recipe dishes' provides an inestimable help in the daily chore of feeding ourselves and our families. However, I fervently hope that in the future we will have the good sense to manage our lives so that we still have time to relish the joy of cooking. If the predictions of the pollsters do not come true, it will be mainly because we have learned to accept the right kind of help from technological kitchen assistants such as the microwave. By doing the time-consuming work that is an essential element in any kind of food preparation, they can leave us free to perform only those more pleasurable parts that we can fit comfortably into our particular ways of life. ∎

Making Friends with the Microwave

Unless you are interested in matters electrical, the arrival in the kitchen of any new appliance can seem on first sight to be a menace rather than a comfort. The blender and the food processor – even the freezer – have seemed in their time to be intruders with hidden powers that one does not feel competent to control.

But the microwave can be the most disturbing of all – on first acquaintance. Like many household appliances it often comes with a variety of controls that seem bewildering rather than helpful and in addition it has the ability to produce the somewhat mysterious and undoubtedly powerful microwaves.

However, as with some people, the microwave oven improves on closer acquaintance. You cannot install one in the kitchen and expect it to become a part of your life without some effort on your part to get to know it. The first thing to do is to learn the basic principles of microwave cookery. It is not necessary to know the full scientific story but only that part needful to use the tremendous capabilities of the machine to their fullest extent. In this book I have tried to lay down only the guidelines to success, as there are many reference books which tell the complete story. In addition,

each machine comes with an instruction book. Read it through. It won't make a lot of sense at first, but as you take your first tentative steps to using it, the information will fall into place and before very long you will be punching in times and power levels as though it were an automatic reflex – like preheating a regular oven or turning on the power, top of stove. It is important, however, to learn the reasons behind the different techniques you need – like covering, shielding, rearranging and standing, which are peculiar to this form of cookery. Gradually you will begin to see it as your friend, helping you in a dozen different ways to prepare both everyday and special-occasion meals. You will learn to adjust your cooking time-scale so that you take for granted such little miracles as a baked potato that cooks in five minutes, butter that softens to just the right texture in 30 seconds, or poached trout for two that can be on the table 15 minutes after you hang up your hat.

You will delight in a method of preparing food that can completely bypass the pan stage, with the dish cooked and served in the same elegant casserole. You will revel in the freedom you are offered by automated meal preparation so simple that any member of the household can operate it without any cookery training. You will relish the flavour of fresh vegetables cooked in their own juices without any loss of colour, texture or water-soluble food nutrients. You will have found a new and welcome friend.

The Oven for Your Lifestyle

Almost daily I am asked the same question: 'What microwave shall I buy?'

There is no simple answer because so much depends on your temperament, the size of your family and your lifestyle. The manufacturers do not make it any easier to come to a decision because they often give different names to the same or similar features, which makes it very difficult to compare and contrast the different models. It is also extremely difficult to quantify the benefits to you of the different features if you have never used a microwave. However, I will try and put the matter into perspective.

If you are turned off by high technology, then it is not sensible to buy a very sophisticated machine with features that you will never use – it is rather like buying a washing machine with ten programmes when, in practice, you rarely use more than two or three.

If you are buying a machine for one or two people and plan to use it mainly for defrosting and reheating, then you may well prefer a small machine with a low loading (400–500 watt output). You will also have no need for variable power – that is only useful if you intend to do 'prime' cooking (i.e., cooking raw food from scratch). However, the vast majority of the recipes can be cooked successfully without variable power.

If you intend to use the microwave for cooking a fairly large proportion of your food then you will want a larger machine – minimum size 1 cu ft – with an output of 650–700 watts. It should be equipped with variable power, which allows you to cook the wide range of food that can benefit from different levels of power. No more than five (including a keep-hot cycle) are really necessary.

As the distribution of microwave power is very erratic, it is essential that the machine is equipped with either a turntable or some kind of stirrer fan – it has the same effect of promoting even cooking. Otherwise food has to be turned by hand at regular intervals and this negates any saving in time or convenience that is achieved by the faster cooking time. In addition, if your budget will allow, it is very useful to have an 'auto-sensor' which works out the time and power level required to cook a particular item of food, for example, a dish of potatoes or a stew, or to reheat a cold soup or casserole. (In the subsequent recipe section, this timing is already worked out for you.) A machine that works out defrosting times and levels according to weight is also extremely useful. Touch control, which is now available on many less expensive models, is quicker and more accurate than manual control, particularly when it comes to cooking in seconds.

The next big leap forward in convenience and cost is to machines that can brown food in some way – the one function that the basic microwave does not carry out as well as a conventional oven. This browning facility can be as simple as a grill sited in the top of the machine, or it can be the ability to convert it into a convection oven that can be used like a regular oven, or in tandem with microwave power. The main advantage of this type of oven is its ability to produce perfect roasts, pies and cakes in something like fifty per cent of the normal time. However, there are only a few very expensive models with this kind of flexibility that are as large as a normal oven and so most of them cannot be used as a direct replacement. If your present oven is functioning well, you may well wish to wait until it is time to replace it, or buy one of these smaller 'combination ovens' simply to complement it. I am confident that in five years' time all domestic ovens will include a microwave facility.

When you are ready to buy a microwave, it is wise to go to a showroom which stocks a range of models (rather than different models from one manufacturer) and ask for an explanation of their capabilities. Alternatively, and this is often the best policy, you can seek advice from several friends who have been using their particular machines long enough to give you the pros and cons. As with freezers, when it comes to quality and reliability, there is little to choose between the different reputable makes. Magazines such as *Which* are also helpful in recommending 'good' buys and listing the latest models.

Here is a check-list of features included in the top-of-the range model from one of the major manufacturers. It might be useful to compare this with the usage you envisage for your own oven and then weigh the benefits against the price you are prepared to pay:

> *Variable power from 70–700 watts*
> *Cyclic defrost – eliminates stand time*
> *Multi-stage memory*
> *Auto-sensor cooking (8 programmes)*
> *Touch more or less (adjusting the above to*
> *personal idea of 'doneness')*
> *Convection cooking (40–250°C) with*
> *auto-preheat Grill heater (1.5kw) with self-clean*
> *lining above element*
> *6 pre-set combination programmes*
> *6 auto-weight combination programmes for meat*
> *– just tell the oven the type of food, the*
> *weight of the food in kilos or pounds and*
> *ounces, press start, the correct microwave*
> *power and oven temperature will be*
> *selected to give a traditional roasted result*
> *Dual-level cooking*
> *Auto-weight defrosting*
> *Ceramic turntable*
> *Stove-enamel lined 1.1 cu ft oven*

The Safety Factor

There are two main worries that bother most people when they are considering bringing a microwave oven into their home. Can there by any danger to health from the radiation generated by the oven and is it possible for microwave energy to leak from the cooker itself?

To put these worries into perspective, it is essential to understand the type of radiation that is actually produced by microwaves.

There are two types of radiation. The first, particle radiation, is produced by atomic and hydrogen bombs and need not concern us in this connection. The second, electro-magnetic radiation, is subdivided into ionizing and non-ionizing radiation. Ionizing radiation produces very high frequency rays such as X-rays, gamma rays and ultra-violet rays, which can, indeed, cause chemical changes in the cellular structure of any organism with which they come into contact. Non-ionizing rays on the other hand – they include radio and television waves as well as microwaves – do not effect any chemical change, but only produce a change in temperature. So long as microwaves are contained within the oven cavity they do not present any danger to human tissue.

That is why the door of a microwave oven is precision designed by engineers so that the minute amount of microwave leakage that occurs is kept well below strictly regulated levels. There are also interlocks on the door of the oven which prevent the machine being switched on unless it is properly closed and which will switch the machine off instantly when the door is opened for any reason.

There is a British Standard covering microwave safety and to ensure that this is maintained, models are independently tested at the Electricity Council Appliance Testing Laboratories for both the electrical safety and microwave leakage. Tests include opening and closing the door of the oven 100,000 times, with measurements taken after every 10,000 operations. In addition the interlocks on the door are tested in the same way. These tests replicate the wear that would occur if the oven was used seven hours a day, seven days a week, fifty-two weeks a year for close on forty years.

Microwave ovens are designed to ensure that if only one of the interlocks fails, microwave energy cannot be switched on. In addition, the machine can only be operated when the power is switched on and the level of power and length of cooking time has been selected. As soon as the cooking time has elapsed or the door catch is moved by even the tiniest amount, the generation of microwaves is instantly halted. There is no possible way that microwaves can be present when the door is opened.

Microwaves do not make food radioactive as they simply pass through it causing the internal temperature to rise. If the microwave has been dropped or damaged in some way, or the machine has been in constant use for a continuous period (some authorities say after a year), it is a wise precaution to have the oven checked by a qualified microwave service engineer. To do this he will use a special meter which registers the level of emission when the oven is in operation.

The How and Why of Microwave Cookery

Microwaves, as their name implies, are very short, electro-magnetic waves converted from electrical energy by a tube in the machine called a magnetron. However, the magnetron will only produce microwaves when the oven door is closed, the power is switched on and a timer is set. As soon as the pre-set time has elapsed or the door is opened at any time during the cooking period, the magnetron is automatically turned off and microwaves are no longer produced so that cooking by microwave energy stops at once.

It is essential to understand just how microwaves behave if you are going to utilize their energy in the most successful way. They actually penetrate the food from the top and the bottom as well as the sides, but only to a depth of about 2 inches (5 cm). However, the heat they generate can then be transferred by conduction to those parts of the food which are too far away from their point of entry to receive the microwave energy direct. That is why even-sized pieces of food less than 4 inches (10 cm) thick, such as a chicken's leg or a sprout, will start to cook immediately from internal heat, rather than, as in the case of conventional methods of cookery, by external contact with hot or moist air or boiling liquid.

The microwaves generate heat in food by 'agitating' the molecules of water, sugar or fat it contains. This causes the molecules to jostle together thousands of millions of times a second, thus generating heat in the food by friction in much the same way as rubbing two sticks together can cause them to burst into flames.

Cooking dishes made from materials that do not contain any water, or only small amounts of it, do not absorb the microwaves which simply pass through them into the food. These dishes therefore remain surprisingly cool – except where they are in contact with hot food. Thus the handles of a soup bowl will remain cool but the bowl will be heated by contact with the hot soup. This gives enormous flexibility in the kind of cooking utensils that can be used.

Microwaves cannot penetrate metal (and that includes china with gold, silver or platinum decoration as well as lead crystal) but are reflected by it, rather like a mirror reflects light. That is also why many ovens have a metal interior which reflects the microwaves so that they can use all their energy to penetrate the food. And why a ready-prepared meal in a shallow foil container will take longer to heat up in a microwave than one in a container made from a material such as plastic, paper, glass, ceramic, plastic film or wood, through which microwaves can pass rather like light through a window.

Will it Microwave?

There are certain types of food and food processes, in particular those that rely on oven browning for their taste, texture and eye appeal, that cannot be satisfactorily translated to an oven without any kind of browning facility and that therefore rely on microwave power alone. These include many cakes and biscuits, as well as roast poultry and braised joints. Add to this list soups that need a long simmering period to draw out extractives from tough, if flavourful, cuts of meat or bones, casseroles that demand the thorough pre-browning of the meat (you can of course do that top of the stove if you wish) as well as biscuits, cakes and yeast bread that need a conventional oven to develop crunch. Soufflés and Yorkshire pudding are disaster areas, as a veritable rise and fall situation occurs in the microwave. Tough connective tissue cannot be broken down in meat however long it is cooked, so use only well hung, tender joints for roasts and first-cut braising steak for casseroles. That is not to say it is impossible to cook any of this food in the microwave but that it cannot be done to what I consider an acceptable standard.

Adapting Conventional Recipes

However, in addition to those dishes for which I give detailed recipes there are many other conventional recipes that can be happily and easily adapted for the microwave oven. These include many soups and starters, casseroles and stews as well as poached and baked fish dishes, vegetables, fruit compotes and certain cakes.

The first step is to find a recipe similar to the one you wish to adapt in this book, or in the instruction book that comes with your machine, and use it as a guide to power levels and cooking times. If you cannot find a similar *type* of recipe in this book, it is probably because I have found it does not adapt well to the microwave. Beware also of trying to cook larger quantities of food than specified in a recipe, as foodstuffs absorb microwave energy and, as only a finite amount of energy can be produced by your machine, the greater the food load the longer it will take to cook so that there will be no saving of time.

As there is so much less evaporation than in a conventional oven, particularly if the dish is tightly covered, you may have to adjust the amount of liquid, for example, in a *casserole*. As a rough guide, allow 10 fl oz (275 ml/1¼ cups) of liquid to each pound of meat. You will notice that most of my casseroles use 15 fl oz (425 ml/2 cups) of total liquid to 1½ lb (675 g) of meat, which is sufficient

for 4 good portions. When preparing *soups* use only enough of the measured liquid in the recipe to cover the vegetables as they cook. In this way you can save even more cooking time as liquid absorbs microwaves and a large quantity of liquid slows down the cooking process. The remainder can be added as hot stock when the solid ingredients have finished cooking. Two pints/1 litre/5 cups is the largest quantity of soup that will show a saving of time.

Add herbs and spices at the beginning of the cooking period but do not add the salt until the end as it has a toughening effect, particularly on protein food such as fish and meat.

Finally, make sure you use the shape and size of dish recommended for the microwave recipe you are using as your guide (see page 25 for pictures of the most useful shapes and sizes of dish).

Cooking Dishes

So many of the dishes used for conventional cooking are both safe and suitable for the microwave that there is some debate as to whether it is worth buying any of the dishes specially made for the purpose.

I am sure that when you look at the list below you will discover that you already possess many of the dishes recommended for use in the recipes. Normal heatproof bowls and jugs, lasagne and gratin-type dishes and shallow-lidded casseroles can all be used in the microwave provided they are made of a suitable material such as heatproof glass, ceramic, china or pottery.

So before you buy any new equipment check what you already have in stock. However, if you intend to make full use of your microwave it is worth investing in any of the dishes recommended as you will find them extremely convenient to use, particularly if they have their own lids to cover the contents instead of clingfilm.

In addition, you will be able to make use of certain plastic dishes that are sold as microwave safe as well as containers made of wood and wicker

16

that you would not use in a conventional oven.

To check if a particular dish is safe in the microwave you need only do the following test: place the dish in the oven with a glass (not lead crystal) half filled with cold water beside it. Microwave on 100% power for 1 minute. If the water is warm at the end of this period and the dish feels cool, it is suitable for use. If the dish and the water are both lukewarm it can still be used but it will take longer for food to cook in it as it will be absorbing some of the energy. If, however, the dish is hot but the water remains cool, do not use it as it will absorb too much of the total microwave energy. It may also overheat and break or even burn your hands. Glass and plastic containers can be tested in the same way but heat on 100% power for only 15 seconds before testing.

Next, consider the shape: for most purposes a shallow dish is to be preferred to a deep one as it will enable the microwave energy to heat the food up evenly.

For recipes that include a fairly high proportion of liquid such as casseroles and soups, a deeper dish will of course be necessary but the heat will then have to be evenly distributed by regular stirring.

Round dishes are to be preferred to square or rectangular ones as sharp corners can be bombarded from several directions by the microwaves causing those parts of the contents to be overcooked.

For baking cakes, pliable plastic dishes are an excellent investment. They do not last for as long as more durable materials but they represent a much smaller initial investment.

Jugs are particularly important both for mixing and cooking so it is worth seeking out ones that are bowl-shaped as well, as this will double their function.

I have kept the list on page 19 as brief as possible. It is compiled from the dishes I found were in constant and comfortable use when I was developing the recipes for this book.

Getting it Right

After the theory comes the practice. Here is a check-list of points to remember as well as some special techniques you will need whenever you use your microwave.

AVOID dishes made of metal, or china that is decorated in any way with silver, gold or platinum. Metal reflects microwaves, causing them to bounce off its surface and so prevents their absorption by the food. It may also cause 'arcing' — a rather frightening phenomenon — when sparks are produced that can damage the oven as well as permanently blacken any metal decorations. Exceptions are:

Small amounts of aluminium foil used for shielding purposes
Shallow foil containers, providing they are not also covered with foil
Dishes recommended by the manufacturers for use on certain programmes in combination ovens

USE dishes as near as possible in depth, width and liquid capacity to those recommended in the recipe. This will ensure that the food is cooked as quickly and evenly as possible, that liquid such as soup and sauces will have plenty of 'headroom' and will not overflow.

PIERCE plastic cooking bags before placing them in the oven if their contents are to be cooked for longer than 5 minutes. This will prevent them bursting through a build-up of steam. Remember also to replace any metal closures with rubber bands or a knot in the plastic. Many authorities also advise piercing the clingfilm used to cover a dish. This is mainly to avoid the danger of scalding from a build-up of steam. However, I do not find this necessary for short-term cooking provided the film is punctured after cooking and then removed with care from the side furthest from you. Clingfilm coverings for dishes cooked by autosensor should definitely not be pierced as this will distort the timing that depends on the measurement of the steam.

PRICK whole vegetables and fruit in their skins to prevent them from bursting as their liquid content heats up and expands. This applies in particular to potatoes, tomatoes, aubergines and apples. For a similar reason, prick the surface membrane covering the yolks of eggs that are to be poached or baked (do not attempt to microwave eggs in the shell or they will explode).

COVER food tightly when cooking or reheating, unless advised otherwise. This helps to speed up the cooking process by keeping any steam that is generated trapped in the cooking dish. It also prevents reheated food from drying out. Suitable coverings include microwave-safe lids, film and plates. Baked goods such as pastry, biscuits and rolls that are to be reheated should be lightly wrapped in a paper napkin, paper towel or one of the special coated plastics made for the purpose in order to absorb moisture drawn to the surface by the heat which would otherwise make them soggy. A piece of absorbent paper, e.g., kitchen roll, laid on top of a dish can also prevent hot fat or liquid spattering the oven surfaces. Foods that should not be covered include those with a high water content such as puddings and cakes, which need to dry out as they cook to achieve the correct texture, and those sauces whose flavour needs to be intensified by the reduction of their liquid content.

SHIELD thinner parts of a large piece of food, for instance the tail of a whole salmon or the shorter ends of a rectangular cake baking dish, with small pieces or strips of aluminium foil. Take care to ensure that the foil does not touch the metal sides, top or (in the case of an oven without a turntable) floor and you will avoid any danger of damage to the oven.

ARRANGE individual items of food of even thickness such as potatoes for baking, rolled fish fillets or meatballs so that they are evenly spaced out round the edge of a round or oval container.

Arrange food of uneven thickness such as chicken joints or chops with the thicker part towards the outside of the dish. This helps to ensure more even penetration by the microwaves and therefore more even cooking.

REARRANGE food which is arranged in a single layer in the dish half way through the cooking period. This will allow the food from the centre to receive its share of the microwave energy.

STIR liquids such as soup and stews as directed in the recipe to ensure even heat distribution and thickening.

CALCULATE cooking times for amounts of food greater or smaller than the recipe by this rule of thumb: allow between a third and a half extra cooking time when doubling the quantity. For example, allow 5 minutes for one potato but 7 minutes for two. Conversely, allow a third less time for a smaller quantity of food. For example, two trout may take 6 minutes to cook but one trout takes only four minutes. There are tables to help you in the Lexicon and probably in your oven instruction book.

LIMIT the initial cooking time for delicate foods such as fish, chicken and cakes as well as 'dense' foods such as potatoes, roasts and poultry to the minimum recommended. Test for doneness as suggested in the recipe. Then, if necessary, add extra cooking time in 30-second bursts. However, before adding on extra time, allow the full standing time (see below) which may be sufficient in itself to complete the cooking process. The food can always be put back in the machine afterwards.

STAND all food for the time recommended in the recipe. Most food will continue to cook for 5 or even 10 minutes after it has been taken out of the oven, as the heat generated on the outer surfaces where the microwaves have penetrated is slowly conducted to the centre. If you remove the food from the oven only when it is completely cooked through to the centre, you will probably find that the outside has overcooked and become tough and dry.

REHEAT casseroles of chicken, meat and fish until the liquid is bubbling throughout. This will guard against any danger of food poisoning.

THAW frozen cooked and uncooked food following the instructions on commercial packs or in your instruction book. Never attempt to hurry the process by using a higher power level than recommended or you may find – particularly in the case of raw fish, meat or chicken – that the outer surface has actually begun to cook before the centre is thawed.

Always allow the full standing time for the same reason. If you intend to do a lot of thawing, it is worth investing in a microwave that calculates and controls the process for you.

How to Use the Book

In the front of the book there is a collection of recipes divided into chapters from starters to desserts and cakes, in the conventional way.

Each recipe is complete in itself and is preceded by a brief description, followed by numbered cooking steps. In only one or two cases is it necessary to refer to another page in the book – perhaps for a special sauce.

At the back of the book is a lexicon – 'A Guide for the Perplexed', which gives basic cooking techniques and times for everyday food, such as fruit and vegetables, as well as factual background information on food and food processes. This Lexicon is in alphabetical order so that if you have a query of any kind you can find the information you need quickly without having to look up a page reference in the index. In this way I hope that when you wish to cook a recipe there will be no extraneous material to distract you. On the other hand when you do have time to browse, the Lexicon will give you plenty of food for thought.

Dishes Recommended for Use in the Recipes

(For numbered illustrations, see page 25.)

Deep-lidded casseroles or bowls
1: 7 pint (4 litre/1 gallon) microwave-safe, plastic-lidded casserole, approximately 10 inches (25 cm) in diameter
*use for cooking chicken and fish stock, casseroles and stuffed vegetables
*the lid can be used (with a trivet) as a roasting dish

2: 5 pint (3 litre/12½ cup) heatproof glass bowl
*use for cooking soup, stock or preserves

3: 3½–4 pint (2–2.25 litre/9–10 cup) lidded casserole, 7½–8 inches (18–20 cm) in diameter
*use for cooking and serving soup, casseroles, rice, grain and certain vegetables

4: 1–2 pint (550 ml–1.25 litres/2½–5 cups) heatproof glass bowl
*use for mixing and cooking certain sauces

5: 10–15 fl oz (275–425 ml/1¼–2 cup) lidded-soup cup or microwave-safe bowl
*use for melting chocolate, butter, etc

Shallow casseroles or dishes
6 & 7: 8 inch (20 cm) round dish 2–3 inches (5–7.5 cm) deep; 10–11 inch (25–27 cm) baking dish 2–3 inches (5–7.5 cm) deep (both made of microwave-safe ceramic with a heatproof glass lid)
*multi-purpose dishes used for chicken, fish, chops, vegetables and fruit arranged in a layer not more than 2–2½ inches (5–7 cm) high. They can also double as serving dishes.

8: 9–10 inches (22.5–25 cm) round dish 1–1½ inches (2.5–4 cm) deep (usually made of heatproof pottery, china or ceramic, e.g., a quiche dish)
*use for cooking a whole salmon, baking apples

9: Assorted oval entrée and rectangular lasagne-type dishes used in conventional cookery, providing they do not have any metal decoration: for example:

10 × 8 × 2 inches (25 × 20 × 5 cm)
11 × 8 × 2 inches (27.5 × 20 × 5 cm)
12 × 9 × 2 inches (30 × 22.5 × 5 cm)

*use for certain baked casseroles as well as poached and sauced fish dishes

Jugs

10: 1 pint (550 ml/2½ cup) and
11: 2 pint (1 litre/5 cup), both usually made of heatproof glass
12: 3½ pint (2 litre/9 cup) usually made of microwave-safe plastic
*for cooking sauces and custard and general mixing purposes

Dishes for Baking

13: 8 inch (20 cm) round dish 2 inches (5 cm) deep, usually made of heatproof glass or plastic
*use for baking regular cakes and cheesecakes

A variety of microwave-safe plastic baking dishes, e.g.,
14: 11 × 6 × 3 inches (27.5 × 15 × 8 cm)
*use for cakes such as streusel kuchen and chocolate walnut squares
15: 8 × 6 × 2 (20 × 15 × 5 cm)
*use for baking bar biscuits like the date bars
16: 8 × 6 × 3 (20 × 15 × 8 cm)
17: 9 × 5 × 3 (22.5 × 12.5 × 8 cm)
*use for baking tea bread or cooking gefilte fish terrines

Miscellaneous

18: 8 inch (20 cm) plastic ring mould
*use for cakes and gefilte fish ring

19: 5 fl oz (150 ml/⅔ cup) or 4 fl oz (125 ml/½ cup) capacity non-metallic ramekins
*use for cooking custard-based dishes

20: Microwave-safe roasting dish and trivet

Microwave Power Settings

The majority of the recipes in the book are cooked on 100% (full) power. Reference is made, however, to other settings such as 70–80% power (for roasting), 50% (for simmering) and 30% (for defrosting or cooking dishes containing eggs or soft cheese such as custard and cheesecake).

Variable power settings give flexibility of cooking temperature similar (but not identical) to that in a conventional oven. Just as in conventional cooking, you select the temperature (expressed in microwave cooking as percentage power) that is best suited to the food or mixture to be cooked. All the recipes in the book give recommended power levels based on a 650 watt oven (see page 21 for how to adapt these levels to lower or higher wattage machines).

As there is, as yet, no universally accepted method of expressing power levels – for the same power level, some manufacturers may use a number, others a term such as 'high' or 'roast' – I have chosen to use percentages of the total power hoping to make the recipes easy to follow, no matter how these power levels are described for your particular machine.

The guide to comparative power settings I give below will help you to find the power settings on your machine that correspond with those that I give in the book. Compare this table with the one given at the front of the instruction book for your machine.

Variable power settings give flexibility of cooking temperature similar, but not identical, to that in a conventional oven. Just as in conventional cooking, you select the temperature (expressed in microwave cooking as percentage power) that is best suited to the food or mixture to be cooked. All the recipes in the book give recommended power levels. The table below is meant for general guidance, particularly when adapting conventional recipes.

To Adjust Cooking Times in this Book for Different Powered Ovens

This is an approximate guide only. Experiment at first with simple dishes and you will soon be able to judge how much extra or less time you will need to allow.

Terms used to express power levels in different makes of microwave ovens.

Power settings used in this book	Alternatives	Used for
100%	High, full power	To bring liquid and sauces to the boil; cook soups, fruit, vegetables, fish, poultry up to 3 lb (1.5 kg) in weight. Also to 'sweat' vegetables, cook minced meat and small pieces of meat and to cook most cakes
80%	Medium high, roast	Roasting joints, reheating cooked food and leftovers; cooking delicate food containing cream, milk, cheese
50%	Medium, simmer	Defrosting small items such as rolls; defrosting and reheating casseroles and cooking egg custard
30%	Low, defrost	Defrosting solid food such as raw roasts, chops and minced meat; pot roasting, softening butter for spreading.

(Note: the timings in the book are based on a 650 watt machine).

When using a 600 watt machine:
Add 5 seconds per minute of cooking time e.g., if the recipe in the book takes 6 minutes, cook it in your machine for 6½ minutes

When using a 500 watt machine:
Add 20 seconds per minute of cooking time. e.g., if the recipe in the book takes 6 minutes cook it in your machine for 8 minutes

When using a 700 watt machine:
Subtract 5 seconds per minute of cooking time e.g., if the recipe in the book takes 6 minutes, cook it for 5½ minutes

Cooking times: *minimum* cooking times are always given. Any food, if underdone when checked, can be given additional time, whereas food overcooked in a microwave may be inedible, e.g., fish or chicken becomes hard and dry, cakes become rubbery in texture.

Use of other appliances: certain recipes suggest *grilling* the dish to brown or crispen it at the end of the microwave cooking time. This can be done with a *conventional grill* or *one sited in the microwave itself.*

The boiling of water for stocks etc., is done most quickly and cost effectively in an *electric kettle.*

Microwave-safe dishes: all cooking dishes and coverings must be selected from those materials recommended as safe to use in the microwave (see pages 19 and 20).

How to Use the Recipes

All the recipes in this book were developed and tested on a machine with 650-watt output, a turntable (a stirrer fan or other mechanism for assisting the even distribution of microwaves will serve the same purpose) and variable power. No other features are required to produce superb results. However, a machine with touch control is more convenient to use and is also more accurate for fine-tuning the cooking times.

If your machine has only 2 settings and no turntable or stirrer fan, and the manufacturers recommend turning the dish at frequent intervals during the cooking period, you will not get satisfactory results from most of the recipes in this book.

Adapting Recipes to a Multi-Function or Combination Oven

If you have a multi-function or combination oven it will include many features not mentioned in the recipes. These may include a multi-stage memory, autosensor cooking, convection cooking, grill heater, pre-set combination programmes and auto-weight combination programme for defrosting raw food and roasting meat.

Each of these add-on features introduces even more variations in method and time. Unfortunately, there is no standardization between the different makes either of features or cooking methods, so I have not attempted to give detailed guidance. All the recipes in the book produce superb results on machines without any of these extra functions. But if you wish to adjust them for use in *your machine* consult the manufacturer's handbook.

Weights and Measures

*SOLID MEASURES are first given in spoons, pounds and ounces.

*LIQUID MEASURES are first given in spoons, pints or fluid ounces. Within the brackets that follow these measures, the first figure given is the metric equivalent and the second is the American equivalent measure in cups, e.g.

   3 oz (75 g/⅓ cup) – solid measure
   5 fl oz (150 ml/⅔ cup) – liquid measure

*AMERICAN EQUIVALENT INGREDIENTS are given on page 25.

*LENGTH MEASUREMENTS are first given in inches and then in centimetres, e.g.

   2 inches (5 cm)

*SPOON MEASURES: as I find the use of millilitres to express spoon capacity unnecessarily complicated, I have used standard imperial tablespoons and teaspoons throughout. (The tablespoon has a capacity of 20 ml, the teaspoon 5 ml, ½ teaspoon 2.5 ml and ¼ teaspoon 1.25 ml capacity.) All spoon measures are level. As the difference in volume is so small I have assumed British and American spoons to be interchangeable; however, some adjustment in the quantity of seasonings may be necessary to suit individual tastes. A 'speck' or 'pinch' is the amount of powdered spice that can be picked up between the finger and thumb.

*In calculating the METRIC EQUIVALENTS of ounces or fluid ounces, I have worked out the *exact* equivalent in grams or millilitres, and then rounded it up or down to the nearest multiple of 25. For instance, 8 ounces exactly equals 226.80 g, which I have given as 225 g; 10 fluid ounces equals 284.10 ml, which I give as 275 ml. In no case is there more than half an ounce or half a fluid ounce difference between the imperial and metric measures as stated, and this is not enough to make other than a trifling difference (in, for example, seasoning) to the recipe. However, it is not advisable to use a mixture of imperial and metric measures in the same recipe, as this may cause an imbalance in the proportions of solid to liquid ingredients.

Ingredients

*BUTTER is slightly salted, unless unsalted is specified.

*SUGAR is granulated unless caster, icing or a variety of brown sugar is specified. There is no standardized nomenclature for brown sugar, but providing some kind of soft light or medium brown sugar is used (*not* the granular demerara sugar unless specified), the exact shade of brown is not important. However, unless specified, the very dark brown molasses sugar should *not* be used as its treacly flavour and colour can overwhelm the other ingredients in a dish.

*EGGS are 'standard' (number 3) size (approximately 2 oz/60 g) in weight. The egg size is only critical when 4 or more eggs are used in a recipe, in which case, extra large or small eggs can upset the ratio of liquids to solids.

*FLOUR is plain unless self-raising flour is specified and white, unless a brown flour is specified. 'Special' (sometimes called 'supreme') self-raising flour is fine-milled from soft wheat and produces cakes of a very fine texture. If it is not available, a regular white self-raising flour can be used instead. American readers should use 'cake' flour, plus baking powder. 4 oz (125 g/1 cup) plain flour plus 1 level teasp baking powder = 4 oz (125 g/1 cup) self-raising flour.

*MARGARINE is a soft variety labelled 'high in polyunsaturates' unless a block or firm margarine is specified.

*DISH sizes are particularly important in microwave cookery to ensure even cooking of all the ingredients, and these are given in each recipe. See also page 26 for drawings of all the cooking dishes used in the book.

Food Storage Times

The recommended storage times given in the recipes are based on certain assumptions:

*IN THE FREEZER: all food, whether cooked or raw, is stored in airtight containers, freezer storage bags or foil packages to prevent freezer 'burn'. The exceptions are soft or fragile foods that are 'open frozen' until firm, and must then be packaged in the same way.

The recommended storage time is based on the maximum period after which deterioration of flavour or texture may take place. If food is frozen for longer than recommended, it will not be dangerous to eat but it will be past its prime.

*IN THE REFRIGERATOR: all cooked and prepared food is stored in airtight containers and covered with clingfilm or foil to avoid dehydration and the transference of flavours and smells from one food to another. All raw fruit and vegetables are stored in plastic bags or containers, according to variety. *The recommended storage time* is based on the maximum period during which the food is pleasant and *safe* to eat.

*Fuller details on food storage can be found in my *Entertaining Cookbook* (Robson Books).

In Stock

These are the (mostly dried) staples I try to keep always in stock. Having to hand, with the exception of a few perishable foods, all the ingredients needed to make any of the dishes in the book saves me a great deal of time and aggravation.

All the fresh herbs listed below can be grown without too much difficulty even in a small garden but it is only worth drying the bay leaves, mint and dill. The essential oils in the other varieties do not develop enough intensity of flavour in a temperate climate. I prefer to buy dried herbs such as marjoram, oregano, tarragon and basil that have been matured under a southern sun. Fortunately, fresh herbs can now be bought throughout the year but the dried ones add more flavour to casseroles and stews.

To ensure that my dried herbs and spices do not become stale before I have time to use them, I only buy them in minimal quantities. Every few weeks I check the stock (by smelling each variety) to reassure myself that they are still worth using. If the aroma has faded I discard them ruthlessly.

Staples in Stock

HERBS, fresh in season
or dried:
basil
bay leaves
chives
dill
fines herbes
herbes de Provence
Italian seasoning herbs
marjoram
mint
oregano
parsley
tarragon

SPICES:
cardamom
cinnamon, ground
cinnamon sticks
cloves
coriander
cumin
ground ginger
mixed sweet spice
turmeric
vanilla essence, vanilla
pods

sea salt, cooking salt
fish seasoning salt
white pepper, ground
black peppercorns
cayenne
paprika

stock cubes – fish, beef,
chicken, vegetable

Madras (medium) curry
powder
mild curry paste or
powder
soy sauce–light and rich
chilli powder or chilli
sauce
dry mustard, made-up
mustard, Dijon
mustard
Worcestershire sauce
minced dried onion
minced dried garlic
fresh garlic

Basmati rice
vermicelli
lentils
self-raising flour
fine-milled, plain
wholemeal flour
plain flour
cornflour
potato flour
sponge self-raising flour
cake flour
80% extraction wheatmeal,
self-raising flour
baking powder

medium matzo meal
dry breadcrumbs
porridge oats

desiccated coconut
plain dessert chocolate
dark coffee granules

extra virgin olive oil

sunflower oil
butter, margarine
oriental sesame seed oil

tomato ketchup
Passata (sieved
tomatoes)
tomato purée – tins or
tubes
cans chopped tomatoes
whole tomatoes
sweet red peppers
(pimentos)
anchovy fillets
tuna
pineapple

eggs, size 3

almonds, whole and
flaked
ground almonds
walnuts
pine kernels
pistachios
sesame seeds
cashews
hazelnuts
pecans

olives, black and green

Amontillado sherry
brandy (3***)
orange juice
lemon juice
dry white wine
red wine
evaporated milk

vinegar – white or red
wine, red fruit such
as raspberry

redcurrant jelly
peanut butter
honey – mild liquid
tahina – sesame seed
paste
chutney – peach,
mango and ginger

sugar – granulated (or
granular sweetener)
caster
soft light brown
soft medium brown
dark brown
demerara

dried fruit
tenderized prunes
raisins
sultanas

In the Refrigerator

lemons
spring onions
carrots
leeks
fresh ginger root

*Some dishes recommended for use in the recipes,
see pages 19 and 20.*

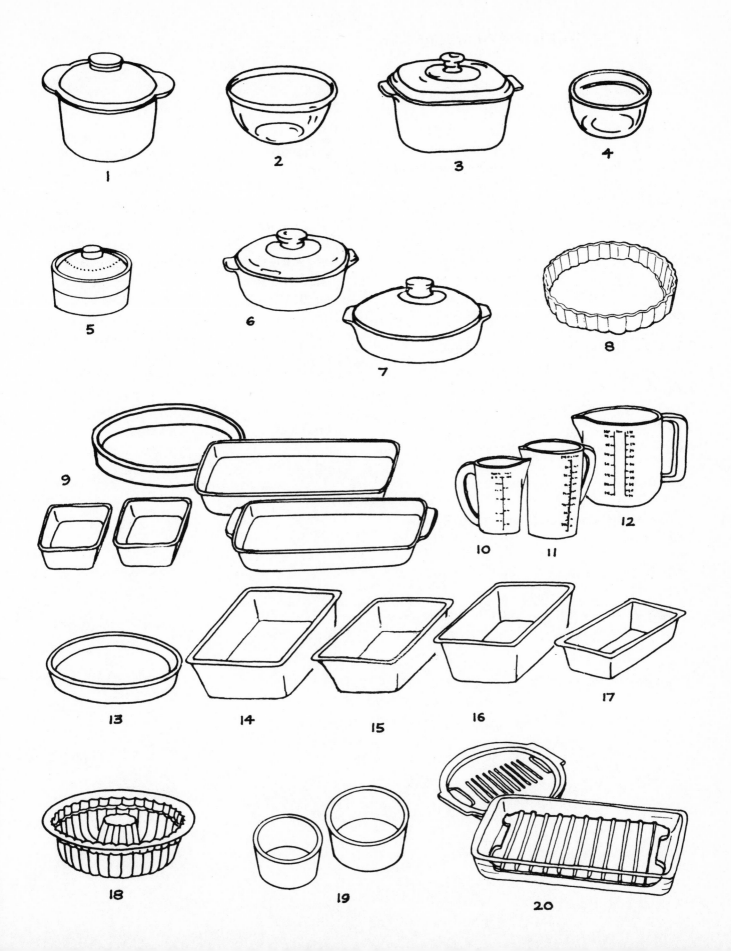

Glossary of British and American Terms

I give here the US equivalents of British food and cooking terms:

UK	US	UK	US
plain flour	all-purpose flour	aubergines	eggplants
special sponge self-raising flour	cake flour plus baking powder	courgettes	zucchini
wholemeal flour	wholewheat flour	mangetout	snow peas
cornflour	cornstarch	petit pois	spring peas
		spring onions	green onions/scallions
caster sugar	superfine sugar		
icing sugar	confectioners' sugar	Galia, Ogen or Charentais melon	musk melon or canteloupe
demerara sugar	brown sugar	morello cherries	sour red cherries
golden syrup	corn syrup		
		digestive biscuits	graham crackers
bicarbonate of soda	baking soda	biscuits	cookies
		minced meat (beef, veal or lamb)	ground meat (beef, veal or lamb)
desiccated coconut	dried and shredded coconut		
		to grill	to broil
hazelnuts	filberts	the grill	the broiler
pine kernels	pine nuts		
sultanas	white raisins		
drinking chocolate	instant chocolate		
plain chocolate	semi-sweet chocolate		
vanilla essence	vanilla extract		
single cream	light cream		
whipping or double cream	heavy cream		

SOUPS

INTRODUCTION

Delicate and creamy vegetable soups, hearty, rib-sticking potages, recipes that are equally successful using chicken or vegetable stocks, and a quartet of variations on the theme of chicken soup . . . you will find them all in this chapter – ready for the table in a fraction of the usual time. But though this speed in preparation can only be achieved by bypassing the traditional techniques, all these soups without exception are the equal in flavour of soups made by more conventional methods. You will not, however, find any meat-based soups in this chapter because the chemical process by which their flavours are released during a long period of simmering cannot take place in the microwave.

Providing you have a suitable dish – a lidded casserole or a small soup tureen of 3½–4 pint (2 litre/9 cup) capacity – your soup can go straight from the microwave to the table. Or you may prefer to cook it in a heatproof bowl and serve it from the kitchen – the choice is yours.

To save the maximum time and effort in preparing these recipes, you do need a food processor to chop or slice the vegetables before cooking and in most cases to purée them afterwards. Otherwise, I do not think they will fit into a practical time-scale – you are better advised to buy a packet or a can instead.

Cooking a soup in the microwave is not simply a question of transferring a conventional recipe intact for even the most sophisticated machines are not designed to mimic a conventional cooker – that is not their role in the kitchen. So here are some of the new ploys you will need:

Substitute minced dried onion for the sautéed onion which is the flavour base for most soups, especially vegetable ones – it works equally well.

Minced dried garlic is more convenient than fresh – and works well in any dish such as soup where it can be simmered in liquid.

As a large amount of liquid slows down cooking in the microwave, add only a small amount of the measured stock for the initial cooking of the vegetables then add the rest when they are tender. You will also save cooking time if this extra stock is added hot. The easiest way to do this is to use meat or vegetable cubes (or a vegetable paste) plus boiling water. If, however, you are using home-made chicken stock from the refrigerator or freezer, heat it in a large jug covered with a plate in the microwave before adding it to the other ingredients.

Many vegetable soups are based on vegetable purées combined with a roux-based sauce. Making this type of sauce is extremely tedious in the microwave. A far better method is to use cornflour for thickening and, for a glossy appearance, add a knob of butter or margarine to the soup itself.

You will notice that in the recipes for the more delicately flavoured soups, a power level of 50% is recommended – this helps bring out their more elusive flavours.

All soups reach their full flavour potential several hours after they are prepared. But only in the case of one or two of the heartier varieties is this maturing time absolutely essential and this is indicated in the recipe.

Whilst for most occasions it is more practical to make chicken stock in quantity on top of the stove, if only four portions are required it can be prepared with great success in the microwave. But you must leave this stock to mature, or the alchemy that changes the pale liquid into a golden soup will not take place.

Cooking knaidlach (matzo meal dumplings) in the microwave works extremely well, resulting in firm but tender balls that are a delight to eat. ■

MICROWAVE BORSCHT

Serves 5–6
Beet juice keeps 4 days under refrigeration,
complete soup 2 days
Freeze beet juice 3 months.
Do not freeze complete soup

This elegant pale pink soup, with its intriguing sweet/sour flavour, can either be served hot with boiled potatoes or cold with a dollop of soured cream.

Generous 1 lb (450 g) raw, old beets or 2 bunches raw, young beets
1 small (3 oz/75 g) carrot
1 small (4 oz/100 g) onion
1½ pints (850 ml/3¾ cups) boiling water
1 tbsp granulated sugar or granular sweetener
2 vegetable stock cubes
10 grinds black pepper
½ teasp salt
To thicken soup
2 tbsp lemon juice
2 eggs
To garnish
5 fl oz (150 ml/⅔ cup) soured cream or creamed smetana or sprinkle of paprika

1   Cut the peeled vegetables in roughly one inch (2.5 cm) chunks and chop finely in a food processor.
2   Put into a 3½ pint (2 litre/9 cup) lidded casserole, or bowl, with the sugar and 1 pint (575 ml/2½ cups) of the hot stock, cover, then cook on 100% power for 12 minutes or until the vegetables feel tender.
3   Meanwhile put the eggs and lemon juice into the food processor and process until evenly mixed, about 3–4 seconds.
4   Pour the hot vegetables and liquid through a coarse sieve into a large jug.

5   With the machine on, pour the hot beet juice on to the egg mixture and process until evenly blended – with a small machine only part of the liquid should be added.
6   Return this liquid and the remaining stock to the cooking dish and cook uncovered on 50% power for 5 minutes, stir, then cook for a further 5 minutes or until steaming hot and slightly thickened.
7   Allow to stand 5 minutes before serving hot.
8   To serve cold, chill thoroughly then whisk in 5 fl oz (150 ml/⅔ cup) soured cream or creamed smetana, or top each serving with a spoonful of cream and a tiny sprinkle of paprika.

A VELOUTÉ OF CARROTS

Serves 4–6
Keeps 3 days under refrigeration
Freeze 3 months

Rich and satisfying in both texture and flavour.

8 oz (225 g/1½ cups) carrots, peeled
white part of 1 fat leek (3 oz/75 g)
1 medium onion
2 stalks of celery
1 medium (5 oz/150 g) potato
1 oz (25 g/2 tbsp) butter or margarine
15 fl oz (425 ml/2 cups) hot vegetable stock (water plus cubes or paste)
1 teasp dried garlic granules
1 level teasp salt
10 grinds black pepper
2 teasp cornflour
15 fl oz (425 ml/2 cups) milk

1   Slice all the vegetables using the fine slicer of the food processor. Put into a 3½ pint (2 litre/9 cup) lidded casserole or bowl with the garlic, fat and 5 fl oz (150 ml/⅔ cup) of the hot stock. Cover

and cook on 100% power for 13 minutes, stirring halfway, until all the vegetables are tender.

2   Purée in the blender or food processor together with the remaining stock and seasonings.

3   Put the cornflour in the cooking dish and mix to a thin cream with 4 tbsp of the milk. Stir in the remaining milk, cover and cook for 4 minutes, stirring halfway, then whisk in the vegetable purée. Cook uncovered on 50% power for 6 minutes or until bubbly, stirring once.

4   To reheat from cold, cook covered at 100% power for 8 minutes, stirring once.

CURRIED CREAM OF BROCCOLI SOUP

Serves 4–5
Keeps 3 days under refrigeration
Freeze 3 months

A pale green soup with an unexpected but very agreeable 'bite'.

12 oz (350 g/2½ cups) very green broccoli (trimmed weight, with leaves and coarse stalk removed)
3 tbsp water
15 fl oz (425 ml/2 cups) vegetable stock (boiling water plus 1 cube or 1 teasp vegetable paste)
nut of butter or margarine
1 tbsp minced dried onion
½ teasp salt
8 grinds black pepper
⅛ teasp ground nutmeg
1 teasp mild curry powder or paste
1 tbsp cornflour
15 fl oz (425 ml/2 cups) milk
For the garnish
1 oz (25 g/¼ cup) toasted pine kernels (see below)

1   Spread pine kernels on a plate and cook on 100% power for 2 minutes, stirring once, until golden. Set aside.

2   Cut the broccoli stalks off the heads, trim the ends and slice about ⅜ inch (1.5 cm) thick. Put into a lidded casserole with 3 tbsp water (the broccoli heads towards the centre of the dish, the stalks around them), cover and cook on 100% power for 8 minutes or until the stalks are just tender when pierced with a slim pointed knife.

3   Turn into a sieve and drench with cold water to 'set' the colour.

4   Purée in a blender or food processor with the stock, the butter or margarine and the seasonings.

5   Put the cornflour in a 3½ pint (2 litre/9 cups) lidded casserole, soup tureen or bowl and mix to a thin cream with 4 tbsp of the milk. Stir in the remaining milk, cover and cook on 100% power for 4 minutes, stirring once, then uncover and whisk in the vegetable purée. Cook uncovered on 50% power for 5 minutes or until barely bubbling.

6   To reheat from cold, cover and cook on 100% power for 8 minutes, stirring once.

CARROT, ORANGE AND CORIANDER SOUP

Serves 6
Keeps 2 days under refrigeration
Freeze 1 month

A wonderful combination of flavours.

1 medium (5 oz/150 g) onion
1 lb (450 g) carrots, peeled
1 oz (25 g/2 tbsp) butter or margarine
1 clove of garlic, chopped
1¼ pints (725 ml/3 cups) hot vegetable stock (water plus cube or paste)
pinch white pepper
½ teasp salt
1 teasp ground coriander

7 fl oz (200 ml/¾ cup plus 2 tbsp) orange juice

2 strips orange peel

3 fl oz (75 ml/⅓ cup) single cream or evaporated milk

1 rounded tbsp chopped parsley or fresh coriander

To garnish

1 oz (25 g/¼ cup) toasted flaked hazelnuts (see below)

1   To toast the hazelnuts, spread on a plate and cook on 100% power for 2 minutes, stirring once.

2   Slice all the vegetables using the fine slicer of the food processor.

3   In a 3½ pint (2 litre/9 cup) lidded casserole or large bowl, melt the butter on 100% power for 1 minute then add the sliced vegetables and garlic, stir well to coat with the fat, then add 5 fl oz (150 ml/⅔ cup) of the hot stock, cover and cook for 13 minutes, stirring halfway, until the vegetables feel tender when pierced with a slim pointed knife.

4   Purée in the blender or food processor together with the pepper, salt and ground coriander.

5   Return to the dish and whisk in the orange juice. Add the peel, cover and cook on 100% power for 5 minutes.

6   Uncover then lift out the peel and stir in the cream or milk and the herbs. If possible, leave for several hours or overnight to mature in flavour.

7   To reheat, cover and cook on 100% power for 8 minutes or until bubbling round the edge.

8   Serve topped with a sprinkle of hazelnuts.

COURGETTE AND LETTUCE SOUP

Serves 6
Keeps 2 days under refrigeration
Freeze 3 months

A beautiful pale green soup with a surprisingly rich flavour. It contains no dairy products and no added fat or starchy thickening.

1 lb (450 g) fresh or frozen courgettes, unpeeled and thinly sliced

1 tbsp minced dried onion or 1 teasp onion salt

1½ pints (850 ml/3¾ cups) hot vegetable stock (hot water plus cubes or paste)

1 medium lettuce, any variety, finely shredded

½ teasp salt (omit if onion salt has been used)

15 grinds black pepper

2 teasp chopped parsley or snipped chives

extra stock if necessary

1   Into a 3½ pint (2 litre/9 cup) lidded casserole, bowl or soup tureen, put the courgettes, the onion and 10 fl oz (275 ml/1¼ cups) of the hot stock.

2   Cover and cook on 100% power for 8 minutes.

3   Add the shredded lettuce, stir, re-cover and cook for 3 minutes.

4   Liquidize or process until smooth, then pour back into the dish.

5   Pour the remaining 1 pint (575 ml/2½ cups) stock into the machine with the salt and black pepper and process briefly to clean down the sides, then add to the purée with the herbs, stirring well.

6   Cover and cook on 100% power for 3 minutes or until barely bubbling.

7   To reheat from cold, thin down with extra stock if necessary to a creamy consistency, then cover and cook on 100% power for 8 minutes.

DANISH CAULIFLOWER SOUP

Serves 4
Keeps 3 days under refrigeration
Freeze 3 months

A rich and creamy soup with the cheese adding an extra flavour dimension.

1 very fresh, white medium-sized cauliflower or 1 lb (450 g) pre packed cauliflower florets
1 tbsp minced dried onion
15 fl oz (425 ml/2 cups) hot vegetable stock
1 oz (25 g/2 tbsp) butter or margarine
½ teasp salt
½ teasp dried fines herbes
pinch white pepper
¼ teasp ground nutmeg
1 tbsp cornflour
15 fl oz (425 ml/2 cups) milk
2 oz (50 g/½ cup) blue cheese, finely crumbled
To garnish
3 tbsp reserved cooked cauliflower

1   Cut the cauliflower away from the stalk then divide into small florets. Wash well then put into a lidded 3½ pint (2 litre/9 cup) casserole or bowl with the minced onion and 5 fl oz (150 ml/⅔ cup) of the hot stock.
2   Cover and cook on 100% power for 12 minutes.
3   Set aside 3 tbsp of the cauliflower florets then purée the remainder together with the rest of the stock, the butter or margarine and the seasonings in a blender or food processor.
4   Put the cornflour into the same casserole and stir to a cream with 4 tbsp of the milk. Stir in the remainder of the milk, cover and cook on 100% power for 3 minutes, stirring once, then uncover and whisk in the cauliflower purée.
5   Cook uncovered on 50% power for 5 minutes. Remove from the oven and add the cheese,

whisking well until it has dissolved. Stir in the reserved cauliflower. Cover and leave for 3 minutes then serve.
6   To reheat from cold, cook, covered, at 100% power for 8 minutes, stirring once.

COURGETTE AND LEEK SOUP WITH GARDEN HERBS

Serves 4–5
Keeps 2 days under refrigeration
Freeze 3 months

Fresh tarragon adds a pleasing piquancy to this smooth, delicate soup with a creamy texture.

1 lb (450 g) fresh or frozen courgettes, unpeeled and thinly sliced (in the food processor)
white part of a fat leek (3–4 oz/75–125 g), thinly sliced (in the food processor)
1½ tbsp minced dried onion
1½ pints (850 ml/3¾ cups) hot vegetable stock (water plus cubes or paste)
½ teasp salt
15 grinds black pepper
1 tbsp cornflour
3 fl oz (75 ml/⅓ cup) single cream, evaporated milk or extra vegetable stock
2 teasp finely snipped fresh tarragon

1   Into a 3½ pint (2 litre/9 cup) lidded deep casserole, large soufflé dish, bowl or tureen, put the courgettes, onion, leek and 8 fl oz (225 ml/1 cup) of the hot stock.
2   Cover and cook on 100% power for 13 minutes.
3   Liquidize or process until smooth, together with the remaining stock, the salt and pepper and the cornflour mixed to a cream with the single cream, evaporated milk or vegetable stock.
4   Return to the dish and cook uncovered on

A Consommé of Forest Mushrooms

100% power for 6 minutes, stirring once, until bubbly round the edge. Stir in the tarragon.

5 To reheat from cold, cover and cook on 100% power for 8 minutes.

CREAM OF GREEN PEPPER SOUP

Serves 6
Keeps 3 days under refrigeration
Freeze 3 months

This soup varies enormously in colour and taste according to the kind of peppers used. Red peppers give it the sweetest flavour but green ones produce a soup that could almost be mistaken for asparagus.

1 very large or 2 medium green peppers, or a mixture of green, yellow and red, coarsely chopped (9–10 oz/250–275 g total weight)
1 medium (5 oz/150 g) onion, coarsely chopped
1½ oz (40 g/3 tbsp) butter or margarine
15 fl oz (425 ml/2 cups) hot vegetable stock (water plus cubes or paste)
2 tbsp and 2 teasp cornflour
15 fl oz (425 ml/2 cups) milk
1 teasp salt
10 grinds black pepper
good pinch powdered nutmeg
1 teasp dried fines herbes or herbes de Provence

1 Halve, deseed and remove any white pith from the peppers then cut in roughly 1 inch (2.5 cm) pieces and coarsely chop in the food processor together with the peeled onion.

2 In a 3½ pint (2 litre/9 cup) lidded casserole or bowl melt the fat on 100% power for 1 minute, add the chopped vegetables, stir well to coat with the fat then cover and cook for 7 minutes.

3 Purée in the food processor with a third of the stock, add the remaining stock and pulse to clean down the sides of the bowl. Return the purée to the casserole.

4 Put the cornflour in a 3½ pint (2 litre/9 cup) jug and mix to a thin cream with 4 tbsp of the measured milk then stir in the remainder together with the seasonings and herbs. Cover with a plate and cook on 100% power for 3 minutes. Uncover and stir thoroughly to ensure the sauce thickens evenly, then cover and cook for a further 2 minutes. Uncover, stir well, then cook uncovered for a further 2 minutes until thickened and bubbly.

5 Stir into the vegetable mixture, cover and cook on 100% power for 5 minutes, stirring once. Stand for 5 minutes, stir well, then serve, or allow to stand for several hours.

6 Reheat, cover and cook on 100% power for 8 minutes, stirring halfway.

A VELOUTÉ OF LETTUCE

Serves 4
Keeps 3 days under refrigeration
Do not freeze

A gently flavoured pale green soup with a creamy texture. It can be served hot or cold.

2 medium potatoes (10 oz/275 g total weight), peeled and thinly sliced
1½ tbsp minced dried onion
1½ pints (850 ml/3¾ cups) hot vegetable stock (made with cubes or paste)
1 large Webb or Iceberg lettuce (including the outside leaves) washed and finely shredded
1 oz (25 g/2 tbsp) of butter or margarine
scant teasp salt
¼ teasp nutmeg
10 grinds black pepper
pinch sugar
1 sprig parsley

Aubergine and Yoghurt Mezze, Israeli Vegetable Ragout, Mushrooms in White Wine, Turkish Style

1 small bay leaf
5 fl oz (150 ml/⅔ cup) single cream, smetana or
    evaporated milk
To garnish
1 tbsp chives

1   Put the potatoes, minced onion and 10 fl oz
(275 ml/1¼ cups) of the hot measured stock in a
deep 3½ pint (2 litre/9 cup) lidded casserole or
bowl, cover and cook on 100% power for 8
minutes or until the potatoes feel tender when
pierced with a sharp knife.
2   Add the lettuce, re-cover and cook for a further
3 minutes, stirring once.
3   Purée in a blender or food processor and return
to the dish with the remaining stock, the butter or
margarine, seasonings, parsley and bay leaf.
4   Cook uncovered on 50% power for 5 minutes,
stir well, then add the cream, smetana or
evaporated milk, and cook a further 1 minute or
until bubbling round the edges.
5   Remove the parsley sprig and bay leaf and
stand covered for 3 minutes, then serve.
6   To reheat from cold, cook covered on 100%
power for 8 minutes, stirring once.
7   To serve, sprinkle with the chives.

ITALIAN MUSHROOM SOUP

Serves 6
Keeps 3 days under refrigeration
Freeze 3 months

A subtly flavoured soup that makes an ideal starter
for a main course of cold poached salmon. If
possible allow the soup to mature for several hours
before serving.

1½ oz (40 g/3 tbsp) butter or margarine
8 oz (225 g/2½ cups) very fresh open cap
    mushrooms, thinly sliced

bulbs of 3 spring onions, finely sliced
small clove garlic, peeled and crushed
10 fl oz (275 ml/1¼ cups) hot vegetable stock
    (water plus cube or paste)
1 rounded tbsp chopped parsley
3 tbsp cornflour
1¼ pints (725 ml/3 cups) milk
1 teasp salt
few shakes white pepper
¼ teasp ground nutmeg
2 tbsp Amontillado sherry
4 tbsp single cream or evaporated milk (optional)

1   In a 3½ pint (2 litre/9 cup) lidded casserole or
bowl melt the butter on 100% power for 1 minute.
Add the mushrooms, spring onions and garlic, stir
well to coat with the fat then cover and cook on
100% power for 4 minutes. Stir in the hot stock
and the parsley and set to one side.
2   Meanwhile, put the cornflour in a 3½ pint (2
litre/9 cup) jug and mix to a thin cream with 4
tbsp of the measured milk. Stir in the remaining
milk together with the seasonings, cover with a
plate and cook on 100% power for 3 minutes,
uncover and stir very well, particularly round the
edges of the jug, to ensure the sauce thickens
evenly, then re-cover and cook for a further 3
mintes. Uncover and cook for 4 more minutes or
until bubbling, stirring once.
3   Give the sauce a final stir then add to the
mushroom mixture.
4   To serve now, stir in the sherry and the cream
(if used), cover and heat on 100% power for 5
minutes or until steaming hot, stirring halfway.
5   To reheat from cold, cook, covered, on 100%
power for 8 minutes, stirring halfway.

WEST AFRICAN PEANUT SOUP

Serves 5–6
Keeps 3 days under refrigeration
Freeze 3 months

Simple but very tasty and, because of its high proportion of vegetable protein, excellent for vegetarians.

8 oz (225 g/1 cup) smooth peanut butter
1 pint (575 ml/2½ cups) hot vegetable stock
10 fl oz (275 ml/1¼ cups) milk
10 grinds sea salt
10 grinds black pepper
pinch nutmeg
2 teasp Madras curry powder

1   Put the peanut butter into a 3½ pint (2 litre/9 cup) lidded casserole or large bowl and whisk in the stock followed by the milk and the seasonings.
2   Cover and cook on 100% power for 6 minutes, stirring halfway.
3   Leave covered for 2–3 minutes before serving.
4   To reheat from cold, cover and cook on 100% power for 8 minutes, stirring halfway.

SPINACH AND GREEN PEA SOUP WITH FRESH MINT AND TOASTED PINE KERNELS

Serves 6
Keeps 3 days under refrigeration
Freeze 3 months

A soup with a positive health bonus – and a wonderfully satisfying taste – that is how I would describe this deep green soup that would make a perfect starter to a spring dinner party. Another bonus for weightwatchers – it is thickened naturally by the spinach and the peas, so it needs neither flour nor cornflour. The pine kernels add a touch of luxury but toasted slivered almonds can be used instead. Serve the soup with warm wholemeal pitta bread. To avoid the bread drying up when it is reheated, sprinkle the surface lightly with cold water, then grill briefly until warm to the touch.

1 oz (25 g/2 tbsp) butter
1 tbsp minced dried onion
7 oz (200 g) packet frozen chopped spinach, defrosted
12 oz (350 g/2 ¼ cups) frozen garden peas
15 fl oz (425 ml/2 cups) hot vegetable stock (water plus cube or paste)
1 bunch fresh mint leaves (1½ cups leaves loosely packed), washed then destalked
1 teasp salt
8 grinds black pepper
15 fl oz (425 ml/2 cups) milk
1 oz (25 g/¼ cup) toasted pine kernels (see page 182)

1   In a 3½ pint (2 litre/9 cup) lidded casserole or bowl, melt the butter on 100% power for 1 minute then add the onion, thawed spinach and garden peas, stir well, cover and cook on 100% power for 7 minutes.
2   Purée in a blender or food processor with the hot stock, mint leaves, salt and pepper (a blender produces the smoothest texture).
3   Put the milk into the cooking dish, cover and cook on 100% power for 5 minutes or until steaming. Add the vegetable purée, whisking well.
4   Cover and cook on 100% power for 5 minutes, stirring once.
5   To serve later, allow to stand for several hours then cover and cook on 100% power for 8 minutes, stirring once.
6   Garnish each serving with sprinkle of pine kernels.

GOOD CHICKEN STOCK

Makes about 2 pints (1.25 litres/5 cups)
Keeps 3 days under refrigeration
Freeze 3 months

This method cuts the normal cooking time by two-thirds. It is also easier to wash up a large heatproof glass bowl than a pan. This makes a marvellous basis for the Traditional Chicken Soup but it does need 24 hours 'rest' to allow it to mature in flavour and deepen in colour (see below). The carcase from a roast bird (frozen until required) definitely enriches the flavour.

1 roast chicken carcase, broken up
1 lb (450 g) giblets (not the liver) or 2 lb (900 g–1 kg) raw carcases, broken
1 large (8 oz/225 g) onion, unpeeled but halved
1 fat carrot, peeled and quartered lengthwise
3 parsley sprigs
1 bay leaf
10 black peppercorns
1–2 squashy tomatoes, halved
2 fat stalks of celery cut in 3 inch (8 cm) lengths
1¾ pints (1 litre/4½ cups) hot water (enough to cover the solids)
1 teasp sea salt

1   Put all the ingredients, except for the salt, into a 5 pint (3 litre/12½ cup) bowl and cover with the hot water from the kettle. Cover the bowl with a large plate and cook on 100% power for 20 minutes, then reduce to 50% power and simmer a further 20 minutes.
2   Add the salt, allow to stand until cool enough to handle, then pour through a strainer, pressing down hard on the solids to extract all the liquid.
3   Put in the freezer until the fat can be lifted off with a slotted spoon (about 2 hours).
4   Refrigerate or freeze until required.

TRADITIONAL CHICKEN SOUP

Serves 4
Keeps 3 days under refrigeration
Freeze 3 months

With time to mature, the Good Chicken Stock (above) will metamorphose into a beautiful golden soup to serve with lokshen (fine vermicelli) or knaidlach (Matzo Meal Dumplings, see page 40) or mandlen (soup nuts).

1 small (2 oz/50 g) carrot cut in ⅜ inch (1 cm) cubes
1 inch (2.5 cm) length of white part of a leek, finely shredded
1 recipe Good Chicken Stock (see above), defrosted overnight, if frozen, or 2 pints (1.25 litres/5 cups) hot water plus two chicken stock cubes
1–2 additional chicken stock cubes (let taste be your guide)
2 teasp chopped parsley (optional)

1   Put the carrot and leek into a lidded soup cup or small bowl with 2 tbsp of the stock. Cover and cook on 100% power for 5 minutes, stirring once. Add to the remaining stock, taste, and add extra stock cubes, if necessary. Allow to mature overnight.
2   To reheat the soup, cover and cook on 100% power for 12 minutes until barely bubbling.
3   Stir in the chopped parsley.

CURRIED CHICKEN SOUP

Serves 4–5
Keeps 2 days under refrigeration
Freeze 3 months

This unusual version of the familiar chicken soup is thickened by rice to give extra body.

2 pints (1.25 litres/5 cups) hot chicken stock (see page 38) or boiling water plus cubes
1 teasp salt
1 tbsp minced dried onion
4 oz (125 g/¾ cup) carrots, peeled and cut in small chunks
2 sprigs parsley with stalks
3 teasp mild curry paste or powder
1 small bay leaf
4 tbsp long grain rice (Patna or Basmati)
4 oz (125 g/⅔ cup) chicken-breast meat
4 oz (125 g/¾ cup) frozen petit pois
sea salt and black pepper to taste

1   In a 3½ pint (2 litre/9 cup) lidded deep casserole, bowl or small tureen, put 10 fl oz (275 ml/1¼ cups) of the chicken stock, the salt, the onion, carrot, parsley, curry paste or powder and bay leaf, the rice and the chicken. Cover and cook on 100% power for 7 minutes, take out chicken, then re-cover and cook for a further 8 minutes.
2   Leave to rest for 5 minutes then lift out the parsley and bay leaf with a slotted spoon and discard. Pour the remaining mixture into a blender together with the remaining stock and purée until absolutely smooth.
3   Return to the soup pan together with the peas and the chicken cut into strips. Cover and reheat for 6 minutes until bubbly.
4   Leave to stand, covered, for 5 minutes, then re-season and serve or allow to go cold. To reheat, cover and cook on 100% power for 8 minutes.

CHICKEN AND TOMATO SOUP WITH FINE LOKSHEN

Serves 4–6
Keeps 3 days under refrigeration
Freeze 3 months

This richly flavoured soup can also be made using vegetable stock. Then it is ideal to serve for a light supper snack, topped with grated cheese and accompanied by buttered rye or granary bread.

1 tbsp olive oil or sunflower oil
Finely chopped in the food processor
1 medium (5 oz/150 g) onion
1 fat clove of garlic
1 medium carrot (about 2 oz/50 g),
1 fat stalk of celery
1 × 14 oz (400 g) can chopped tomatoes
sprig parsley
small bay leaf
1 teasp salt
1–2 teasp light brown sugar (according to acidity of tomatoes)
10 grinds black pepper
1¼ pints (725 ml/3 cups) hot chicken soup (see page 38) or good strong stock made from cubes
small handful of fine vermicelli, broken up (1½ oz/40 g approx)

1   In a 3½ pint (2 litre/9 cup) lidded casserole or bowl put the oil and the finely chopped onion, garlic, carrot and celery, mix well, cover and cook for 5 minutes on 100% power.
2   Add the tomatoes, herbs and seasonings, stir, then cover and cook for a further 8 minutes on 100% power, stirring halfway, until the vegetables are tender.
3   Remove the bay leaf and parsley and purée in a blender or a food processor.
4   Return to the dish, add the hot stock (whirled

briefly in the blender or food processor to clean down the sides), stir well, cover and bring back to the boil (about 4 minutes on 100% power).

5   Uncover and add the pasta, then cook uncovered for a further 5 minutes.

6   Cover again and leave for 5 minutes, re-season if necessary and serve.

7   To reheat from cold, cover and cook on 100% power for 8 minutes.

TO COOK KNAIDLACH (MATZO MEAL DUMPLINGS)

Serves 4
Keeps 2 days under refrigeration
Freeze 1 month

In the microwave, these light and fluffy dumplings cook in approximately half the normal time. For a large quantity, however, it is probably more convenient to cook them on top of the stove.
As with the conventional method you have a choice of cooking liquid – water or chicken soup. The latter is the most delicious but be warned that the knaidlach will absorb almost a quarter of the soup.

For the knaidlach (this produces firm but tender dumplings)

1 large egg
1 very slightly rounded tbsp rendered chicken fat, chicken-flavoured vegetable fat or soft margarine
2 tbsp warm chicken soup or water
½ teasp salt
speck white pepper
pinch ground ginger
1 rounded tbsp ground almonds
2½ oz (65 g/4 heaped and 1 rounded tbsp) matzo meal

1   Whisk the egg until fluffy then stir in the soft fat, tepid soup or water, seasonings, ground almonds and matzo meal and mix thoroughly. The mixture should look moist and thick but should not be quite firm enough to form into balls. If too soft, add a little more meal; if too firm, add a teaspoon or two of water. Chill for at least an hour, but overnight will do no harm.

2   To cook in water: put 1½ pints (850 ml/3¾ cups) boiling water plus 1 teasp salt in a 3½–4 pint (2–2.5 litre/9–10 cup) deep lidded casserole or bowl. Cook covered on 100% power for 5 minutes until boiling.

3   Meanwhile take pieces of the chilled mixture the size of walnuts and roll into balls between wetted palms. Place in the boiling water, cover and cook at 100% power for 5 minutes, then reduce to 50% power for a further 10 minutes. Leave to stand (covered) for 5 minutes, then drain and put in chicken soup.

4   To cook in chicken soup (see page 38): put 2 pints (1.25 litres/5 cups) soup in a 3½ pint (2 litre/9 cup) deep lidded casserole or bowl, cover and cook on 100% power for 11 minutes until boiling (7 minutes if hot soup is used). Place the knaidlach in the boiling soup, cover and cook at 100% power for 7 minutes, then at 50% power for a further 10 minutes. Leave to stand covered for 5 minutes then serve at once.

5   To reheat soup and knaidlach from cold: cover and cook on 100% power for 12–13 minutes until bubbling around the edges.

A CONSOMMÉ OF FOREST MUSHROOMS

Serves 6
Keeps 4 days under refrigeration
Freeze 3 months, but expect the mushrooms to toughen a little

This elegant clear soup makes an ideal starter for a dinner party before a hearty main course.
NOTE: It is important to make the soup 24 hours in advance to allow the flavour to develop to the full.

8 oz (225 g/2½ cups) 'exotic' mushrooms (if possible, a mixture of shii-take and oyster mushrooms)
4 oz (125 g/1¼ cups) large flat mushrooms
1 oz (25 g/2 tbsp) butter or margarine
4 fat spring onion bulbs, trimmed and finely sliced
2 pints (1.25 litres/5 cups) strong vegetable stock or chicken stock (made with cubes or preferably home-made, see page 38)
1 teasp fresh thyme leaves, chopped, or pinch dried thyme
3 tbsp finely snipped chives
3 tbsp brandy
10 grinds black pepper
½ teasp salt
Optional garnish for dairy version
1 × 5 fl oz (150 ml/⅔ cup) carton soured cream
a few reserved snipped chives

1   Trim any tough stalks from the mushrooms, wipe with a damp cloth then cut into strips about ⅜ inch (1 cm) wide and 1 inch (2.5 cm) long.
2   In a 3½ pint (2 litre/9 cup) lidded casserole or bowl, heat the fat on 100% power for 1 minute, add the spring onion bulbs and the mushrooms together with 2 tbsp of the measured stock. Stir well, cover and cook on 100% power for 5 minutes, stirring once.
3   Add the thyme, half the chives, the brandy, the seasoning and the stock. Cover and cook on 100%

power for 6 minutes, stirring once. Cool and refrigerate.
4   Just before serving, cook covered on 100% power for 8 minutes or until barely bubbling, then stir in the remaining chives, taste and re-season if necessary.
5   For a dairy version, top each bowl of soup with a spoonful of cream and sprinkle with the reserved chives.

LENTIL AND CUMIN SOUP

Serves 4
Keeps 4 days under refrigeration
Freeze for 3 months

This is a gently spiced soup that is very satisfying on a cold night.

4 oz (125 g/½ cup) brown or red lentils, soaked for 15 minutes in double their volume of boiling water
1 tbsp olive oil
Coarsely chopped in the food processor
½ onion
1 small red pepper
3 oz (75 g/¾ cup) carrots
1 × 7 oz (200 g) can tomatoes, chopped
1 teasp dark brown sugar
½ teasp salt
10 grinds black pepper
½ teasp minced dried garlic
1 bay leaf
½ teasp dried fines herbes
1½ pints (850 ml/3¾ cups) vegetable or meat stock
For the garnish
1 tbsp snipped chives

1   In a 3½ pint (2 litre/9 cup) lidded casserole, soup tureen or bowl, put the onion, pepper, carrots and the olive oil. Cover and cook on 100% power for 7 minutes, stirring once.

2   Mix in a jug half the stock, the chopped tomatoes, the seasonings and herbs.

3   Uncover the vegetables, add the well rinsed and drained lentils and the seasoned liquid, cover and cook on 100% power for a further 10 minutes.

4   Blend or process until puréed then return to the soup dish.

5   Add the remaining stock to the processor, process for 2 seconds to clean down the sides then add to the soup pan. Re-cover, then heat on 100% power for 4 minutes until barely bubbling. Taste for seasoning and stir in the chives.

6   Serve at once or leave several hours (covered) then reheat for 8 minutes on 100% power.

TOMATO AND ORANGE SOUP WITH TINY DUMPLINGS

Serves 4–5
Keeps 3 days under refrigeration
Freeze for 3 months

The depth of flavour of this very tasty soup belies the speed with which it is prepared.

For the soup

1 × 5 oz (150 g) can or tube of tomato purée or 2 heaped tbsp

½ teasp onion salt or 3 teasp minced dried onion

½ teasp garlic granules

2 teasp dark brown sugar

2 strips of thinly pared orange peel

1 bay leaf

10 grinds black pepper

½ teasp salt

1 teasp herbes de Provence or Italian seasoning herbs

1½ pints (850 ml/3¾ cups) strong hot vegetable or meat stock (see Lexicon page 186)

For the dumplings

1½ oz (40 g/3 tbsp) soft butter or margarine

1 egg

1½ oz (40 g/6 tbsp) self-raising flour

2 tbsp ground almonds (optional)

good pinch of salt

pinch of white pepper

OR

For dumplings made with matzo meal

1 oz (25 g/2 tbsp) rendered chicken fat or soft margarine

1 egg

2½ oz (65 g/5 tbsp) medium matzo meal

2 tbsp warm water

2 tbsp ground almonds (optional)

¼ teasp salt

few shakes white pepper

For the garnish

2 teasp chopped parsley or snipped fresh basil

1   To make either type of dumplings, put the soft fat in a mixing bowl and cook for 15 seconds on 80% power. Then stir in the rest of the ingredients in the order given. Freeze to allow the mixture to firm up whilst the soup is prepared and cooked.

2   To make the soup, put all the ingredients into a 3½ pint (2 litre/9 cup) bowl or lidded casserole, cover and cook on 100% power for 8 minutes. Stir well then leave covered whilst the dumpling mixture is formed.

3   Roll the dumpling mixture into marble-sized balls between wetted palms and put into the soup. Cover and cook for 5 minutes. If possible, leave several hours for the flavour to develop.

5   Reheat, covered, for 8 minutes on 100% power (2½ minutes for an individual bowl).

6   Stir in the parsley or basil just before serving.

STARTERS

INTRODUCTION

As the starter sets the mood of the meal, it needs to be both appealing to the eye and stimulating to the appetite, but not so satisfying that it overshadows the main dish that is to follow.

With this 'specification' in mind, most of the dishes in this chapter feature vegetables that are colourful and tasty but fairly light in substance.

Whilst all these dishes are cooked more speedily than usual, as with any similar recipe prepared in the conventional way, they still need some hours in which to develop their full flavour.

It may surprise you to see globe artichokes heading the list, but the microwave cooking method makes them a practical proposition even for an everyday meal because it avoids all the usual hassle and uncertainty in preparing these delicately flavoured, if cumbersome, vegetables. As for the Hollandaise sauce – that bogeyman of even the professional chef – cooking by microwave makes it certain of complete success.

I have included some aubergine recipes in this chapter because the flesh becomes especially sweet and creamy without any of the attention that is needed when it is grilled in the traditional way.

Mushrooms take particularly kindly to the microwave and, by using 'instant' herbs and spices, aromatic dishes such as Champignons à la Grecque can be prepared and cooked in less than fifteen minutes.

In a dish such as the Israeli vegetable ragout, the action of the microwave develops flavour at the same time that it preserves a little 'bite' in each vegetable – something that can normally only be achieved by cooking each individual variety in a separate pan and combining them all just before serving. The chapter concludes with two very special dishes of marinated fish. ■

GLOBE ARTICHOKES WITH A TARRAGON HOLLANDAISE SAUCE

Serves 4–6
Best eaten the same day

What a joy to prepare artichokes this way without a vast pan of bubbling water steaming up the kitchen – the artichokes are left quietly steaming in their own moisture. The microwave method of preparing a Sauce Hollandaise puts this perhaps most difficult sauce within the reach of anyone who can press a button!

If preferred, a herb vinaigrette can be served with the artichokes in place of the Hollandaise.

4–6 fine globe artichokes (each weighing 8–12 oz/225–350 g)
For the sauce
4½ oz (140 g/½ cup plus 1 tbsp) unsalted butter or margarine
2 egg yolks
1 tbsp lemon juice
2 teasp wine vinegar
½ teasp caster sugar
pinch salt
speck white pepper
½ teasp grated lemon rind
1 tbsp fresh tarragon, snipped

1   To prepare the artichokes, bend the stalk so that it breaks off and pulls out the coarse filaments at the base, which may then need to be trimmed off level with a knife. Turn the artichoke on its side on a board and cut off the top ⅔ inch (2 cm) using a strong sharp knife. Trim off the points of the remaining leaves of the artichoke with a pair of scissors.
2   Wash well, then tightly wrap in microwave clingfilm. Place in a circle on the turntable or a large plate.

3   Cook at 100% power for 15 minutes for 4 artichokes, or 19 minutes for 6 artichokes. (2 artichokes will take just 10 minutes.)
4   Remove from the oven and leave for 5 minutes, then puncture the film with a knife to release any build-up of steam and carefully unwrap.
5   Leave to cool at room temperature while you prepare the sauce.
6   Not more than 1 hour before serving, melt the butter or margarine in a small basin, loosely covered with a paper towel, on 100% power for 1½ minutes.
7   Meanwhile, using a balloon whisk, whisk the egg yolks in a medium (1 pint/575 ml/2½ cup) basin with the lemon juice, wine vinegar, sugar and seasonings.
8   Slowly whisk in the hot melted butter, then cook on 30% power for a further 2 minutes, stirring after 1 minute.
9   Remove and stir in the lemon rind and tarragon. The sauce should resemble a thick coating custard. It will thicken further on standing.
10   To serve, put each artichoke on a separate large plate (special grooved artichoke plates are ideal) with an individual cocotte, or schnapps glass, filled with dressing at the side.
11   The leaves are plucked out one at a time, dipped in the sauce, then sucked to remove the juicy flesh at the base. When all the leaves have been pulled out, the thistle-like 'choke' will be revealed. This must be cut off with a small sharp knife to reveal the tender heart, which is then cut up with a knife and fork and dipped in the sauce. (If preferred, the choke can be removed in the kitchen before serving.)

AUBERGINE AND TAHINA MEZZE

Serves 4–5 as a starter, 8 as a dip
Keeps 1 week under refrigeration
Do not freeze

This microwave version of the Middle-Eastern classic dish may lack the charred flavour of the original (which you only achieve if the aubergines are grilled over charcoal), but it is a delicious dish by any reckoning, unctuous in texture with a wonderfully piquant flavour.

2 medium glossy aubergines (total weight approximately 1 lb/450 g)
large sprig parsley
1 fat clove of garlic, peeled and halved
1 tbsp fresh lemon juice
2 rounded tbsp tahina (sesame seed paste)
½ level teasp salt
8 grinds black pepper
pinch cayenne or chilli powder
½ teasp ground cumin

1 Cut off and discard the prickly green calyx then prick the aubergines all over, place on 2 layers of paper towelling and cook on 100% power for 10 minutes.
2 Allow to stand for 1 minute, then pierce with a skewer. If not completely tender, cook for a further 2 minutes.
3 When cool enough to handle, halve lengthwise and scoop out the flesh, then purée in a food processor or blender together with the parsley and garlic. Add all the remaining ingredients and process until smooth and creamy.
4 Cover and chill for several hours.
5 To serve, spoon into a pottery dish or 4 individual cocottes. Serve with a dish of black olives and warm pitta bread or sticks of raw carrot and green pepper.

AUBERGINE AND YOGHURT MEZZE-*VARIATION*

This is somewhat milder in flavour and very refreshing on a hot day.

2 medium glossy aubergines (total weight approximately 1 lb/450 g)
1 medium (5 oz/150 g) green pepper
3 teasp olive oil
1 clove garlic, peeled and halved
large sprig parsley
1 tbsp lemon juice
1 tbsp olive oil
½ teasp salt
8 grinds black pepper
5 fl oz (150 ml/⅔ cup) strained Greek-style yoghurt, fromage frais or creamed smetana

1 While the cooked aubergines are cooling, halve, deseed and remove the white pith from the green pepper, and cut into ½ inch (1.25 cm) dice. Put in a small bowl with the olive oil, cover with pierced clingfilm and cook on 100% power for 4 minutes.
2 Purée with the aubergine flesh, as before, with all the remaining ingredients except the yoghurt, fromage frais or creamed smetana.
3 When the purée is smooth, pulse in Greek-style yoghurt, fromage frais or creamed smetana.

CHAMPIGNONS À LA GRECQUE

Serves 4–6
Keeps 5 days under refrigeration

These tiny mushrooms in their fragrant juice can be served as a light starter. They look most appetizing arranged in small porcelain cocottes or they can be spooned into one gratin dish to accompany cold meat or fish in a buffet. The cooked mushrooms should be allowed to marinate for at least 12 hours before serving.

1½ lb (575 g/6 cups) button mushrooms
4 tbsp olive oil
4 tbsp water
1½ tbsp lemon juice
1½ tbsp wine vinegar
1 teasp tomato purée or bottled sun-dried tomatoes
10 grinds black pepper
½ teasp ground coriander
¼ teasp Italian seasoning
1 bay leaf or ¼ teasp ground bay leaf
1 teasp salt
½ teasp caster sugar
½ teasp garlic granules
1 tbsp coarsely chopped parsley

1 Trim the stalk of each mushroom level with the cup then rinse and drain them well.
2 In a large basin, put all the other ingredients except the parsley, cover with a plate and cook on 100% power for 3½ minutes.
3 Add mushrooms, toss to coat with the juices, cover and cook on 100% power for a further 6½ minutes, stirring once.
4 Remove to a serving dish, or individual cocottes, with a slotted spoon.
5 Cook the sauce, uncovered, on 100% power for 5 minutes to thicken it and intensify the flavour, then pour over the mushrooms and stir in the parsley.

MUSHROOMS IN WHITE WINE, TURKISH STYLE

Serves 4–6
Keeps 5 days under refrigeration

This is lighter and fruitier than the more familiar Greek dish. But it does need 12–24 hours to develop its full flavour potential. It looks suitably rustic garnished with sprigs of flowering thyme and either served in individual pottery dishes or in one larger dish.

1½ lb (575 g/6 cups) button mushrooms
2 rounded teasp tomato purée
1 tbsp minced dried onion
5 fl oz (150 ml/⅔ cup) dry white wine
½ teasp freshly ground coriander
½ teasp garlic granules
3 tbsp olive oil
pinch cayenne pepper
1 teasp salt
¼ teasp white pepper
large bunch parsley
1 bay leaf
small sprig fresh lemon thyme (if available)
4 tbsp sultanas
1 large unpeeled lemon, thinly sliced and the slices halved
For the garnish
2 oranges, peeled and sectioned
4–6 tiny sprigs of thyme (in flower if you grow your own herbs)

1 Trim the mushroom stalks level with the base of the cups then wipe with a damp cloth.
2 In a large basin, put all the ingredients (except for the mushrooms, sultanas and lemon slices), mix well, cover with a plate and cook on 100% power for 3½ minutes.
3 Add the remaining ingredients, stir well, then re-cover and cook for 6 ½ minutes, stirring once.

4   Chill for several hours, or overnight. Remove the parsley and bay leaf. Shortly before serving, divide between small cocottes or place in one larger dish and garnish with the sections of orange and sprigs of fresh thyme.

ISRAELI VEGETABLE RAGOUT

Serves 4–6
Keeps under refrigeration for 3 days

First cousin to the Provençal ratatouille, this luscious vegetable stew is equally delicious served hot with plainly grilled or roast meat and poultry, or cold as a starter, with plenty of black bread or challah to mop up the savoury juices. The exact amount of each vegetable is not important – I use what is on bargain offer on the day, or whatever vegetable I find lurking in a corner of the fridge. (The total weight should of course be the same.) But do use olive oil – both for its unique fruity flavour and for the special succulence it gives to this kind of dish, especially when it is served cold. The flavour improves with standing so even if the ragout is to be served hot, it will taste better if made earlier and reheated.

1 large (8–12 oz/225–350 g) aubergine, cut in ½-inch (1.25 cm) thick slices
2 medium courgettes, unpeeled and cut in ½-inch (1.25 cm) thick slices
4 tbsp olive oil
1 × 5 oz (150 g) onion, peeled, halved and finely sliced
1 fat clove of garlic, finely chopped
1 each red and green pepper, seeded and cut in ½-inch (1.25 cm) wide strips (9–10 oz/ 250–275 g total weight)
half a 15 oz (425 g) can chopped tomatoes
2 rounded teasp tomato purée
1 teasp Italian seasoning
1 teasp brown sugar or substitute
1 teasp salt

15 grinds black pepper
1 tbsp chopped parsley
1 tbsp shredded fresh basil leaves or 1 teasp dried

1   Put the sliced aubergine and courgettes in a colander, or salad spinner, sprinkle thickly with salt and leave for 30 minutes. Rinse well and dab or spin dry.
2   Put the oil in a 3½ pint (2 litre/9 cup) lidded casserole or bowl and heat for 2 minutes. Then add the onion, garlic and pepper strips and cook uncovered at 100% power for 5 minutes.
3   Stir well, add the dried aubergine slices, cover and cook for a further 8 minutes.
4   Uncover and add the courgettes, tomatoes, purée and seasonings. Cover and cook for a further 8 minutes, stirring once or twice.
5   Uncover. The sauce should be thick but juicy. If it is at all watery, cook uncovered for a further 3 minutes.
6   Stir in the herbs and serve warm or at room temperature.

SALADE PROVENÇALE

Serves 4–6
Keeps 3 days under refrigeration

The fennel and broad beans add pleasant variety to this dish of lightly braised vegetables strewn with fresh herbs.

2 tbsp extra virgin olive oil
2 medium onions, peeled, halved and sliced paper thin
1 fat clove of garlic, peeled and coarsely chopped
1 each medium-sized red and green pepper, halved, seeds and pith removed and cut in ⅜ inch (1 cm) thick strips (9–10 oz/250–275 g total weight)

1 fat bulb of fennel, halved, stalk end removed,
    then cut in very thin slices

2 medium shiny courgettes, cut in ½-inch (1.25
    cm) thick slices, each of which is then halved

4 oz (125 g/1 cup) frozen broad beans

1 large sprig parsley

1 small sprig thyme

1 bay leaf

2 canned Italian tomatoes, drained on paper
    towelling then seeds discarded and flesh cut in
    strips

1 teasp salt

15 grinds black pepper

2 tbsp chopped fresh herbs – a mixture of parsley,
    tarragon, marjoram or oregano and chives

8 fresh basil leaves, finely shredded

5 fl oz (150 ml/⅔ cup) vinaigrette dressing

1   In a 10 inch (25 cm) lidded casserole or large
bowl, heat 1 tbsp of the oil on 100% power for 1
minute.

2   Add the onion and the garlic, cover and cook
for a further 3 minutes.

3   Add the peppers, fennel, courgettes and broad
beans and tuck in amongst them the sprigs of
parsley, thyme and the bay leaf. Sprinkle with half
a tbsp of the remaining oil, cover and cook on
100% power for 8 minutes.

4   Uncover and lay the tomato strips on top of the
vegetables and sprinkle with the remaining oil.
Re-cover and cook a further 3 minutes, then leave
to stand, covered, for 5 minutes.

5   Remove and discard the parsley, thyme sprigs
and the bay leaf, then sprinkle with salt and pepper
and toss gently together. Chill for several hours.

6   Sprinkle with the fresh herbs just before
serving and pass the vinaigrette dressing separately.

HERRINGS SOUSED IN SPICED CIDER VINEGAR

Serves 4
Keeps 4 days under refrigeration

This old-fashioned favourite takes on a new
dimension when it is cooked in the microwave for
10 minutes instead of the traditional 3 hours. Of
course it will not have caramelized in this short
time but the flavour and texture are still excellent.

4 fine fat herrings, filleted

salt and white pepper

1 medium onion, peeled and finely sliced

For the sousing liquid

½ teasp salt

1 teasp sugar

4 tbsp boiling water

5 fl oz (150 ml/⅔ cup) cider vinegar

2 teasp pickling spice

1 bay leaf

3 rounded teasp golden syrup

1   Wash and scale the herrings with a sharp knife
then split lengthwise (if large), lay skin side down
on a board and sprinkle the flesh lightly with salt
and pepper. Strew with some of the onion, then
roll up from the head end to the tail. Arrange like
the spokes of a wheel round the edge of a 10 inch
(25 cm) shallow-lidded casserole.

2   Put the salt and sugar into a jug, pour on the
boiling water and stir well to dissolve them. Stir in
the vinegar, pickling spice and bay leaf and pour
over the herrings. Finally, dribble a little golden
syrup on the top of each fillet. Strew the remaining
onion on top.

3   Cover and cook for 10 minutes. Leave to cool
with the lid on then refrigerate until ready to serve.

TROUT IN WHITE WINE

Serves 6
Keeps 3 days under refrigeration
Do not freeze

This is my adaptation, using the more delicate pink-fleshed rainbow trout instead of mackerel, of the classic *Macquereau au Vin Blanc*. It makes a perfect starter, flavourful but light in texture, to serve before roast or grilled meat or poultry. It needs to marinate for at least 12 hours before serving.

3 × 8–10 oz (225–275 g) trout, filleted (bones and heads reserved) and well washed

For the fish stock

1 medium onion

1 medium carrot

1 unpeeled lemon

⅓ bottle (approx 10 fl oz/275 ml/1¼ cups) dry white wine, e.g. Muscadet

4 fl oz (125 ml/½ cup) hot water

1 peeled clove of garlic

1 teasp mixed pickling spices (including a dried chilli pepper)

½ teasp salt

1 teasp sugar

sprig of dill or fennel

sprig of parsley

½ teasp Dijon mustard

For the garnish

1 orange, peeled, pith removed and segmented

extra sprigs of dill or fennel

1   Thinly slice the onion, carrot and lemon.

2   To make the fish stock, put the fish bones and the heads into a 3 pint (2 litre/9 cup), 10 inch (25 cm) shallow lidded casserole, add all the remaining ingredients, except the filleted trout and the mustard, cover and cook on 100% power for 5 minutes or until bubbling, then reduce to 50% power and simmer for a further 15 minutes. Leave covered to cool, then strain into a basin or jug and discard the débris.

3   Meanwhile, cut the unskinned fillets lengthwise in two, then arrange side by side in the casserole. Strain the stock over them, cook on 100% power for 6 minutes (the liquid should be barely trembling), then leave until the stock is cold.

4   Lift the fillets out of the liquid, carefully strip off the skin then arrange side by side in the washed cooking dish.

5   Cook the liquid uncovered in a 2 pint (1.25 litre/5 cup) jug on 100% power for 5 minutes until it has a good strong flavour. If it tastes rather acid, add another teaspoon of sugar.

6   Stir the mustard into half this liquid then spoon over the fish to coat it lightly. (The remaining stock can be frozen for later use.) Chill for at least 12 hours.

7   Just before serving, garnish with the orange sections and the sprigs of fresh herbs.

FISH

INTRODUCTION

All manner of fish and fish-based recipes – poached, braised, baked and sauced – take kindly to the microwave. Apart from the saving of time common to all foods, it is also much easier to cook the fish exactly to your particular taste, without any fear of hard or dried-out flesh. And as results, similar to conventional poaching, are achieved by cooking completely without fat, it gives the microwave technique a big dietary plus over many other forms of fish cookery. You will see that in some cases I have given a choice of cooking times. Allow the minimum, then test every 30 seconds until the fish is the right degree of 'doneness'. If a resting time is given, allow this before testing.

Whole fish, steaks and fillets need slightly different methods of arranging on the cooking dish. A whole salmon, for instance, which is generally too long to fit most machines, can be curled round the inside of a quiche or similar circular dish. Steaks should be arranged so that the thicker end is to the outside of a round dish to get the main impact of the microwave energy. Small whole fish, such as trout, should be arranged head end to tail to ensure even heat penetration, and rolled fillets arranged in a circle or oval for a similar reason.

The most useful dish for fish cookery is a 10–11 inch diameter (25–27.5cm) round casserole about 2 inches (5 cm) deep with a slightly domed lid that increases its height to 3 inches. This will serve for both cooking and serving the different variations of gefilte fish, as well as all the sauced dishes you will find in this chapter. It will also do splendidly (covered with film) for cooking a whole salmon to silky perfection. An oval gratin dish is also useful for cooking a number of trout that cannot be fitted into a round dish.

Gefilte fish cooks extremely well in the microwave. Provided you follow the instructions exactly, you will find that the stock is equal in flavour to the one achieved when it is simmered on top of the stove, and there are no fishy odours to fill the kitchen. Fish stock is also useful to 'stockpile' in the freezer, as the foundation for poaching and saucing many of the dishes.

Family-style dishes are given in quantities for four, but the more elegant ones are sufficient for six. ■

FISH STOCK

Freeze for 2 months

This is a well flavoured stock that can be used as a poaching liquid or, when stored in small cartons, can form the basis for any fish sauce.

2 lb (900 g) white fish heads and bones
2 carrots
1 large onion
some mushroom stalks
1 fat stalk celery
a large sprig of parsley (with the stalk)
a bay leaf
10 peppercorns
1¾ pints (1 litre/4½ cups) boiling water

1   Chop all the vegetables finely in the food processor.
2   Wash the fish heads and bones thoroughly (any blood will make the stock bitter), break up into 2 inch (5 cm) pieces then put in a 7 pint (4 litre/1 gallon) lidded casserole or bowl, together with all the other ingredients. Cover and cook on 100% power for 10 minutes then reduce to 50% power and continue to cook for another 10 minutes.
3   Strain through a fine sieve and use as required or freeze in portions of 5 fl oz (150 ml/⅔ cup) for further use.

POACHED SALMON STEAKS WITH DILL SAUCE

Serves 4
Leftovers keep 2 days under refrigeration
Do not freeze

A most elegant dish with the slightly tart butter sauce contrasting with the delicate flavour of the fish, which can be served hot or cold. The sauce can be made up to an hour ahead – it should be tepid or at room temperature when it is served.

4 × 6 oz (175 g) salmon steaks
5 fl oz (150 ml/⅔ cup) fish stock (see above)
squeeze lemon juice
salt
white pepper
For the sauce
4½ oz (140 g/½ cup plus 1 tbsp) slightly salted   butter or margarine
2 egg yolks
1 tbsp lemon juice
2 teasp white wine vinegar
½ teasp caster sugar
pinch salt
speck of white pepper
½ teasp grated lemon rind
1 tbsp fresh snipped dill or 1 teasp dried dill
For the garnish
1 fine lemon, sliced
1 spray of dill

1   Arrange the washed steaks round the edge of a shallow lidded casserole with the thin parts to the centre. Pour on the stock and lemon juice and cover, then cook on 80% power for 8 minutes, turning the fish over after 4 minutes (the liquid should just have come to the simmer).
2   Leave to stand for 5 minutes, then sprinkle lightly with salt and pepper. Drain off the stock and freeze for later use.

3   Carefully remove the skin from each steak and arrange the salmon on a serving dish.

4   To make the sauce, melt the butter in a small basin loosely covered with a paper towel on 100% power for 1½ minutes.

5   Meanwhile, using a balloon whisk, whisk the yolks in a medium basin with the lemon juice, wine vinegar and seasonings. Whisk in the hot melted butter gradually, then cook on 30% power for a further 2 minutes, stirring half way. It will resemble a thick custard and will thicken further on standing. Stir in the rind and dill.

6   Serve garnished with lemon slices and dill.

WHOLE SALMON with Hungarian Cucumber Salad

Serves 6–8 (or 4 plus leftovers)

Whole cooked salmon can be kept for 3 days in the refrigerator but its texture is at its peak about two hours after cooking. If salmon is to be served warm, allow it to rest in the kitchen for 15–30 minutes for the delicate flavour can be muted if the fish is too warm. This method keeps the flesh moist and light in texture.

NOTE: A 5 lb (2.25 kg) fish should be cooked in a 10 inch (25 cm) dish and will take 12 minutes, resting for 5 minutes. Always check 'doneness' by nicking the flesh to the bone with a slim sharp knife. If it still looks a darker pink near the bone, give it a further minute's cooking – it will continue to cook as it cools down.

1 × 3½ lb (1.5 kg) salmon
salt
white pepper
a little chopped fresh tarragon if available
4 tbsp water
For the salad dressing
2 level tbsp caster sugar or granular sweetener
2 tbsp boiling water
4 tbsp red wine vinegar or red fruit vinegar such as raspberry or blackcurrant
1 teasp salt
15 grinds black pepper
2 tbsp fresh snipped dill or chives
For the salad
1 fat cucumber
1 lb (450 g) small tomatoes
2 teasp salt
2 canned red peppers, drained on paper towels and cut in small squares
For the garnish
½ large cucumber, sliced

1   At least 2 hours before serving, slice the unpeeled cucumber very finely either on a mandoline or in a food processor using the crinkly slicer. Set on one side. Halve or quarter the tomatoes (according to size) and put in a bowl sprinkled with the two teaspoons of salt. Leave.

2   For the dressing, dissolve the sugar in the water (use cold water with granular sweetener), then stir in the remaining dressing ingredients. Add the cucumber slices and chill.

3   An hour before serving, drain all the liquid from the tomatoes and add them to the cucumber together with the red peppers.

4   Select a 9 inch (22.5 cm) quiche dish or shallow casserole. Remove the head from the salmon and sprinkle the well washed body cavity with salt, pepper and fresh tarragon. Curl the fish round in the dish, add the water then cover with a double thickness of pierced clingfilm (or a single thickness of freezer quality clingfilm) and cook on 100% power for 9 minutes.

5   Uncover, cover the tail section with a scrap of foil to prevent it drying out, then re-cover the dish and cook on 100% power for a further 1½ minutes.

6   Leave the fish to stand, covered, until it is cool enough to be handled as follows:

7   Using a long, thin-bladed knife, cut through the skin along the length of the backbone, across the tail and around the head. Using the blade of

the knife, peel off the skin and pull off the fins. With the back of the knife, scrape away the shallow layer of brown-coloured flesh over the centre of the fish.

8 Turn the salmon over and repeat, and then cut down along the backbone. Turn the knife flat, ease the fillet gently from the bone and lift off (with a large fish this may have to be done in two pieces).

9 At the head and tail, cut through the bone with scissors and peel the bones away. Replace upper fillet.

10 Garnish with the thinly sliced cucumber, arranged in overlapping slices, rather like scales, over the surface of the fish.

11 Serve surrounded by the salad.

NOTE: If the fish is to be served warm, do not fillet but, after skinning, lift carefully on to a warm platter ready to serve.

TROUT WITH ALMONDS

Serves 4
Keeps 2 days under refrigeration
Freeze 1 month

The microwave cooks delicate fish like trout so that the flesh stays light and moist and it does save preheating a conventional oven, particularly useful in the summer. For a dieter, simply omit the fried almond garnish, pouring the lemon juice alone over instead. If more convenient the fish can be cooked earlier in the day, then the garnish can be poured over and the fish reheated on 75–80% power for 2 minutes.

4 × 8 oz (225 g) trout
1 tbsp fresh tarragon, chopped, or ½ teasp dried
½ teasp salt
For the garnish
2 oz (50 g/¼ cup) butter or margarine
2 oz (50 g/½ cup) flaked almonds
3 tbsp lemon juice
10 grinds black pepper

1 Have the fish cleaned and the heads removed. Wash the body cavity, sprinkle with the herbs and salt, then lay in a shallow serving dish, side by side but head to tail. Cover and cook on 100% power for 8 minutes.

2 Leave to stand, covered, for 5 minutes while you prepare the garnish.

3 In a medium bowl, melt the butter on 100% power for 1½ minutes (cover with a paper towel to avoid splashing). Add the almonds and cook uncovered on 100% power for 3½ minutes until golden brown, then stir in the lemon juice and black pepper.

4 Uncover the fish and carefully remove the top skin, then pour over the sauce and reheat, uncovered, on 100% power for 1 minute. Serve at once.

NOTE: For a completely fatless dish, omit the butter, spread the almonds on a plate and cook on 100% power for 3½ minutes then mix with the lemon juice.

TROUT WITH ANCHOVY SAUCE

Serves 4

A simple but very tasty sauce to accompany plainly cooked trout. The sauce can be prepared ahead then reheated until steaming when required.

4 × 8 oz (225 g) trout
½ teasp salt
speck of white pepper
1 tbsp lemon juice
For the sauce
1 can (2 oz/50 g) anchovy fillets, well drained
1½ oz (40 g/3 tbsp) butter
6 fl oz (175 ml/¾ cup) dry white wine such as Graves or Chablis
2 teasp chopped parsley
10 grinds black pepper

1   Have the fish cleaned and the heads removed. Wash the body cavities, sprinkle each lightly with the salt and pepper and 1 teasp of lemon juice. Lay side by side in a shallow serving dish, cover and cook on 100% power for 9 minutes. Leave to stand, covered, while you prepare the sauce.

2   Chop the anchovies roughly. Melt the butter in a jug or bowl on 100% power for 1 minute, then add the anchovies and cook uncovered on 50% power for 1½ minutes. Stir well so they 'melt' into the butter, then add the remaining ingredients and cook for a further 2 minutes.

3   To serve, remove the top skin from the trout and pass the sauce separately.

HALIBUT CREOLE

Serves 6

The spicy sauce keeps the fish beautifully moist and the grilled topping provides a crunchy contrast.

1 oz (25 g/2 tbsp) butter
1 small onion, finely chopped
1 clove garlic, finely chopped
1 medium green pepper, seeded and cut in ½ inch (1.25 cm) squares
1 small can (7 oz/200 g) plum tomatoes, drained and chopped (4 large tomatoes)
10 grinds black pepper
1 teasp salt
1 teasp brown sugar
pinch cayenne pepper or 1 teasp mild chilli sauce
butter for greasing the dish
4 × 6 oz (175 g) halibut steaks
For the topping
4 heaped tbsp coarse dry breadcrumbs, mixed with 1½ oz (4 g/3 tbsp) melted butter and 2 tbsp grated cheese

1   In a medium jug or bowl melt the butter on 100% power for 1 minute then add the onion, garlic and pepper and cook uncovered on 100% power for 3 minutes.

2   Add all the remaining ingredients except the halibut, stir well and cook uncovered on 100% power for a further 4 minutes until the mixture is thick and juicy.

3   Lightly butter a lidded casserole or shallow baking dish and arrange the fish steaks in it, side by side. Divide the sauce between the steaks, cover and cook on 100% power for 8 minutes or until the fish flakes easily.

4   Spread the breadcrumb topping evenly over the steaks and grill under moderate heat until the topping is crisp and golden brown.

GRATIN OF FISH À LA CRÈME

Serves 4
Do not freeze

The cream soaks into the fish and potatoes, creating a wonderful sauce as it draws out their flavours.

1½ lb (675 g) new potatoes (or equivalent in best quality canned potatoes, drained)
4 × 5 oz (150 g) fillets of lemon sole, baby halibut, rolled, or 1¼ lb (575 g) fillet of hake cut in 4
butter for greasing the dish
1 oz (25 g/2 tbsp) butter
8 fl oz (225 ml/1 cup) whipping cream
1 teasp salt
speck of white pepper
2 tbsp minced dried onion
2 rounded tbsp grated mature Cheddar cheese

1   Put the scrubbed (or, if you prefer, scraped) potatoes in a dish with 2 tbsp water, cover with a lid or pierced clingfilm and cook on 100% power for 12 minutes, or until cooked, drain and leave

until cool enough to handle, then cut in ⅜ inch (1 cm) slices.

2   Have the fish skinned, then wash lightly, salt the skinned side and fold in two (seasoned side inside).

3   Generously butter the bottom and sides of an entrée dish 1½ inches (4 cm) deep and just wide enough to hold the folded fillets side by side. Arrange the sliced potatoes evenly on the bottom, sprinkle lightly with some of the salt, then lay the fish on top, and dot with the butter.

4   Mix the cream, seasonings and onion in a 2 pint (1.25 litre/5 cup) jug, cover and cook on 100% power for 3 minutes until steaming. Pour over the fish.

5   Cover and cook on 100% power for 6 minutes, uncover and sprinkle evenly with the cheese, then cook uncovered on 100% power for a further 2 minutes.

6   Brown under a hot grill until golden.

FISHERMAN'S CASSEROLE

Serves 4
Leftovers keep 1 day under refrigeration
Do not freeze

A simple dish that brings out the natural flavour of prime fish.

1 oz (25 g/2 tbsp) butter
½ medium onion, grated
1 medium carrot, grated
1 lb (450 g) thick hake or haddock fillet, skinned and cut in 4
4 tbsp boiling water or fish stock (see page 53)
1 small bay leaf
6 black peppercorns
2 teasp cornflour
5 fl oz (150 ml/⅔ cup) single cream, evaporated milk or milk

½ teasp salt
speck white pepper
about 6 oz (175 g/1 cup) leftover cooked peas (optional)
2 teasp chopped parsley

1   In a shallow lidded casserole, or gratin dish large enough to hold the pieces of fish side by side, melt the butter on 100% power for 1 minute.

2   Add the grated onion and carrot, mix well and cook uncovered for a further 4 minutes.

3   Add the fish, turning each piece in the buttered vegetables to coat it on both sides. Add 4 tbsp boiling water, or fish stock, and tuck the bay leaf and peppercorns in a corner under a piece of fish. Cover and cook on 70–80% power for 6 minutes.

4   Put the cornflour in a small bowl and mix smoothly with 4 tbsp of the cream or milk then gradually stir in the remainder, together with the salt and pepper and any cooking liquid from the fish. Pour over the fish and cook uncovered for a further 3 minutes until bubbly.

5   Add the cooked peas (if used), cover and heat through for a further 3 minutes.

6   Sprinkle with the parsley and serve.

PARTY FISH (Fillets of Fish in a Mushroom and Sour Cream Sauce)

Serves 4–6
Leftovers keep 1 day under refrigeration
Do not freeze

A dish to prepare early and cook 'à la minute' just before serving.

6 × 4 oz (125 g) fillets of lemon sole or plaice, skinned
salt
butter for greasing the dish

white pepper

1 oz (25 g/2 tbsp) butter

8 oz (225 g/2½ cups) button mushrooms, sliced

squeeze lemon juice

pinch nutmeg

6 medium very ripe tomatoes, sliced

2 × 5 fl oz (150 ml) cartons sour cream

½ teasp salt

8 grinds black pepper

tomato ketchup

4 tbsp cheese, grated

1 can anchovies (optional)

1   Wash and lightly sprinkle the fish with 1 teasp salt and leave to drain in a colander.

2   Butter the sides and bottom of a 2 inch (5 cm) deep lidded casserole or gratin dish, large enough to hold the rolled fillets side by side.

3   Take each fillet in turn and sprinkle with a little pepper, roll up and lay side by side in the buttered dish.

4   Finely slice the mushrooms, cover and cook in a small bowl with the 1 oz butter on 100% power for 3 minutes. Stir in the lemon juice and nutmeg.

5   Arrange the tomato slices and mushroom mixture around the fish, making sure it is all packed together.

6   Mix the sour cream in a small bowl with ½ teasp salt and 8 grinds black pepper and enough tomato ketchup to turn it pale pink.

7   Pour the cream over the fish, scatter with 3 tbsp grated cheese and decorate with the anchovy fillets if used. Cover and microwave on 100% power for 5–6 minutes (depending on the thickness of the fillets).

8   Remove cover and sprinkle with the remaining cheese. Cook, uncovered, on 100% power for a further 2 minutes.

9   Grill gently until golden brown.

FILLETS OF SOLE IN THE PROVENÇALE MANNER

Serves 4

Leftovers keep 2 days under refrigeration

Do not freeze

A delicious low fat dish with a punchy flavour.

4 × 5 oz (150 g) fillets of lemon sole, each cut lengthwise in two

For the sauce

1 tbsp sunflower oil

1 tbsp minced dried onion

½ teasp garlic granules

15 fl oz (425 ml/2 cups) Passata (sieved tomatoes) or a 14 oz (400 g) can chopped tomatoes

2 teasp tomato purée

4 tbsp dry white wine (optional)

1½ teasp sugar

½ teasp salt

10 grinds black pepper

4 oz (125 g/1¼ cups) small mushrooms, thinly sliced

½ teasp herbes de Provence

For the garnish

1 tbsp chopped parsley or finely snipped basil

1   Put all the sauce ingredients into a large jug or bowl and cook on 100% power for 5 minutes until slightly thickened.

2   Arrange the rolled fillets of fish in a lidded casserole or quiche dish large enough to hold them side by side. Pour over the sauce, cover and cook on 100% power for 7 minutes.

3   Leave, covered, for 5 minutes before serving.

SALMON STEAKS
BRAISED WITH FRESH BASIL

Serves 4
Leftovers keep 1 day under refrigeration
Do not freeze

An unusual French treatment of salmon perfumed with fresh basil.

1 tbsp olive oil

1 bunch spring onion bulbs, trimmed and very
   thinly shredded

1 clove garlic, peeled and crushed

1 large branch of large-leafed basil

5 fl oz (175 ml/⅔ cup) fish stock, homemade (see
   page 53) or using a cube

4 × 6 oz (175 g) salmon steaks

2 canned Italian tomatoes, drained well on paper
   towelling then cut in small cubes

¼ teasp white pepper

½ large lemon, thinly sliced

½ teasp salt

For the garnish

several small sprigs of basil

1   In a shallow lidded casserole or gratin dish large enough to hold the steaks of fish, put the olive oil and heat uncovered on 100% power for 3 minutes.
2   Add the spring onions and garlic, cover and cook for a further 3 minutes.
3   Leave covered while you strip the leaves of basil from the stalks (which you should save), shred them coarsely, then gently pat them on both sides of each fish steak.
4   Add the fish stock to the onions in the casserole together with the basil stalks (cut in 2 or 3). Arrange the fish steaks narrow end to the centre of the dish and scatter with the tomatoes. Sprinkle them with the pepper.
5   Cover and cook for 3 minutes, then carefully turn over the fish, arrange the slices of lemon on

top, re-cover and cook for a further 3 minutes, adding an extra 30 seconds if necessary.
5   Sprinkle lightly with salt and garnish with sprigs of basil. Serve from the casserole, spooning some of the delicious juices over each fish steak.
FOR 6: Use 6 steaks, 3 tomatoes, a whole lemon. Cook the fish 5 minutes on one side and 4 minutes on the other.

SALMON KEDGEREE

Serves 4
Keeps 2 days under refrigeration
Do not freeze

A flavoursome light supper dish, studded with nuggets of juicy salmon.

1 oz (25 g/2 tbsp) butter

small bunch spring onion bulbs, finely sliced

1 pint (575 ml/2½ cups) fish stock (see page 53)
   or made with a cube

1 tbsp lemon juice

½ teasp salt

8 grinds black pepper

8 oz (225 g/1⅓ cups) long grain rice (Patna or
   Basmati) or 7 oz (200 g/1 cup plus 1 tbsp)
   packet rice and wild rice mix

8 oz (225 g) piece fresh salmon fillet, skinned and
   cut into ½ inch (1.25 cm) chunks

4 eggs, hardboiled and coarsely chopped

1 tbsp chopped parsley

1 oz (25 g/¼ cup) flaked toasted almonds

1   In a 3½–4 pint (2 litre/9 cup) lidded casserole or bowl melt the butter on 100% power for 1 minute then add the spring onion bulbs. Stir and cook, uncovered, for 3 minutes.
2   Measure the stock in a jug, then add the seasonings and lemon juice and pour into the

casserole. Add the rice, mix well and cook covered on 100% power for a further 10 minutes.

3   Stir well, add the salmon chunks, cover and cook for a further 5 minutes. Leave to stand, covered for 5 minutes.

4   Mix in the chopped egg and parsley gently with a fork, taste for seasoning, then sprinkle with the almonds and serve.

5   To reheat, sprinkle the surface with a little cold water, cover and cook on 100% power for 3–4 minutes or until steaming. Fluff up with a fork and serve as freshly cooked.

seasonings and mix to a smooth cream with 4 tbsp of the milk. Gradually stir in the remaining milk. Cover and cook on 100% power for 3 minutes, whisking once.

3   Uncover, drop in the butter and cook uncovered on 100% power for 1½ minutes. Then whisk in the cream (if used) and the cheese.

4   Drain any liquid off the fish, salt it very lightly, then mask completely with the sauce. Serve immediately, or grill for 2–3 minutes until golden and bubbly.

HADDOCK MORNAY

Serves 4–5
Do not freeze

Simple and tasty.

1½ lb (675 g) filleted haddock, cut into 4 or 5 slices
1 tbsp lemon juice
For the sauce
1 tbsp cornflour
½ teasp salt
speck of white pepper
good pinch dry mustard
good pinch nutmeg
good pinch cayenne pepper
10 fl oz (275 ml/1¼ cups) milk
1 oz (25 g/2 tbsp) butter
2 tbsp single or soured cream (optional)
3 oz (75 g/¾ cup) mature cheddar, grated

1   Arrange the pieces of fillet round the edge of a quiche dish or lidded casserole, sprinkle with the lemon juice, cover and cook on 100% power for 6 minutes. Leave to stand for 3 minutes with the lid on while you make the sauce.

2   Put the cornflour in a jug or bowl with all the

FILLETS OF SOLE IN CIDER SAUCE

Serves 4–6
Leftovers keep 2 days under refrigeration
Do not freeze

Poached fish is coated with a delicious sauce, its fruitiness reinforced by a garnish of poached apples.

4–6 × 5–6 oz (150–175 g) fillets of lemon sole, baby halibut or plaice, skinned, lightly salted and rolled
2 tbsp shallots or spring onion bulbs, chopped
8 fl oz (225 ml/1 cup) dry cider (2 tbsp reserved to mix with cornflour)
1 teasp fish seasoning salt
4 oz (125 g/1¼ cups) mushrooms, thinly sliced
1 tbsp cornflour
4 tbsp double cream
For the garnish
2 eating apples, peeled, cored and sliced into 8
squeeze of lemon juice

1   First prepare the garnish by arranging the apple slices in a shallow dish, sprinkling with the lemon juice, covering and cooking on 100% power for 3 minutes. Allow to stand until required, then drain.

2   Arrange the fillets in a shallow lidded casserole or quiche dish. Sprinkle the onion around them then cover with the cider mixed with the seasoning salt. Cover and cook on 100% power for 6–8 minutes, then lift out on to a plate using a slotted spoon.

3   Strain the cooking liquid into a jug or basin, add the mushrooms and cook uncovered on 100% power for 5 minutes to concentrate the flavour.

4   Meanwhile, wipe out the dish and return the fish to it.

5   Add the cornflour, mixed smoothly with the reserved cider, to the cooking liquid and cook on 100% power for 2 minutes until thickened and bubbly.

6   Stir in the cream, taste and re-season if necessary. Pour over the fish and garnish with the drained poached apples.

PAUPIETTES OF SOLE WITH A SAUCE DUGLÈRE

Serves 6
Keeps 2 days under refrigeration
Do not freeze

You can serve the fish, hot or cold, under or over the delicious sauce – as you prefer.

6 × 5 oz (150 g) block fillets of lemon sole, skinned and each cut lengthwise in two
pinch salt and pepper
4 fl oz (125 ml/½ cup) dry white wine
½ teasp fish seasoning salt
For the sauce
1 oz (25 g/2 tbsp) butter
white part of 4 spring onions, finely chopped
4 oz (125 g/1¼ cups) button mushrooms, finely sliced
8 oz (225 g) can chopped tomatoes or 8 fl oz (225 ml/1 cup) Passata (sieved tomatoes)
1 level tbsp tomato purée or 1 rounded tbsp tomato ketchup
1 teasp sugar
pinch dried oregano
pinch dried tarragon
10 grinds black pepper
½ teasp salt
1 tbsp finely chopped parsley

1   Lightly season each strip of sole then roll up with the seasoned side on the inside. Arrange side by side in a shallow lidded casserole, quiche or gratin dish.

2   Mix the wine and fish seasoning salt, pour over the fish, cover with a lid or pierced clingfilm and cook on 100% power for 6 minutes or until the fish flakes easily with a fork. Add extra cooking time if necessary in 30-second steps.

3   Lift out the fish and drain on crumpled kitchen paper.

4   Cook the remaining liquid uncovered on 100% power for 4 minutes until reduced by half. Set to one side.

5   To make the sauce, put the butter and spring onions in a bowl, cover and cook on 100% power for 3 minutes.

6   Add all the remaining sauce ingredients (except the parsley), then stir in the reduced stock. Cover and cook on 100% power for 5 minutes.

7   Meanwhile, wash out the fish dish and spoon the sauce over the base. Arrange the fish on top and scatter with the parsley.

8   Reheat on 80% power for 2 minutes then serve. If made earlier in the day, cover and reheat from room temperature on 80% power for 5 minutes.

SOLE LUCULLUS

Serves 4–5 as a main course, 8 as a starter
Leftovers keep 2 days under refrigeration
Do not freeze

This is one of the most delectable of fish dishes,
whether served hot or cold, as the smoked salmon
filling gives it an unexpected yet subtle flavour.
The pink and white paupiettes of sole arranged on
the pale green watercress sauce form a particularly
pretty presentation. If the fish is to be served hot,
prepare the sauce first, then reheat if necessary just
before serving.

For the filling
4 oz (125 g) mild smoked salmon (or gravlax)
2 oz (50 g) unsalted butter
5 grinds black pepper
2 teasp snipped dill
½ teasp finely grated lemon rind
4–5 block fillets of lemon sole (weight 5–6
    oz/150–175 g each), skinned then cut in half
    lengthwise
For the watercress sauce
1 bunch or 3 oz (75 g) pack of watercress, stalks
    removed
6 fl oz (175 ml/¾ cup) fish or vegetable stock (see
    page 53)
4 fl oz (125 ml/½ cup) dry white wine e.g.
    Muscadet
¼ teasp salt
pinch of white pepper
1½ tbsp cornflour
4 fl oz (125 ml/½ cup) single or whipping cream

1   Place the filling ingredients in the bowl of the
food processor and process until smooth. Spread
the skinned side of each fillet with a thin layer of
the smoked salmon butter then roll up into a
'pinwheel'. Arrange these pinwheels in a circle
around the rim of a 10 or 11 × 2 inches (25 or 27½
× 5 cm) dish, cover and cook on 100% power for 6

minutes or until the sole flakes easily with a fork.
2   To make the sauce, process the watercress and
the stock in a blender or food processor for 1
minute. Pour into a microwave-safe jug. Add the
cornflour slaked with the wine. Cover and cook at
100% power for 4 minutes, stirring halfway.
3   Uncover and stir in the cream, salt and pepper.
Reheat if necessary.
4   Serve the fish on a pool of watercress sauce.

SOLE VÉRONIQUE

Serves 6
Leftovers keep 2 days under refrigeration
Do not freeze

Rolled fillets of white fish with grapes in a creamy
wine sauce, this is a classic dish that uses a modern
technique.

2 tbsp spring onion bulbs, finely sliced
6 × 6 oz (175 g) fillets of lemon sole (or baby
    halibut), skinned, seasoned and rolled
5 fl oz (150 ml/⅔ cup) dry white wine
5 fl oz (150 ml/⅔ cup) fish stock (see page 53) or
    made with a cube
small bay leaf
6 peppercorns
For the sauce
the strained cooking liquid
½ teasp salt
pinch white pepper
1½ oz (40 g/3 tbsp) butter and 1 oz (25 g/¼ cup)
    flour creamed together on a plate (beurre
    manié)
4 tbsp double cream
8 oz (225 g/1½ cups) green grapes, pipped

1   To cook the fish, scatter the finely sliced onion
bulbs on the base of a gratin dish. Divide each fillet
in two lengthwise. Lay the rolled fish on top, cover
with the wine, fish stock and spices, and cook

covered on 100% power for 8 minutes.

2   Lift the fish out with a slotted spoon and drain on kitchen paper.

3   Strain the liquid into a basin and wash out the dish. Return the fish to the dish.

4   To make the sauce, heat the liquid, covered, in a microwave-safe jug on 100% power for 3 minutes. Uncover and whisk in the beurre manié a teasp at a time, then cook covered on 100% power for 1½ minutes.

5   Whisk in the cream, taste and re-season if necessary. Scatter the grapes over the fish, saving a few for garnish, then mask the dish with the sauce.

6   To reheat later, cook covered on 80% power for 5 minutes.

SALMON STEAKS IN SOUR CREAM SAUCE

Serves 4
Leftovers keep 1 day under refrigeration
Do not freeze

An unctuous partnership of silky salmon and delicate sauce.

| 4 × 6 oz (175 g) salmon steaks, ¾ inch (2 cm) thick |
| 1 level teasp salt |
| 2 shallots or 4 spring onion bulbs, finely chopped |
| 1 tbsp lemon juice |
| 1 bay leaf, crumbled |
| 3 fl oz (75 ml/⅓ cup) dry white wine (such as Chablis) |
| 4 fl oz (125 ml/½ cup) fish stock (see page 53) or made with a cube |
| 1 oz (25 g/2 tbsp) butter and 1 tbsp flour creamed together on a plate (beurre manié) |
| 5 fl oz (150 ml/⅔ cup) crème fraîche, soured cream or Greek-style yoghurt |
| *For the garnish* |
| chopped parsley |

1   Wash the salmon steaks, then drain well. Arrange them in a shallow lidded casserole or quiche dish wide enough to hold the fish in one layer, with the thicker part of each steak to the outside.

2   Put the shallots, lemon juice and bay leaf in a jug with the wine and fish stock, then stir well and pour over the fish. Cover with a lid or pierced clingfilm, then cook on 80% power for 8 minutes, turning each steak over half way through. Check that it is cooked right through. Add extra cooking time, if necessary, 30 seconds at a time.

3   Let the fish stand, covered, for 3 or 4 minutes, then lift out of the baking dish with a slotted spoon and strain the cooking liquid into a jug or bowl. Skin the fish (but leave on the bone) and return to the washed baking dish.

4   Cook the fish liquor, covered with a plate, at 100% power for 3 minutes, then uncover and add the beurre manié a teasp at a time, whisking all the time.

5   Re-cover and cook on 100% power for a further 1½ minutes until bubbly. Stir in the cream.

6   Taste, then pour over the steaks, masking them completely. Grill for 3 minutes until golden brown.

7   Sprinkle with parsley and serve.

GEFILTE FISH TERRINE WITH A PINK MAYONNAISE SAUCE

Serves 8–10
Keeps 3 days under refrigeration
Freeze 3 months

The refrigerated sauce keeps as long as ordinary mayonnaise but does not freeze.

This stunning new presentation of an old favourite is baked in a loaf shape decorated with vegetable 'flowers'. It is simpler to prepare than the traditional balls and easy to slice at the table with a serrated knife.

For the terrine
1 large (7 oz/200 g) onion, peeled
2 eggs
2 teasp salt
pinch of white pepper
2 teasp sugar
1 tbsp oil
2 tbsp cold water
2 oz (50 g/½ cup) medium matzo meal (or cream crackers crushed to coarse crumbs)
1 oz (25 g/¼ cup) ground almonds (optional)
1 lb (450 g) each of filleted and skinned haddock and hake, minced or chopped in the food processer
oil for greasing the dish
For the decoration
1 thin 'finger' carrot
1 green pepper
For the sauce
5 rounded tbsp mayonnaise
2 rounded tbsp tomato ketchup
3 teasp white horseradish sauce

1   Prepare the gefilte fish in the usual way by mixing the puréed onion, eggs, seasoning, oil and water (most easily done in the food processor) and then adding the matzo meal and ground almonds (if used) in a large bowl. Add the minced or processed fish and mix well with a fork until evenly blended. Set to one side.

2   Choose a loaf-shaped container made of glass or microwave-safe plastic measuring approximately 9 × 5 × 3 inches or 8 × 6 × 3 inches (22 × 12 × 7.5 cm or 20 × 15 × 7.5 cm), grease it with oil and bottom-line with a strip of silicone paper.

3   Meanwhile, peel the carrot and cut into thin rounds; cut the green pepper into a similar number of thin 'stalks'. Blanch the carrots, covered, with 3 tbsp boiling water for 3 minutes, and then blanch the strips of pepper for 30 seconds in the same way. Put both into a colander and drench with cold water to set the colour then pat dry.

4   Spoon the fish mix into the dish, levelling the surface. Cover with a piece of microwave-safe pierced clingfilm, tucking it inside the dish. Cook on 100% power for 10 minutes or until the surface feels spongy to gentle touch.

5   Chill for 1 hour then remove the cover, run a knife round the edges and carefully turn out on to a long dish or tray and lift off the strip of silicone paper. Arrange the decoration on top, pressing it lightly into the fish. Serve at room temperature.

6   To make the sauce, mix all the ingredients together and put in a decorative bowl. Leave both the sauce and the terrine for several hours for the flavours to develop and the terrine to firm up.

GEFILTE FISH

Serves 4–6 with 14 small patties or 7 larger ones
Keeps 3 days under refrigeration
Freeze raw patties 3 months

While I do not think the flavour is quite as deep as when the fish is stewed in the traditional manner, this is a marvellous way of cooking just enough fish for one meal, using your own ready frozen gefilte fish balls. Both the stock and the fish can be prepared in the microwave in 30 minutes. However, you will need to leave the dish overnight if you wish the sauce to 'jell'. The fish is still delicious even if no fish skins and bones are available for the stock.

For the stock (sufficient for two occasions)

2 lb (900 g) fish heads, skins and bones, well washed

1 medium onion, thinly sliced

2 medium carrots, sliced ¼ inch (0.5 cm) thick

2 level teasp sugar

2 level teasp salt

boiling water to cover the bones (about 1½ pints 850 ml/3¾ cups)

14 small patties, or 7 large patties, of raw gefilte fish mix (half the quantity of fish mix given for the Gefilte Fish Terrine, see page 64)

1   Put the well washed heads, skins and broken-up bones into a large bowl or lidded casserole, barely cover with boiling water, then cook, covered, on 100% power until boiling – about 10 minutes.

2   Uncover, skim the top, then add the remaining ingredients for the stock. Cover and cook on 50% power for 10 minutes. Strain. Measure ½ pint (275 ml/1¼ cups) and freeze the remainder.

3   Arrange the fish patties in a round or oval dish, positioning them in a ring, then pour over the stock with the carrots. Cover with a lid or pierced clingfilm, then cook on 100% power for 5 minutes.

4   Turn each ball over, then cook on 50% power for a further 7 minutes.

5   Leave to stand, covered, until cold, then refrigerate until required.

GEFILTE FISH RING - *VARIATION*

This makes a delicious summer dish with salad and 'chrane' (beetroot and horseradish sauce) and is particularly popular with those who like gefilte fish but not the jellied stock.

1   Instead of making fish patties, approximately 1½ lb (675 g/3 cups) fish mix can be used to fill a microwave-safe ring mould, 8 inches (20 cm) approx in diameter. There is no need to make any stock.

2   Lay a paper towel on top of the ring and cook it on 100% power for 5 minutes, then cook on 50% power for a further 8 minutes.

3   Insert a knife and if it comes out almost clean, the ring is done. Otherwise give it 2 minutes more, repeating the test until it is done.

4   Leave covered until cold.

GEFILTE FISH BALLS IN A LEMON SAUCE

Serves 4–6
Keeps 3 days under refrigeration
Do not freeze

One of the classic sauces of the Anglo-Jewish cuisine, light, refreshing and so easy and quick to prepare.

14 small or 7 larger patties of gefilte fish, made from half the quantity of Gefilte Fish Terrine mix (see page 64), based on 1 lb (450 g) filleted fish

For the poaching liquid

½ onion, thinly sliced

2 teasp sugar

1 teasp salt

speck of white pepper

10 fl oz (275 ml/1¼ cups) boiling water

For the sauce

2 teasp potato flour or cornflour
4 tbsp fresh lemon juice
2 eggs
3 tbsp sugar
8 fl oz (225 ml/1 cup) strained poaching liquid (see above)

1   Divide the fish mix into 7 or 14 pieces, and, with wetted hands, form each piece into an oval patty. Arrange the patties in a circle or oval in a shallow gratin dish, or lidded casserole.

2   Put all the ingredients for the poaching liquid into a jug or bowl and cook covered on 100% power until bubbling, about 2 minutes.

3   Pour the liquid around the patties, cover with a lid or pierced clingfilm, then cook on 100% power for 5 minutes.

4   Turn each ball over, re-cover, then cook on 50% power for a further 5 minutes. Leave to stand, covered, for 5 minutes.

5   Lift the patties from the dish, then strain 8 fl oz (225 ml/1 cup) of the poaching liquid into a jug. Freeze any remaining liquid. Return the patties to the washed dish.

6   Put the potato flour or cornflour into a bowl or jug and gradually stir in the lemon juice, then whisk in the eggs, sugar and poaching liquid until smooth (or mix for 10 seconds in a blender or food processor, then pour into a jug).

7   Cook uncovered on 50% power for 2 minutes, stir and cook for a further 2–3 minutes until thickened to the consistency of a coating custard. Pour over and round the patties, cover and chill until required.

HALIBUT IN LEMON SAUCE - *VARIATION*

Instead of the gefilte fish balls, use 1½ lb (675 g) of steaked halibut cut ¾ inch (2 cm) thick. The fish (still on the bone) is then cut into 4–6 portions. Cook the fish, covered in the same poaching liquid but on 100% power for 8 minutes, or until the fish flakes easily with a fork.

GEFILTE FISH PROVENÇALE

Serves 4–6
The cooked dish keeps 3 days under refrigeration
Do not freeze

A 10 inch (25 cm) round dish with a glass lid makes a perfect cooking and serving dish, or you can use an oval gratin dish covered with clingfilm. I like to leave the fish in the sauce for several hours to allow it to absorb the wonderful flavours. If you are using frozen raw patties, let them defrost overnight in the refrigerator, or in the microwave defrost on 30% power for 14 minutes, turning the patties over once. Leave to stand for 20 minutes.

8 fish patties (total weight approx 2 lb (900 g)

For the sauce

1 can or tube (5 oz/150 g) tomato purée (or 2 rounded tbsp)
10 fl oz (275 ml/1¼ cups) boiling water
2 teasp olive or sunflower oil
1 teasp onion salt
2 canned sweet red peppers, drained and cut in thin strips
1 tbsp tomato ketchup
1 bay leaf
10 grinds black pepper
½ teasp dried Italian herbs or herbes de Provence
1 teasp brown sugar

Gefilte Fish Terrine with a Pink Mayonnaise Sauce, Paupiettes of Sole with a Sauce Duglère

1   Whisk all the sauce ingredients together in a 2 pint (1.25 litre/5 cup) microwave-safe jug or bowl until smooth. Heat the sauce, covered, on 100% power for 3 minutes.

2   Arrange the raw patties side by side in a casserole, pour over the sauce, and cook on 100% power for 6 minutes.

3   Remove the lid, baste the fish with the sauce, then re-cover and cook on 50% power for a further 5 minutes.

4   Leave covered for 10 minutes, then remove clingfilm, if used, and refrigerate until required.

5   Leave at room temperature for 1 hour before serving.

TUNA LASAGNE

Serves 4
Leftovers keep 2 days under refrigeration
Freeze 3 months

A very tasty 'store-cupboard' dish. If it is more convenient, prepare one day and cook the next. But either allow to come to room temperature or cook on 100% power for 3 minutes extra, if straight from the refrigerator.

a nut of butter for greasing the dish
9 strips lasagne (no-cooking-required type)
For the sauce
2 tbsp cornflour
1¼ pints (725 ml/3 cups) milk
2 oz (50 g/¼ cup) butter
2 teasp minced dried onion
2 canned pimentos, well drained and cut in ½ inch (1.25 cm) squares
½ level teasp mustard
¼ teasp nutmeg
1 level teasp salt
¼ teasp white pepper
1 tbsp parsley, chopped

7 oz (200 g) can tuna, drained and roughly flaked
2 hardboiled eggs, sliced
3 tbsp single cream or top of milk
3 oz (75 g/¾ cup) grated cheese

1   Put the cornflour into a large jug or bowl and mix to a cream with 4 tbsp of the milk, then slowly stir in the remainder. Cook covered on 100% power for 4 minutes, whisk thoroughly to ensure even thickening, then cook for a further 3 minutes. Whisk again then stir in the seasonings and parsley.

2   Stir into the sauce, the tuna, eggs and cream with ⅔ of the cheese (reserve ⅓ for topping).

3   Select a casserole approximately 10 inches × 8 inches × 2 inches (25 × 20 × 5 cm) and butter it.

4   To assemble, put a thin layer of sauce on the bottom of the dish, cover with 3 strips of lasagne, then a layer of sauce. Repeat twice, finishing with the remaining sauce. Sprinkle with the rest of the cheese.

5   Cook uncovered on 100% power for 3 minutes then cook on 50% power for 10 minutes, until bubbling round the edges.

6   Brown under the grill until golden brown. Allow to stand for 5 minutes before serving.

Potatoes Baked in Cider, Chicken Breasts in a Honeyed Orange and Raisin Sauce

BEEF AND LAMB

INTRODUCTION

Lamb and minced beef are the stars of microwave meat cookery – they cook quickly and brilliantly in a dozen different dishes. Tougher cuts of meat, which demand long slow cooking to tenderize them and develop their flavours, do not fare so well. However, top quality braising beef will produce a superb casserole if it is cooked for part of the time on a lower power level – equivalent to conventional simmering – though you probably will not save more than three-quarters of an hour of total cooking time. On the other hand, all the lamb casseroles will cook to tender perfection in under half an hour. However, your microwave casserole, whether made of beef or lamb, will demand the minimum of attention and, providing the meat is cooked in a richly-coloured sauce, like all the dishes in this chapter, you will be delighted with the results.

In all these casseroles I have not used more than 1½ lb (675 g) trimmed weight of boned-out shoulder (the sweetest lamb cut) or beef braising steak (top rib is excellent). Larger quantities take too long to cook to be practicable. I have not attempted to brown the meat in the usual way – if you wish, you can do this on top of the stove beforehand – but have used deep-coloured sauces, often based on tomatoes, which produce an attractive result even from unbrowned meat. The exception to this is minced meat. Because it is so finely divided and includes a proportion of fat, it does brown extremely well and the Bolognese sauce produced in this way is quite superb. Mincemeat balls, which are pre-browned mainly to prevent their flavour leaching out into the cooking liquid, are put straight into the simmering sauce that seals them in a similar way. Minced meat also works well in a meatloaf to be served both hot or cold, and as a juicy filling for a particularly succulent dish of stuffed peppers. By using a typical barbecue-type sauce, I have also managed to produce a dish of glazed lamb chops (they look anaemic cooked in any other way), which are every bit as successful as when cooked over a far greater time-span in the oven. And for the day when you have ten minutes, half a pound of grilling steak and a few assorted vegetables, what about a stir-fry, Chinese style?

Unless you have a combination oven, you cannot truly 'roast' in the microwave but you can produce a good-looking tender joint with the help of glazes and other little tricks that also enhance the flavour. The method suggested for cooking the beef and lamb roasts in this chapter produces succulent joints, providing you use only prime meat, which in the case of beef should be well hung.

No special cooking dishes are needed for meat cookery. All the casseroles and the meatball recipes were cooked in a 3½–4 pint (2–2.25 litre/9–10 cup) lidded casserole, though I know many people use a similar sized bowl covered with clingfilm. But if you have invested in one of the very large 7 pint (4 litre/9 US pint) microwave-safe plastic lidded casserole, you will find it excellent not only for casseroles of meat and meatballs, but also for the stuffed vegetables (it gives more room for basting). The lid also makes an excellent 'roasting dish' when fitted with a trivet to keep the joint raised above the fat and juices that exude during the cooking time. ∎

ROAST BONED RIB OF BEEF WITH A THREE-PEPPER COATING

Serves 4–5
Keeps 3 days under refrigeration
Freeze 3 months

If the beef is well hung by the butcher, usually for a minimum of 14 days, microwave cooking will produce a tender joint that is as pink as you please within a crusty brown outside. The mixture of peppers give the meat a wonderful richness of flavour but, if you prefer, simply sprinkle it with freshly milled black or Sichuan pepper. Do not salt until after the meat has been cooked, as the surface will be toughened.

It is essential to lift the meat above the base of the dish to prevent it soaking up the fat as it melts. For this purpose, use either a special microwave-safe trivet or an upturned saucer sitting in a quiche-type dish.

1 × 3 lb (1.5 kg) rolled wing rib (first cut), weight when boned
For the coating
1 teasp black peppercorns
1 teasp green peppercorns
1 teasp Sichuan peppercorns
2 small sprigs of thyme (use the leaves stripped from their stalks)
1–2 tbsp olive oil
microwave beef browning and seasoning powder
For the gravy if the meat is to be served hot
3 teasp cornflour
3½ fl oz (90 ml/⅓ cup) full-bodied red wine
10 fl oz (275 ml/1¼ cups) (approximately) good hot beef stock or bouillon
1 teasp Dijon mustard
salt and pepper if necessary

1 Two hours before cooking, crush the peppercorns and thyme to a coarse powder with the end of a rolling pin (or in a mortar and pestle). Brush the meat lightly with the olive oil, then rub in the pepper mixture. Leave at room temperature for 2 hours, then sprinkle lightly with the microwave browning and seasoning powder. Arrange on the trivet or saucer in a shallow dish.

2 The meat can be cooked either by time or temperature but, in either case, it will take about 35 minutes.

3 To cook by temperature: insert the probe into the centre of the meat and cook on 80% power, according to the manufacturer's instructions.

4 To cook by time: allow 11 minutes to the pound (450 g) (medium rare) or 13 minutes to the pound (450 g) (well done). It is important to turn the meat over half way through. A joint of this weight needs 16½ minutes each side.

5 When the cooking time is up, drain off any juices that have collected in the dish and use in making the gravy. Leave the meat to rest for 10–15 minutes, loosely covered with foil.

6 Put the cornflour in a jug and slowly stir in the wine. Add the meat juices made up to 10 fl oz (275 ml/1¼ cups) with the hot beef stock and mustard. Cook on 100% power for 5 minutes, stirring once, until shiny and slightly thickened.

ROAST SHOULDER OF LAMB DIJONNAISE

Serves 6–8
Leftovers keep 3 days under refrigeration
Freeze 3 months

The savoury mustard coating not only gives the roast a rich brown colour but also keeps it juicy without basting.

| 1 × 3 lb (1.25 kg) boned shoulder of lamb |
| 1 tbsp olive oil |
| ½ teasp salt |
| 10 grinds black pepper |
| *For the coating* |
| 4 level tbsp Dijon mustard |
| 1 clove garlic, peeled and crushed |
| ½ teasp dried herbes de Provence |
| ½ teasp dried herb seasoning for lamb (if available) |
| 2 teasp grated fresh ginger |
| 2 teasp olive oil |
| *For the gravy* |
| 2 teasp cornflour |
| 2 tbsp white vermouth or cold water |
| 8 fl oz (225 ml/1 cup) hot lamb or beef stock (including juices from the lamb) |
| ½ teasp finely chopped rosemary sprigs |
| salt and black pepper, if necessary |

1   Two hours before you intend to start roasting the meat (or at any time up to 12 hours in advance) lay the meat, skin side down, on a board, cut out any lumps of fat, cover with greaseproof or silicone paper and pound with a mallet or rolling pin until the meat is of a fairly even thickness.
2   Brush the meat evenly with the olive oil and sprinkle with the salt and pepper, then roll up, securing with string in two or three places.
3   Put all the coating ingredients, except the oil, into a small bowl and stir to blend, then gradually beat in the oil. Paint this mixture all over the lamb with a pastry brush, making sure the underside is coated as well. Arrange on a rack in a roasting dish or on two upturned saucers arranged side by side in a shallow casserole.
4   Cook on 80% power for 30 minutes, turning the meat over carefully half way. Leave to stand, lightly covered with foil, for 15–20 minutes.
5   To make the gravy, put the cornflour in a jug and mix to a liquid with the vermouth or cold water, then stir in the hot stock. Cook on 100% power for 4 minutes, stirring once. Add the rosemary sprigs and seasoning, if required.

ROAST SHOULDER OF LAMB WITH A PIQUANT ORANGE GLAZE

Serves 6–8
Leftovers keep 3 days under refrigeration
Freeze 3 months

Another method of producing a rich brown roast. The fruity sauce and glaze contrasts well with the 'sweetness' of the lamb shoulder meat.

| 1 × 3 lb (1.25 kg) boned shoulder of lamb, unrolled |
| ½ teasp salt |
| 10 grinds black pepper |
| 1 tbsp olive oil |
| 1 teasp finely grated orange rind |
| 1 teasp finely grated lemon rind |
| *For the glaze* |
| 2 oz (50 g/¼ cup) soft brown sugar |
| 2 tbsp lemon juice |
| 3 tbsp orange juice |
| 1 tbsp Worcestershire sauce |
| *For the gravy* |
| 2 teasp cornflour |
| 1 tbsp orange juice |
| juices from the lamb made up to 8 fl oz (225 ml/1 cup) with hot stock |

1   Lay the meat, skin side down, on a board, cut out any lumps of fat, cover with greaseproof paper and pound with a cutlet bat or a rolling pin to equalize the thickness. Season with the salt and pepper, brush with the olive oil, then scatter with the grated rinds. Roll up, securing with string in 2 or 3 places.

2   Mix all the ingredients for the glaze in a jug and cook uncovered on 100% power for 3 minutes.

3   Arrange the meat on a rack in a roasting dish or in a shallow casserole on two upturned saucers.

4   Cook on 80% power for 15 minutes, turn, and spread with the glaze, and cook for a further 15 minutes.

5   Remove from the oven, cover loosely with foil and leave to rest for 10–15 minutes before carving.

6   For the gravy, in a jug mix the cornflour to a smooth cream with the orange juice. Stir in the juices from the lamb, then cook uncovered on 100% power for 3 minutes, stirring halfway, until bubbly.

ROAST SHOULDER OF LAMB WITH A MINTED FILLING AND GLAZE

Serves 6–8
Leftovers keep 3 days under refrigeration
Freeze 3 months

This is particularly delicious when served cold in thin slices for the cooling time allows the herb flavour to permeate the meat.

1 × 3 lb (1.25 kg) boned shoulder of lamb, unrolled
1 teasp salt
20 grinds black pepper
1 teasp Microwave Browner

For the filling
4 tbsp finely snipped chives
2 tbsp chopped fresh mint or 2 teasp dried
1 tbsp olive oil
½ teasp grated lemon rind
½ teasp salt
10 grinds black pepper
For the glaze
2 tbsp mint jelly

1   Mix together all the ingredients for the stuffing in a bowl.

2   Lay the meat, skin side down, on a board, cut out any lumps of fat, cover with silicone or greaseproof paper and pound until it is of a fairly even thickness.

3   Sprinkle the meat with the salt and pepper, then spread evenly with the filling and roll up, securing with string in 2 or 3 places.

4   Sprinkle with the Microwave Browner, arrange on a rack in a roasting dish or in a shallow casserole on two upturned saucers. Cover lightly with paper towels and cook on 80% power for 15 minutes.

5   Turn over carefully, discard the paper towels and cook for a further 5 minutes, then spread with the jelly and cook for a further 10 minutes. Leave to stand for 30 minutes.

BEEF IN BEER

Serves 4–5
Keeps 3 days under refrigeration
Freeze 3 months

The classic Belgian recipe, full of hearty flavour.

2 tbsp sunflower oil
1 large (8 oz/225 g) onion, peeled and very thinly sliced
2 sticks of celery, cut in ½ inch (1.25 cm) lengths

1½ lb (675 g) (weight after trimming) first cut
   braising steak, cut in ¾ inch (2 cm) cubes

1 teasp salt

15 grinds black pepper

1 level tbsp tomato purée

1 teasp brown sugar

1 can (15 fl oz/425 ml/2 cups) brown ale (reserve
   2 tbsp)

1 tbsp soy sauce

1 clove garlic, crushed

2 bay leaves

3 teasp cornflour, dissolved in 2 tbsp ale

1   In a 6–7 pint (3.5–4 litre/8 US pints) deep lidded casserole or bowl heat the oil uncovered on 100% power for 3 minutes, then add the vegetables, stir well and cook uncovered for a further 4 minutes.

2   Stir in the meat seasoned with the salt and pepper, add all the remaining ingredients, except for the cornflour liquid, cover and bring to the boil on 100% power – about 8 minutes.

3   Turn down to 50% power and cook covered for 30 minutes, reduce to 30% power and cook a further 45 minutes until the beef is just tender.

4   Stir in the cornflour liquid and cook uncovered on 100% power for 3 minutes until thickened.

5   Stir well and serve at once, or cover and leave to mature for several hours or overnight.

6   Reheat covered on 100% power for 10 minutes or until bubbly.

BRAZILIAN BEEF

Serves 4–5
Keeps 3 days under refrigeration
Freeze 3 months

A satisfying casserole to come home to, so try and make it one day to serve the next. It will also give the different spices time to mellow.

2 tbsp olive oil

1 medium (5 oz/150 g) onion, finely chopped

1 green pepper, seeded and cut in 1 inch (2.5 cm)
   strips

4 oz (125 g/1¼ cups) mushrooms, thickly sliced

1 can (5 oz/150 g/⅔ cup) tomato purée diluted
   with 2 cans (10 fl oz/275 ml/1¼ cups) water

2 tbsp tomato ketchup

2 bay leaves

1 teasp garlic granules

1–2 teasp sweet chilli sauce

2 teasp paprika

1 teasp medium curry powder or paste

2 teasp Worcestershire sauce

1 teasp salt

10 grinds black pepper

2 teasp cornflour mixed to a cream with 2 tbsp
   cold water

2 lb (900 g) braising steak (1½ lb/675 g trimmed
   weight), cut into cubes

1 can (15 oz/425 g) red kidney beans

For the garnish

1 tbsp chopped parsley

1   In a 4–6 pint (2.5–3.5 litre/10–15 cup) deep lidded casserole or bowl, heat the oil uncovered on 100% power for 3 minutes, then add the onion and mushrooms, stir well and cook uncovered for a further 4 minutes, stirring well.

2   Meanwhile, in a jug mix together all the remaining ingredients, except for the meat and red kidney beans. Then add to the vegetables, stirring well. Add the meat, stir again, then cover and cook on 100% power for 10 minutes until bubbling, reduce to 50% power and simmer for 30 minutes, then reduce to 30% power and simmer for a further 45 minutes until the meat is tender. Stir well.

3   Add the drained beans (if to be served now), cover and cook for a further 5 minutes at 50% power.

4   Stand for 5 minutes then serve, or cover and leave in the refrigerator to mature for several

hours or overnight.

5   To reheat, stir in the drained beans and reheat covered on 100% power for 10 minutes until bubbling.

6   To garnish, sprinkle with the chopped parsley.

SOUTHERN BEEF CASSEROLE

Serves 4–5
Keeps 3 days under refrigeration
Freeze 3 months

The flavour of this colourful casserole is so good, even when freshly made, that it is hard to believe it has not simmered for hours in a conventional oven.

2 tbsp sunflower oil

1 large onion (8 oz/225 g), finely chopped

1 each medium red and yellow peppers, seeds removed and cut into ½ inch (1.25 cm) squares

1 × 15 oz (425 g) can chopped tomatoes

5 fl oz (150 ml/⅔ cup) hot beef stock or fruity red wine

1 teasp minced garlic

1 level teasp dried basil

1 bay leaf

1 teasp salt

15 grinds black pepper

1½ teasp brown sugar

1½ lb (675 g) braising steak (weight after trimming), cut in 1 inch (2.5 cm) cubes

3 teasp cornflour, dissolved in 2 tbsp water

1   In a 6–7 pint (3.5–4 litre/8 US pints) deep lidded casserole or bowl heat the oil, uncovered, on 100% power for 3 minutes, then add the onion, stir well and cook uncovered for a further 4 minutes, stirring once.

2   Stir in all the remaining ingredients, except the meat and the cornflour liquid, then add the meat cubes, stir thoroughly, then cover and bring to the

boil on 100% power – about 8 minutes. Turn down to 50% power and cook covered for 30 minutes, then reduce to 30% power and cook a further 45 minutes, until the meat is just tender.

3   Stir in the cornflour liquid and cook uncovered on 100% power for 3 minutes until thickened.

4   Stir well and serve at once, or cover and leave to mature for several hours or overnight.

5   Reheat covered on 100% power for 10 minutes or until bubbly.

PINEAPPLE BEEF CASSEROLE

Serves 4
Keeps 3 days under refrigeration
Leftovers freeze 3 months

The casserole is delicious served with Savoury Rice (see page 123). Cook the casserole first then leave it standing while the rice is in the oven. A brief reheating (3–4 minutes) will then bring it back to bubbling point again.

2 tbsp sunflower oil

1 medium (5 oz/150 g) onion, finely chopped

2 stalks celery, finely sliced

1½ lb (675 g) (trimmed weight) best braising steak, cut in 1 inch (2.5 cm) cubes

1 medium (15 oz/430 g) can pineapple pieces, drained, juice reserved

5 fl oz (150 ml/⅔ cup) hot beef stock

1 teasp salt

10 grinds black pepper

1½ tbsp cornflour

1 tbsp rich soy sauce

1 tbsp tomato ketchup

3 teasp brown sugar

2 tbsp red wine vinegar

1   In a 4–6 pint (2.25–3.5 litre/10–15 cup) deep lidded casserole or bowl heat the oil uncovered on

100% power for 3 minutes, then add the vegetables, stir well and cook uncovered for a further 4 minutes.

2   Stir in the meat then add the stock, the pineapple juice made up to 10 fl oz (275 ml/1¼ cups) with hot water, and the salt and pepper, cover and bring to the boil on 100% power – about 10 minutes. Reduce to 50% power and cook, covered, for 30 minutes, then reduce to 30% and cook for a further 45 minutes until the beef is just tender.

3   Meanwhile, in a small bowl mix together all the remaining ingredients, including the pineapple. Add to the casserole and cook on 100% power for a further 3 minutes, then stir well.

4   Leave to stand five minutes before serving, or cover and leave to mature in the refrigerator for several hours or overnight.

5   Reheat covered on 100% power for 10 minutes or until bubbly, stirring once.

BEEF SPANISH STYLE WITH ORANGE JUICE AND RED WINE

Serves 4–5
Keeps 3 days under refrigeration
Freeze 3 months

There is a strong Moorish influence in the flavourings of this superb casserole that combines the spices of Arabic cooking with the fruit and wine of southern Spain.

2 tbsp oil
1 medium (5 oz/150 g) onion, finely chopped
1 fat clove garlic, finely chopped
5 fl oz (150 ml/⅔ cup) orange juice (from 2 small oranges)
5 fl oz (150 ml/⅔ cup) fruity red wine plus 5 fl oz (150 ml/⅔ cup) hot beef stock or 10 fl oz (275 ml/1¼ cups) beef stock
3 strips orange peel
2 strips lemon peel
1 cinnamon stick
1 small bay leaf
3 cloves (optional)
1 teasp salt
10 grinds black pepper
2 lb (900 g) best braising steak (weight after trimming), cut in 1 inch (2.5 cm) chunks
3 oz (75 g/¾ cup) large black or green olives, cut away from the stone in large pieces
3 teasp cornflour mixed to a cream with 2 tbsp cold water

1   In a deep lidded 4–6 pint (2.25–3.5 litre/5–7½ US pints) casserole or bowl, heat the oil uncovered on 100% power for 3 minutes, then add the onion, stir well and cook uncovered for a further 4 minutes.

2   Stir in all the ingredients, except the meat, cornflour liquid and olives, then add the meat, stir well, cover and cook on 100% power for 10 minutes or until bubbling. Reduce to 50% power and cook covered for 30 minutes, then reduce to 30% power and cook for a further 45 minutes or until the beef is just tender.

3   Uncover and stir in the olives and the cornflour liquid. Cook on 100% power for a further 3 minutes.

4   Leave to stand for 5 minutes before serving, or cover and leave to mature in the refrigerator for several hours or overnight.

5   Reheat, covered, on 100% power for 10 minutes.

LAMB IN THE PROVENÇALE MANNER

Serves 4
Keeps 3 days under refrigeration
Freeze 2 months

A simple country casserole scented with Mediterranean herbs.

1½ lb (675 g) (trimmed weight) boneless
  shoulder of lamb, cubed

2 tbsp olive oil

Peeled and then finely chopped in the food
  processor

  1 medium onion

  1 large carrot

  1 clove garlic

2 teasp brown sugar

10 fl oz (275 ml/1¼ cups) hot chicken stock plus
  5 fl oz (150 ml/⅔ cup) dry white wine or 15 fl
  oz (425 ml/2 cups) chicken stock

1 scant tbsp tomato purée

1 teasp dried herbes de Provence

¼ teasp ground nutmeg

1 teasp salt

10 grinds black pepper

4 oz (125 g/1¼ cups) button mushrooms, stalks
  trimmed level with the caps

1 tbsp chopped parsley

1   In a 3½–4 pint (2–2.25 litre/9–10 cup) deep lidded casserole or bowl heat the oil, uncovered, on 100% power for 3 minutes, add the chopped vegetables and the brown sugar, stir well and cook uncovered for 5 minutes.

2   Mix the chicken stock and wine (if used) with all the seasonings, then add to the vegetables together with the lamb. Stir well, cover and cook on 100% power for 7 minutes or until bubbling, then cook on 30% power for a further 12 minutes.

3   Uncover, add the mushrooms and cook uncovered on 80% power for a further 8 minutes.

4   Stir in the chopped parsley, cover and leave for 5 minutes, then serve, or leave in the refrigerator to mature for several hours or overnight.

5   Reheat, covered, on 100% power for 8 minutes or until bubbly.

MOROCCAN LAMB AND PRUNE TAGINE

Serves 4
Keeps 3 days under refrigeration
Freeze 2 months

A delightful blend of flavours and textures. This goes well over Savoury Rice (see page 123).

2 tbsp sunflower oil

1 large (8 oz/225 g) onion, peeled and finely
  chopped

1 slightly rounded tbsp honey

15 fl oz (425 ml/2 cups) boiling water

1 teasp salt

10 grinds black pepper

scant teasp cinnamon

½ teasp ground coriander

good pinch of ground ginger

1½ lb (675 g) (trimmed weight) boneless
  shoulder of lamb, cubed

8 oz (225 g/1½ cups) stoned tenderized prunes

For the garnish

2 oz (50 g/½ cup) split whole blanched almonds

1   To prepare the garnish, toast the blanched almonds on 100% power for 4 minutes (or until golden brown), stirring once, then reserve.

2   In a 3½–4 pint (2–2.25 litre/9–10 cup) deep lidded casserole or bowl, heat the oil, uncovered, on 100% power for 3 minutes, then add the onions and the honey, stir well and cook uncovered for a further 4 minutes, stirring once.

3   Add the boiling water and the seasonings, stir well, then add the meat, mixing thoroughly with the liquid. Cover and cook on 100% power for 10 minutes or until bubbling, stir again and cook on 30% power for a further 12 minutes or until the lamb is tender.

4   Add the prunes, stir well and cook uncovered for a further 5 minutes.

5   Cover and allow to stand for 5 minutes before serving, or cover and leave in the refrigerator to mature for several hours or overnight.

6   Reheat, covered, on 100% power for 8 minutes or until bubbling. Sprinkle with the toasted almonds.

NAVARIN AU COINTREAU

Serves 4–5
Keeps 3 days under refrigeration
Freeze 2 months

The meat from a boned shoulder of lamb – considered by connoisseurs to have the finest flavour – is cooked in a very refreshing orange and liqueur sauce. For a simpler version, substitute extra chicken stock for the wine, and orange juice for the liqueur.

1 teasp salt
10 grinds black pepper
1 tbsp sunflower oil
1½ lb (675 g) (trimmed weight) boneless shoulder of lamb, cut in 1 inch (2.5 cm) chunks
1½ tbsp dried minced onion
1 teasp dark brown sugar
10 fl oz (275 ml/1¼ cups) hot chicken stock plus 5 fl oz (150 ml/⅔ cup) medium dry white wine or 12 fl oz (350 ml/1½ cups) hot chicken stock
1 level teasp salt
2 large navel oranges, peeled, pith removed and flesh sectioned (reserve 8 sections)
3 teasp cornflour, smoothly mixed with
3 tbsp Cointreau or orange juice
For the garnish
1 tbsp chopped parsley
8 reserved sections of orange (see above)

1   In a 3½–4 pint (2–2.25 litre/9–10 cup) deep lidded casserole or bowl, heat the wine and stock or the stock on 100% power for 3 minutes or until reduced by half – this concentrates the flavour.

2   Add all the remaining ingredients, except the cornflour liquid, stir well, cover and cook on 100% power for 8 minutes or until bubbling.

3   Stir well, re-cover and simmer on 30% power for a further 12 minutes or until the lamb is tender.

4   Stir in the cornflour liquid and cook uncovered on 100% power for 3 minutes or until the sauce has thickened.

5   Cover and leave to stand for 5 minutes, then serve or leave in the refrigerator to mature for several hours or overnight.

6   Reheat on 100% power in a covered serving dish for 8 minutes or until bubbly, stirring once. Garnish with the reserved orange sections and parsley.

LAMB ROGAN GHOSH

Serves 4–5
Keeps 3 days under refrigeration
Freeze 2 months

A delicious curry by anyone's standards, with a good balance between sweet and hot seasonings.

1 oz (25 g/⅓ cup) desiccated coconut
boiling water to cover the coconut
1 tbsp oil
2 tbsp dried minced onion
2 tbsp Madras (medium hot) curry paste

2 tbsp tomato purée

10 fl oz (275 ml/1¼ cup) hot chicken stock

1 large cooking apple, peeled, cored and chopped

2 tbsp peach chutney

2 oz (50 g/½ cup) sultanas

1½ lb (675 g) (trimmed weight) boneless
   shoulder of lamb, cubed

3 teasp cornflour dissolved in 1 tbsp cold water

1   Put the coconut in a medium bowl. Cover with boiling water and heat on 100% power for 1 minute. Allow to stand for 5 minutes, then drain and reserve.

2   In a 3½–4 pint (2–2.25 litre/9–10 cup) deep lidded casserole or microwave-safe bowl put all the ingredients, except for the lamb and cornflour liquid, and mix well. Stir in the lamb, then cover and cook on 100% power for 8 minutes or until bubbly.

3   Stir well, re-cover and simmer on 30% power for 12 minutes or until the lamb is tender.

4   Stir in the cornflour liquid and cook uncovered for 3 minutes or until bubbling.

5   Cover and leave to stand for 5 minutes, then serve or leave covered in the refrigerator to mature for several hours or overnight.

6   Reheat on 100% power in a covered serving dish for 8 minutes or until bubbly, stirring once.

CANTONESE BEEF AND GREEN PEPPERS IN BLACK BEAN SAUCE

Serves 2 as a main course,
4 with another main dish
Do not freeze

Yes, a stir-fry prepared with great success (and the minimum of oil) in the microwave.

8–10 oz (225–275 g) grilling steak

1 tbsp rich soy sauce

1 tbsp Shao Hsing rice wine or dry sherry

½ teasp sugar

1 teasp cornflour mixed with a little water

1 large or 2 small green peppers, cored and seeded

1 large or 2 small onions

2 tbsp vegetable oil

2 spring onions, cut into short lengths

1 slice ginger root, peeled and chopped

1 green or red, hot chilli pepper seeded and thinly
   sliced (optional)

2 tbsp crushed black bean sauce

1   Cut the beef into thin squares about the size of large postage stamps. Mix the meat with the soy sauce, wine and sugar, add the cornflour paste and marinate for 25–30 minutes.

2   Cut the green peppers and the peeled onions into pieces the same size as the beef.

3   Heat the oil with the spring onions, ginger and chilli in a wide shallow casserole on 100% power for 3 minutes. Add the green pepper, onions and the black bean sauce, mix well and cook on 100% power for 1–2 minutes, stirring once.

4   Add the beef, mix well and continue cooking on 100% power for 2–3 minutes, stirring once or twice, until it has lost its redness.

5   Serve immediately.

LAMB CUTLETS
IN A HONEY GLAZE

Serves 4
Best eaten the same day

The sauce coats the chops with a glistening golden brown sheen. Garnish with orange segments and serve with any remaining glaze spooned over the chops or in a pool at the side.

6–8 first cut lamb cutlets, trimmed of all fat
salt
black pepper
1 egg, beaten
dry breadcrumbs
For the sauce
4 tbsp clear honey
4 tbsp medium brown sugar
3 tbsp concentrated orange juice
2 tbsp red wine vinegar
2 tbsp rich soy sauce
1 tbsp tomato ketchup
1 teasp Dijon mustard
For the garnish
1 orange, peeled, pith removed and segmented
with a serrated knife

1   Season the meat with salt and pepper then dip first in egg and then in fine dry breadcrumbs. Arrange in a casserole large enough to hold the chops in one layer with the eye of each chop to the outside.
2   Cook uncovered on 100% power for 5 minutes. Set aside.
3   Meanwhile, put all the sauce ingredients into a jug or bowl and stir well then cook uncovered on 100% power for 2 minutes or until bubbling. Stir again then pour over the chops.
4   Cook uncovered on 100% power for 6 minutes then turn the chops over and cook for a further 6 minutes, basting once.

5   Serve from the dish, garnished with the orange segments.

SAVOURY MEAT LOAF
WITH PIZZAIOLA SAUCE

Serves 4, twice
Keeps 2 days under refrigeration
Freeze 4 months

A wonderful 'all-purpose' dish – delicious served hot with baked or mashed potatoes but equally good when cold with chips, latkes or salad.

1 medium (5 oz/150 g) onion, peeled and cut in
1 inch (2.5 cm) chunks
2 large slices of brown bread or 2 oz (50 g/1 cup)
fresh breadcrumbs
2 eggs
2 teasp dry mustard
2 teasp tomato ketchup
1 tbsp dark soy sauce
1½ teasp salt
20 grinds black pepper
large sprig parsley
2 tbsp medium matzo meal or porridge oats
2 lb (1 kg) fresh minced beef
For the sauce
1 can (14 oz/400 g) chopped tomatoes
1 tbsp tomato purée
1 tbsp olive oil
1 level teasp salt
1 level teasp sugar
1 level teasp mixed Italian herbs
10 grinds black pepper
1 clove garlic, crushed

1   In a blender or food processor, purée all the ingredients except the matzo meal (or porridge oats) and the meat. Put in a bowl, stir in the meal (or oats), then add the minced meat and mix

thoroughly with a large fork.

2 Turn the mixture into a 2 lb (900 g) loaf tin, 9 × 5 × 3 inches (22.5× 12.5 × 7.5 cm), packing it down well. Then, turn out immediately into a shallow microwave-safe rectangular dish (do not use plastic).

3 Cook uncovered on 100% power for 12 minutes. Remove from the oven. Allow to stand for 10 minutes.

4 To make the pizzaiola sauce while the meat is standing, put all the ingredients into a jug and cook uncovered on 100% power for 6 minutes. Stir well.

5 Serve in slices with the hot sauce.

RAGU BOLOGNESE

Serves 4 with 1 lb (450 g/4 cups) pasta
Keeps 4 days under refrigeration
Freeze 3 months
Reheats well. Total cooking time 45 minutes

You *can* make a reasonable facsimile of a Bolognese sauce in a shorter time but I find the extra simmering vastly improves the flavour.

1 onion
1 carrot
2 stalks celery
1 medium green pepper, deseeded
2 cloves garlic, peeled
1 tbsp olive oil
1 lb (450 g) lean minced beef
10 fl oz (275 ml/1¼ cups) chicken stock or 5 fl oz (150 ml/⅔ cup) each full-bodied red wine and chicken stock
1 × 15 oz can (425 g) chopped tomatoes
2 level tbsp tomato purée
1 bay leaf
1 teasp dried Italian herbs
1 teasp brown sugar
1 teasp salt
15 grinds black pepper

1 Cut the peeled vegetables into roughly 1 inch (2.5 cm) pieces and chop very finely with the garlic in the food processor.

2 In a 4 pint (2.25 litre/10 cup) deep lidded casserole or bowl, heat the oil covered on 100% power for 3 minutes.

3 Add the vegetables and the raw meat, stir well with a fork to break down any lumps, then cook uncovered for 10 minutes, stirring once – the meat will be brown.

4 Meanwhile, mix the remaining ingredients together in a jug or bowl, then add to the meat mixture, stir and cook uncovered on 100% power for 18 minutes. Stir again, then cook uncovered on 50% power for a further 15 minutes, stirring once.

5 Stir well and serve with pasta boiled on top of the stove.

MEXICAN RICE - *VARIATION*

Very tasty, very simple. Good for a light supper after the cinema. It reheats well.

1 recipe Ragu Bolognese
½ recipe Savoury Rice (see page 123) or 3 cups (approx) cooked rice

1 Make exactly as for the ragu but substitute 1 teasp mild chilli powder for the dried Italian herbs.

2 When the ragu is ready, add the rice, stir well with a fork, cover and cook on 50% power for 5–7 minutes until thick and juicy.

3 To reheat, cover and cook on 100% power for 8 minutes or until bubbling.

MEATBALLS IN BARBECUE SAUCE

Serves 4–5
Keeps 4 days under refrigeration
Freeze 3 months

This is a splendid undemanding dish for a casual meal. Serve with Traditional Mashed Potatoes (see page 119)

For the meatballs

⅓ of an 8 oz (225 g) onion, peeled (reserve remainder for sauce)

1 egg

2 medium slices white or brown bread (2 oz/50 g)

½ teasp salt

10 grinds black pepper

1 teasp rich soy sauce

1 lb (450 g) minced beef

For the barbecue sauce

5 oz (150 g) onion (reserved from meatballs) cut in roughly 1 inch (2.5 cm) chunks

1 tbsp sunflower oil

1 tbsp soft dark brown sugar

1 level teasp salt

10 grinds black pepper

1 teasp Dijon mustard

2 teasp soy sauce

1 tbsp lemon juice

5 oz (150 g/⅔ cup) can tomato purée diluted with 2 cans (10 fl oz/275 ml/1¼ cups) hot water

1 To make the meat balls, purée all the ingredients, except the meat, in the food processor. Pour into a bowl, add the meat, then mix with a fork until the mixture is evenly blended. Allow to stand while the sauce is prepared.

2 In the food processor, chop the remaining onion using a pulse action until finely chopped but not watery.

3 Put the onion in a 3½ pint (2 litre/9 cup) deep lidded casserole or bowl and sprinkle with the oil and sugar. Stir well then cover and cook on 100% power for 5 minutes, stirring once.

4 Meanwhile, in a jug or bowl put all the remaining sauce ingredients and whisk to blend. Add to the onion mixture, stir well, then cook uncovered for 4 minutes until bubbling.

5 Form the minced meat mixture into balls about 1½ inches (4 cm) in diameter. Add to the bubbling sauce, cover and simmer on 50% power for 6 minutes.

6 Leave covered for 5 minutes then serve, or reheat later (covered) on 100% power for 8 minutes or until bubbling.

TURKISH MEATBALLS-*VARIATION*

Serves 4–5
Keeps 4 days under refrigeration
Freeze 3 months

A less spicy casserole. Make in exactly the same way as the Meatballs in Barbecue Sauce, but with this sauce:

5 oz (150 g) onion (reserved from meatballs) cut in roughly 1 inch (2.5 cm) chunks

1 tbsp sunflower oil

1 tbsp soft dark brown sugar

5 oz (150 g/⅔ cup) can tomato purée diluted with 2 cans (10 fl oz/275 ml/1¼ cups) hot water

1 teasp salt

10 grinds black pepper

For the garnish

1 oz (25 g/¼ cup) toasted pine kernels (see page 182)

Scatter the pine kernels on top just before serving.

MEXICAN MEATBALLS

Serves 4–5
Will keep 4 days under refrigeration
Freeze 3 months

Because the meatballs do not need to be fried in the conventional way, the microwave method of cooking this superb dish uses only a tablespoon of oil. The sealing of the meatballs' surface is achieved instead by putting them straight into the simmering sauce.

For the meatballs

⅓ of an 8 oz (225 g) onion, peeled (reserve the remainder for the sauce)

2 oz (50 g/2 medium slices) white or brown bread

1 egg

½ teasp salt

10 grinds black pepper

1 teasp rich soy sauce

1 lb (450 g) raw minced beef

1 × 14 oz (400 g) can red kidney beans, drained

For the chilli sauce

5 oz (150 g) onion (reserved from meatballs) cut in roughly 1 inch (2.5 cm) chunks

1 fat clove garlic, peeled and roughly chopped

1 tbsp oil

2 teasp brown sugar

1 × 14 oz (400 g) can chopped tomatoes

2 rounded tbsp tomato purée

5 fl oz (150 ml/⅔ cup) boiling water

1–2 teasp mild chilli sauce

½ teasp each ground cumin and coriander

½ teasp salt

10 grinds black pepper

1 bay leaf

1½ teasp paprika

1   To make the meatballs, purée all the ingredients, except the meat, in the food processor. Pour into a bowl, add the meat, then mix with a fork until the mixture is evenly blended. Allow to stand while the sauce is prepared.

2   In the food processor, chop the onion and garlic using a pulse action until finely chopped but not watery.

3   Put into a 3 inch (7.5 cm) deep lidded casserole approx 7½ inches (19 cm) in diameter (3½–4 pints/2–2.25 litres/9–10 cups) and sprinkle with the oil and sugar. Stir well, then cover and cook on 100% power for 5 minutes, stirring once.

4   Meanwhile, in a jug or bowl put all the remaining sauce ingredients and whisk to blend. Add to the onion mixture, stir well then cook uncovered for 4 minutes until bubbling.

5   Form the minced meat mixture into balls about 1½ inches (4 cm) in diameter. Add to the bubbling sauce, cover and simmer on 50% power for 6 minutes.

6   Take out of the oven and leave covered while you drain the beans. Put in a small casserole, cover and cook on 100% power for 3 minutes.

7   Serve the meatballs and sauce over the hot beans.

STUFFED PEPPERS, HUNGARIAN STYLE

Serves 4
Keeps 3 days under refrigeration
Freeze 2 months

Hungarians rarely use the rather acid green peppers – they prefer the sweeter red ones – and I am now converted to their idea. As the peppers cook, they absorb some of the sauce, which makes for a very succulent dish. Choose a dish – about 9–10 inches (22.5–25 cm) in diameter and 3½ inches (8 cm) deep – in which they can stand or lean against the sides without crowding, so that you can baste them with the sauce.

4 squat medium to large red peppers, about 1½ lb (675 g) total weight
For the sauce
2 teasp dried minced onion
1 tbsp sunflower oil
5 oz can (150 ml/2 rounded tbsp) tomato purée
10 fl oz (275 ml/1¼ cups) hot water
2 tbsp demerara sugar
1½ tbsp lemon juice
½ teasp cinnamon or mixed spice
1 teasp salt
For the stuffing
1 lb (450 g) lean minced beef
1 egg, beaten
2 level tbsp medium matzo meal or porridge oats
1 level teasp salt
10 grinds black pepper
1 teasp paprika pepper
2 teasp minced dried onion

1   Mix all the stuffing ingredients together in a bowl.
2   Slice the tops off the peppers, remove the seeds and ribs and stuff loosely with the stuffing mixture. Any leftover stuffing can be formed into 1 inch (2.5 cm) balls and arranged in the dish. Replace the tops as lids, arrange the peppers in a 5 pint (3 litre/ 12½ cup) deep lidded casserole large enough to hold them side by side.
3   Mix all the sauce ingredients in a jug and cook uncovered on 100% power for 5 minutes or until bubbling.
4   Pour the sauce around the peppers, cover and cook on 100% power for 10 minutes or until bubbling, then reduce to 80% power and cook for a further 15 minutes until the peppers feel tender when pierced with a slim pointed knife.
5   Take out of the oven and stand for 5 minutes before serving.
6   To reheat, cook covered on 100% power for 6–8 minutes or until the sauce is bubbly.

POULTRY

INTRODUCTION

You can poach it, casserole it, stir fry it and glaze it but unless you have a combination oven you cannot roast a chicken to an acceptable standard of brownness in the microwave. However, this is more than made up for by the other glorious dishes that can be cooked in ten short minutes. Brazil, Spain, France, China, Morocco, even Turkey, all include in their cuisines superb recipes that I have converted for the microwave. You may find others that you can adapt yourself, following a similar method and remembering the magic formula: for 4–6 joints use no more than 15 fl oz (425 ml/2 cups) of liquid and allow a total cooking period, for a casserole, of approximately 18 minutes – a shorter time if boneless breasts are used.

If plainly poached chicken is needed for a salad, a risotto or a casserole, the microwave will do it speedily and with splendid results. For these kinds of dishes, it is better to poach the chicken on the bone as the flesh will have more flavour and a superb stock will be produced. However, boneless breasts look more appetizing than joints when cooked in a light-coloured sauce, such as pineapple, orange or mushroom. Several of the dishes in this chapter use marinated chicken which not only augments the natural flavour of the bird but also produces a lovely brown colour even in a normal microwave oven. You will also get excellent results from a microwave stir-fry, such as the Sichuan Chicken with Cashew Nuts, or from the Baked Ginger Chicken and the Chicken Saté, as soy sauce adds colour as well as flavour to this type of recipe.

When several vegetables are used in a casserole, it is always better to use fresh ones and chop them in the food processor, but where only onion is used, I have substituted the minced and dried kind to save time.

The only requirement for any dish that is to be used for cooking poultry is that it should be large enough and deep enough to hold the pieces side by side, and come with its own lid. You will soon work out the most convenient dish for your use. Try to choose one that will also go straight to the table. For even cooking, position the pieces so that the thickest part is to the outside of the dish where it will get the full impact of the microwaves. Whenever it is practicable, pour a hot sauce on the chicken – the cooking time will be less than when a lukewarm one is used. Do not be tempted to increase the recommended cooking times, particularly when the chicken is steamed with a small amount of broth, as even a minute or two too long will tend to dry out the flesh. It is better first to nick a piece and check that it is white right through to the centre – if there is any sign of pink, indicating incomplete cooking, give it another 30 seconds and try again. However, all the recipes have been carefully timed and should only need adjusting if you have a different powered machine (see page 21).■

POULET BASQUAISE

Serves 4–6
Keeps 3 days under refrigeration
Freeze 3 months

The chicken is cooked in a herb-scented sauce studded with fat black olives.

2 tbsp olive oil
1 medium (5 oz/150 g) onion, finely chopped
1 medium green pepper, seeds removed and cut in thin strips
1 medium clove garlic, finely chopped
4–6 chicken breast portions on the bone (approx 2 lb/900 g total weight)
1 × 15 oz can (425 g) chopped tomatoes
2 tbsp tomato purée
2 teasp brown sugar
½ teasp each dried basil, tarragon and oregano, or 1½ teasp herbes de Provence
4 oz (125 g/1¼ cups) button mushrooms, stalks trimmed level with caps
1 teasp salt
15 grinds black pepper
4 oz (125 g/1 cup) black olives

1   In a casserole large enough to hold chicken breasts in one layer, heat the oil on 100% power for 3 minutes, then add the onion, green pepper and garlic. Cover and cook on 100% power for 6 minutes.
2   Add the chicken, spoon the vegetables over and cook uncovered on 100% power for 3 minutes.
3   Meanwhile, put the remaining ingredients, except for the black olives, into a large jug or bowl. Stir well, then pour over chicken breasts, cover and cook on 100% power for 15 minutes.
4   Take the dish out, spoon the sauce over the breasts to coat them evenly and garnish with black olives.
5   Rest, covered, for 5 minutes, then serve with rice or pasta.

CHICKEN BRASILIA

Serves 4–6
Keeps 2 days under refrigeration
Freeze 3 months

A barbecue-style sauce is mellowed by the addition of a little honey.

2 tbsp sunflower oil
1 medium (5 oz/150 g) onion, finely chopped
1 teasp garlic granules
4–6 skinned chicken portions on the bone (approx 2 lb/900 g total weight)
4 oz (125 g/1¼ cups) mushrooms, sliced
half a green pepper, seeded and finely sliced
half a red pepper, seeded and finely sliced
2 tbsp honey
2 teasp brown sugar
½ teasp powdered mustard
½ teasp salt
10 grinds black pepper
3 teasp light soy sauce
2 rounded tbsp tomato purée made up to 15 fl oz (425 ml/2 cups) with hot chicken stock
1 teasp wine vinegar

1   In a casserole large enough to hold the chicken portions in one layer, heat the oil uncovered on 100% power for 3 minutes, then add the onion, green pepper and garlic, cover and cook on 100% power for 6 minutes.
2   Add the chicken joints and mix well with the vegetables.
3   Meanwhile, put all the remaining ingredients into a large jug or bowl, stir well, then pour over the chicken. Cover and cook on 100% power for 18 minutes.
4   Take the dish out, spoon the sauce over the breasts to coat them evenly, cover and allow to rest for 5 minutes before serving.

POLLO ALLA CACCIATORA

Serves 4–6
Keeps 3 days under refrigeration
Leftovers freeze 3 months

A hearty dish, rich with tomatoes and herbs in the Italian manner.

4–6 skinned chicken portions (total weight about 2 lb/900 g)
5 fl oz (150 ml/⅔ cup) dry white wine
10 oz (275 g) (⅔ of a 15 oz/425 g can) chopped tomatoes with their juice
1 teasp salt
1 teasp brown sugar
8 grinds black pepper
1 bay leaf
½ teasp dried Italian seasoning herbs
2 tbsp olive or sunflower oil
1 medium (5 oz/150 g) onion, finely chopped
1 fat clove garlic, peeled and finely chopped
1 green pepper, seeds and pith removed, cut in ½ inch (1.25 cm) wide strips

1 Put the wine in a 2 pint (1 litre/5 cup) jug and cook uncovered on 100% power for 3 minutes until reduced by half – this intensifies the flavour. Add the chopped tomatoes, all the seasonings and herbs and set aside.
2 In a 3½ pint (2 litre/9 cup) lidded casserole, heat the oil uncovered on 100% power for 3 minutes then add the onion, garlic and green pepper and cook covered for 5 minutes.
3 Add the seasoned liquid and stir well, then add the chicken portions and baste with the mixture. Cover and cook for 18 minutes then baste well, re-cover and leave to stand for 5 minutes before serving.
4 To reheat from cold, cook covered on 80% power for 8 minutes or until bubbling.

SUPRÊME DE POULET À LA CHÂTAIGNE

Serves 6
The raw prepared dish keeps 24 hours under refrigeration

This dish has a wonderful combination of flavours, with the rich and spicy glaze contrasting with the sweetness of the chestnuts.

6 × 4 oz (125 g) skinned and boned chicken breasts tossed to coat in 1 oz (25 g/¼ cup) flour
For the marinade
2 teasp minced dried onion
½ teasp garlic granules
½ tbsp light soy sauce
2 tbsp Amontillado sherry
1 tbsp fresh lemon juice
2 tbsp light brown sugar
2 rounded tbsp peach chutney
For the chestnut purée
1 × 15½ oz (440 g) can natural chestnut purée
2 oz (50 g/¼ cup) margarine
½ teasp onion salt
10 grinds black pepper
For the garnish
1 ripe peach or nectarine, thinly sliced just before serving

1 At least 30 minutes before cooking (or up to 24 hours in advance if more convenient), lay the coated chicken breasts side by side in a large dish and slash each breast once or twice to help the marinade soak in.
2 Whisk the marinade ingredients together, then spoon over the chicken. Leave to marinate, basting once or twice.
3 Put the chestnut purée (cut in roughly 2 inch/5 cm chunks) into the food processor together with the soft fat, onion salt and pepper, and process

until smooth, scraping down the sides when necessary to achieve the consistency of mashed potatoes. (This can be done by mashing with a fork but it is tedious.)

4   Arrange the purée in a casserole large enough to hold the breasts in one layer, then arrange the chicken breasts on top, thicker ends towards the outside of the dish, covering and surrounding them with the marinade. Cover and cook on 100% power for 9 minutes.

5   Stand, covered, for 5 minutes then serve from the dish garnished with the slices of peach.

POULET MAROCAIN

Serves 4–6
Keeps 2 days under refrigeration
Freeze 3 months

The prunes add an interesting flavour and texture to the sauce.

2 tbsp sunflower oil
1 medium (5 oz/150 g) onion, finely chopped
4–6 skinned chicken portions on the bone (total weight about 2 lb/900 g), sprinkled with freshly ground black pepper
10 fl oz (275 ml/1¼ cups) hot chicken stock
1 teasp garlic granules
¼ teasp ground turmeric
½ teasp salt
½ teasp ground cumin
½ teasp ground cardamom
1 teasp ground ginger
9 oz (250 g) pack tenderized (ready to eat) prunes
2 teasp cornflour mixed to a cream with 3 teasp lemon juice

1   In a casserole large enough to hold the chicken portions in one layer, heat the oil uncovered on 100% power for 3 minutes, then add the onion,

cover and cook for 5 minutes.

2   Add the chicken joints and stir well with the onion, then arrange in an even layer, breast portions to centre, legs and thighs to outside of dish.

3   Put the stock and all the seasonings and spices into a large jug, stir well, then add to the casserole, cover and cook on 100% power for 18–20 minutes. Uncover, stir in the prunes and the cornflour liquid then cook uncovered on 80% power for 3 minutes until bubbling.

4   Cover and leave to stand for 5 minutes then serve.

5   To reheat from cold, cook covered on 80% power for 8 minutes or until bubbling throughout.

BAKED GINGER CHICKEN

Serves 4
Keeps 3 days under refrigeration
Freeze 2 months

Only 1 teaspoon of fat – and that is polyunsaturated sesame oil – is needed to create this piquant and juicy chicken dish. The secret lies in the savoury but almost fat-free marinade. Serve with rice or baked potatoes. It is also a useful dish to cook for two people (see below).

1 lb (450 g) boneless chicken breast meat
For the marinade
2½ tbsp light soy sauce
1½ teasp peeled and finely chopped fresh ginger root
2 teasp sesame oil
few drops Tabasco sauce or pinch of cayenne pepper

1   Fifteen minutes before you intend to cook the chicken (though longer will do no harm), cut the chicken into strips about 1 inch (2.5 cm) and ¾

inch (2 cm) thick and lay side by side in a shallow casserole.

2   Mix the marinade ingredients in a small basin or jug then pour over the chicken. Stir once or twice before cooking.

3   Cover and cook on 100% power for 5 minutes, turning the chicken pieces over half way. Serve from the dish.

FOR 2: Use half the quantity of chicken and marinade, cover and cook for 3½ minutes.

GLAZED MANGO AND GINGER CHICKEN

Serves 6
The raw prepared dish keeps 24 hrs under refrigeration
Leftovers keep 2 days under refrigeration
Do not freeze

The shiny glaze makes the chicken look most appetizing.

6 unskinned chicken joints (2½ lb/1 kg total weight), washed, dried and dusted lightly with flour
For the marinade
½ medium (5 oz/150 g) onion, grated
2 cloves garlic, crushed or 2 teasp garlic granules
2 tbsp light soy sauce
2 tbsp Amontillado sherry
4 tbsp lemon juice
4 tbsp light brown sugar
2 rounded tbsp mango and ginger chutney
½ teasp mild chilli powder

1   Arrange the coated chicken joints, skin side up and side by side in a shallow microwave-safe casserole. Slash through the flesh at 1 inch (2.5 cm) intervals.

2   Whisk all the marinade ingredients together and pour over the chicken. Leave for up to 2 hours, turning occasionally. (If time is short, reduce it to 15 minutes.)

3 Make sure the joints are skin side up, then cover the dish and cook on 100% power for 12 minutes.

4   Uncover, baste and continue to cook uncovered on 100% power for a further 8–10 minutes, or until the chicken is nicely glazed with the sauce.

5   Serve with Golden Rice (see page 124)

CHICKEN SATÉ

Serves 4–6 as a main dish, 8–12 with cocktails.

Instead of grilling the chunks of chicken in the traditional way, they are cooked in the microwave then served over rice. For a buffet or to accompany cocktails, the pieces can be speared on cocktail sticks and arranged on a platter accompanied by a bowl of the saté sauce.

The spicy marinade keeps each chunk of chicken juicy as it cooks. The delicious peanut sauce is traditional but, for a low-fat diet, a squeeze of lemon juice can be used instead.

1½–2 lb (700–900 g/4–6 cups) boned and skinned chicken breast meat, cut in roughly 1 inch (2.5 cm) chunks
For the marinade
1 teasp minced dried onion
1 clove garlic, crushed
2 tbsp light soy sauce
pinch cayenne pepper
1 teasp ground coriander
1 teasp ground ginger
1 tbsp lemon juice
1 tbsp sunflower oil
For the dipping sauce
2 teasp oil
1 teasp minced dried onion
1 teasp minced garlic
¼ teasp cayenne pepper
½ teasp salt

5 fl oz (150 ml/⅔ cup) chicken stock

1 ½ teasp medium brown sugar

6 tbsp (125 g/½ cup) smooth peanut butter

1 tbsp lemon juice

1   At least 2 hours (or the night) before, whisk all the marinade ingredients together, pour over the chunks of chicken that are arranged in one layer in a shallow lidded casserole. Leave at room temperature for at least 2 hours, basting once or twice. Refrigerate at this point if the dish is not to be cooked at once.

2   Shortly before serving, make the sauce as follows: put all the ingredients (except peanut butter and lemon juice) into a jug, cover and cook on 100% power for 4 minutes. Leave covered for 5 minutes, then uncover and whisk in the peanut butter and lemon juice. The sauce should be of coating consistency. If too thick, whisk in a little more stock. Taste and add salt if necessary.

3   To cook the chicken: cover the dish and cook 1½ lb (700 g) chicken on 100% power for 7 minutes, 2 lb (900 g) chicken for 8 minutes, stirring once to rearrange the pieces. Uncover and check that the chicken shows no sign of pink when a piece is cut. Add extra cooking time if necessary by 30 seconds.

SICHUAN CHICKEN WITH CASHEW NUTS

Serves 2 as a main course, 3–4 with other dishes
Leftovers keep 1 day under refrigeration
Do not freeze

A classic Chinese dish which translates well to the microwave.

10–12 oz (275–350 g/2 cups) chicken breast
  meat, boned and skinned

½ teasp salt

1 egg white, lightly beaten

1 tbsp cornflour, mixed with 1 tbsp cold water

1 green pepper, cored and seeded

2 oz (50 g/½ cup) dry-roasted cashew nuts

2 tbsp vegetable oil

2 spring onions trimmed and cut into 1 inch (2.5
  cm) lengths

1–2 slices ginger root, peeled and chopped

½ teasp sugar

1 tbsp Sichuan chilli bean paste

2 tbsp rice wine or dry sherry

1   Cut the chicken into ¾ inch (2 cm) cubes. Mix first with the salt, then the egg white and, finally, with about half the cornflour paste.

2   Cut the green pepper into pieces the same size as the chicken cubes. Split the cashew nuts in half.

3   Heat the oil on 100% power for 3 minutes in shallow 10 inch (25 cm) round casserole, add the chicken cubes, stir and cook uncovered on 100% power for 4 minutes or until the meat turns white, stirring once or twice.

4   Add the spring onions, ginger, green peppers, cashew nuts, sugar, bean paste and wine, mix well and cook on 100% power for 2–3 minutes, stirring twice.

5   Thicken the liquid with the remaining cornflour paste by mixing well and cooking on 80% power for 40 seconds. Stir well and serve.

POACHED CHICKEN BREASTS IN A MUSHROOM AND WINE SAUCE

Serves 4–6
Leftovers keep 2 days under refrigeration
Do not freeze

A creamy-textured, delicately flavoured sauce to serve with plainly poached breasts of chicken.

4–6 × 4 oz (125 g) skinless and boneless chicken breasts
2 fl oz (50 ml/¼ cup) medium dry white wine
For the sauce
4 spring onion bulbs, trimmed and finely sliced
8 oz (225 g/2½ cups) button mushrooms, thinly sliced
2 tbsp sunflower oil or rendered chicken or turkey fat
1 tbsp cornflour
4 tbsp Amontillado sherry
5 fl oz (150 ml/⅔ cup) hot chicken stock (see page 38) or water plus a cube
3 fl oz (75 ml/⅓ cup) medium dry white wine
pinch salt
pinch nutmeg
pinch white pepper

1   First make the sauce: put the spring onions, mushrooms and fat in a lidded casserole, cover and cook on 100% power for 4 minutes, then uncover, bubble 2 minutes to evaporate some of the liquid, then leave.

2   Meanwhile, mix the cornflour and the sherry in a 2 pint (1.25 litre/5 cup) jug to a smooth cream then add all the remaining sauce ingredients, bring to the boil and cook for 4 minutes stirring halfway, until thickened. Stir in the mushrooms and onions.

3   Arrange the chicken breasts in a casserole large enough to hold them in one layer, thick side of each breast to the outside. Pour on the 2 fl oz (50 ml/¼ cup) of wine, cover and cook on 100%

power for 7 minutes.

4   Lift out with a slotted spoon then pour the cooking liquid into the sauce. Return the chicken breasts to the dish and leave covered while you reheat the sauce until bubbling – about 3 minutes on 100% power. Check that it is of a coating consistency. If not, cook for a further minute then pour over the breasts.

CHICKEN BREASTS IN A HONEYED ORANGE AND RAISIN SAUCE

Serves 4–6
Leftovers keep 2 days under refrigeration
Do not freeze

A delicately flavoured, succulent dish with a very refreshing fruitiness.

4–6 skinned and boned chicken breasts (1½–1¾ lb/675–800 g total weight)
For the sauce
1½ tbsp cornflour
5 fl oz (150 ml/⅔ cup) orange juice
5 fl oz (150 ml/⅔ cup) fruity fairly dry white wine, e.g. Alsatian Riesling
5 fl oz (150 ml/⅔ cup) strong chicken stock or soup (see page 38) or water plus cube
2 teasp grated lemon rind
1 level tbsp mild liquid honey
3 inch (8 cm) stick of cinnamon
3 tbsp Muscatel raisins
nut of margarine
For the garnish
2 oz (50 g/½ cup) toasted slivered almonds
2 navel oranges, well washed and sliced, with the peel left on

1   Arrange the chicken breasts in a 3½ pint (2

litre/9 cup) lidded casserole with the thicker part of the breasts to the outside.

2   In a 2 pint (1.25 litre/5 cup) microwave-safe jug, mix the cornflour to a cream with 4 tbsp of the orange juice, then stir in the rest of the juice and all the remaining ingredients, except the margarine. Cook, covered with a plate, on 100% power for 6 minutes, stirring halfway, then stir in the margarine and pour over the chicken, cover and cook for 10 minutes. Leave to stand, covered, for 5 minutes.

3   Uncover, sprinkle with the toasted nuts and garnish with the orange slices.

CHICKEN BREASTS IN A SWEET AND SOUR PINEAPPLE SAUCE

Serves 6
Keeps 2 days under refrigeration
Freeze 3 months

The shimmering green and gold sauce makes this a particularly beautiful dish.

6 × 5 oz (150 g) skinned and boned chicken breasts (total weight 1½–2 lb/675–900 g)
For the sauce
2 tbsp cornflour
juice from 15¼ oz (430 g) can unsweetened pineapple cubes or rings (reserve the pineapple)
1 teasp salt
10 grinds black pepper
1 tbsp sunflower oil
2 teasp minced dried onion
2 teasp light soy sauce
9 fl oz (250 ml/1 cup plus 2 tbsp) approx hot chicken stock
1 medium green pepper, seeds and pith removed, and flesh cut in ½ inch (1.25 cm) squares
3 teasp brown sugar

1   Arrange the chicken breasts in a 3½ pint (2 litre/9 cup) lidded casserole with the thicker part

of the breasts to the outside.

2   In a 2 pint (1.25 litre/5 cup) microwave-safe jug, mix the cornflour to a cream with 4 tbsp of the pineapple juice, then stir in the rest of the juice and all the remaining ingredients.

3   Cook, covered with a plate, on 100% power for 5 minutes, stirring halfway, then pour over the chicken, cover and cook on 100% power for 10 minutes. Leave to stand, covered, for 5 minutes.

4   To reheat from cold, cover and cook on 80% power for 8 minutes or until bubbling.

SHERRIED CHICKEN OR TURKEY

Serves 4 as an entrée, fills 12 medium or 36 cocktail-size patty cases
Keeps 2 days under refrigeration
Do not freeze
May be reheated

This is a versatile mixture that can be served as a light main dish (over rice or pasta) or used as a filling for patty cases.

12 oz (350 g/2 cups) chicken or turkey breast meat, or 3 chicken breast portions, cooked as described on page 173, or the meat from half a roast or poached fowl, or 12 oz (350 g/2 cups) meat from a cooked turkey
1 canned pimento, cut in ½ inch (1.25 cm) squares
For the sauce
1 tbsp sunflower oil or rendered chicken or turkey fat
4 oz (125 g/1¼ cups) tiny button mushrooms, finely sliced, or 4 oz (125 g/1¼ cups) medium mushrooms, coarsely chopped
1½ tbsp cornflour mixed to a cream with 3 tbsp Amontillado sherry
10 fl oz (275 ml/1¼ cups) strong chicken or turkey stock
1 egg yolk
¼ teasp nutmeg

2 teasp parsley
½ teasp salt
speck of white pepper

1   Cut the poultry meat into chunky bite-sized pieces and put into a bowl with the pimento.
2   In a small lidded soup cup or bowl, heat the oil or fat on 100% power for 1 minute. Add the mushrooms, cover and cook for 3½ minutes. Leave to stand.
3   Put the cornflour and sherry liquid into a 3 ½ pint (2 litre/9 cup) jug or bowl and add the stock. Cover and cook on 100% power for 4 minutes, stirring halfway to ensure even thickening. The mixture should be thick and bubbly.
4   Drop in the egg yolk and whisk vigorously to cook it in the hot sauce then stir in the mushrooms, nutmeg, parsley, salt and pepper (if necessary). Add to the chicken mixture and stir gently together. Cover and reheat on 80% power for 3 minutes or until steaming.
5   To reheat from cold, cover and cook on 80% power for 5 minutes or until steaming.

CHICKEN OR TURKEY RISOTTO

Serves 4–5
Keeps 2 days under refrigeration
Freeze 3 months

A delicious supper dish and one of the best ways to use up the remains of a bird.

1 cup (7 oz/200 g by weight) Basmati rice
2 tbsp oil
4 oz (125 g/1¼ cups) mushrooms, each sliced in quarters
10 fl oz (275 ml/1¼ cups) hot chicken stock (see page 38) or water plus cube
1 rounded tbsp tomato purée
1 tbsp minced dried onion

1 teasp garlic granules
4 fl oz (125 ml/½ cup) medium dry white wine
2 teasp brown sugar
8 oz (225 g/1¼ cups) poached chicken or turkey breast meat (see page 173), or remains of a poached fowl or roast chicken, cut in bite-sized pieces

1   Turn the rice into a sieve and hold under the cold tap until the water runs clear (this removes excess starch).
2   In a 3 pint (1.5 litre/8 cup) lidded casserole, put the oil and mushrooms, cover and cook on 100% power for 3 minutes. Uncover and add the drained rice.
3   Mix all the ingredients, except the chicken, in a jug or bowl, then add to the casserole, stir well, cover and cook on 100% power for 5 minutes, then cook at 80% power for a further 10 minutes.
4   Add the chicken, fluff up with a fork, then cover and stand for 5 minutes before serving.
5   To reheat from cold, sprinkle the surface with a little cold water, cover and cook on 100% power for 4 minutes or until steaming.

CIRCASSIAN CHICKEN (Cerkes Tavugu)

Serves 6 as a main dish, 8 as part of a buffet
Keeps 3 days under refrigeration
Do not freeze

In this interesting Turkish dish, juicy pieces of chicken are coated with a creamy walnut sauce and served on a bed of rice. Cooking the chicken on the bone not only makes it especially succulent but also produces a superb stock to use as the basis for the sauce.

    The dish is served at room temperature, though it can be refrigerated until an hour before it is served.

15 fl oz (425 ml/2 cups) water, or enough to barely cover the chicken

8 grinds black pepper

1 teasp salt

1 × 4 lb (1.75 kg) chicken, cut into 4 or 6 portions, backbone and wing tips trimmed and frozen for later use, or 2 lb 8 oz (1.25 kg) chicken portions

1 carrot, cut in half

½ onion, cut in half

2 sticks celery

3 sprigs parsley

For the sauce

3 thin slices of bread from a large loaf (approx 3 oz/75 g total weight)

10 oz (275 ml/1¼ cups) (approx) of the liquid in which the chicken was cooked

6 oz (175 g/1½ cups) walnut pieces

1 small clove garlic

For the garnish

powdered paprika

3 teasp chopped parsley

a handful of black olives

To serve with the chicken

cold Savoury Rice (see page 123)

1   Measure the water and add the pepper and salt.

2   In a 7 pint (4 litres/17½ cup) deep lidded casserole or very large bowl, arrange the chicken pieces skin side down, with the breast portions to the centre and the legs, thigh pieces and wings around them. Tuck in the carrot, onion, celery and parsley sprigs, pour over the seasoned water, cover and cook on 100% power for 12 minutes till bubbling round the edges, then reduce to 50% power and continue to simmer for a further 10 minutes.

3   Allow the chicken to cool in the stock in the covered dish, then lift out, skin, remove the flesh from the bones and cut into strips each about 3 inches (7.5 cm) long and ½ inch (1.25 cm) wide. Put into a bowl and leave covered.

4   Pass the stock through a sieve into a bowl and put in the freezer for a couple of hours until the fat can be skimmed off.

5   To make the sauce, put the decrusted bread in a small bowl and barely cover with some of the chicken stock, leave for 2 minutes then squeeze out as much liquid as possible. Put the walnuts and the well squeezed bread, together with the garlic clove, into the food processor and process until it forms a smooth paste. Add the stock gradually until the sauce is of a coating consistency. Taste and add a little salt and black pepper if necessary.

6   Stir enough of the sauce into the chicken to coat all the pieces, then arrange in a mound on a bed of the cold rice on a shallow oval platter. Coat with the remaining sauce, sprinkle with the paprika and chopped parsley and garnish with the olives.

CHICKEN AND AVOCADO MAYONNAISE ON A CRUNCHY RICE SALAD

Serves 6–8
Serve the same day
Leftovers keep 2 days under refrigeration
Do not freeze

A delicious blend of flavours.

1–1¼ lb (450–600 g/3–3½ cups) skinless chicken breast meat, poached as described on page 173

1 large or 2 medium ripe avocados

2 tbsp fresh lemon juice

10 fl oz (275 ml/1¼ cups) mild mayonnaise

1 tbsp medium strength curry paste

2 rounded tbsp peach chutney

1 teasp grated fresh ginger root

For the rice salad

8 oz (225 g/1⅓ cups) Basmati (Indian long grain) rice

15 fl oz (425 ml/2 cups) hot chicken stock

4 tbsp vinaigrette dressing

1 large red pepper, seeded and finely diced

3 rounded tbsp seedless raisins

2 oz (50 g/½ cup) dry-roasted cashews, chopped
For the garnish
1 bunch watercress

1   Cut the chicken flesh into bite-sized pieces.
2   Peel, halve and stone the avocado, cut it into pieces of a similar size and mix gently with the lemon juice.
3   In a large bowl, mix the mayonnaise, curry paste, chutney and fresh ginger, then gently stir in the chicken and avocado, cover and chill until required. For an alternative presentation, see photograph facing page 100.
4   To make the rice salad, turn the rice into a sieve and hold under the cold tap until the water runs clear (this removes excess starch). Put the drained rice into a 3 pint (1.5 litre/8 cup) lidded casserole or bowl. Add the hot stock and stir well. Cover and cook on 100% power for 5 minutes until bubbling, then cook on 80% power for a further 8 minutes. Allow to stand for 5 minutes, then fluff up with a fork.
5   Put the hot rice into a bowl and mix gently with the vinaigrette, using a large fork and spoon.
6   Stir in the red pepper dice, raisins and nuts, then refrigerate in a covered container for several hours.
7   Shortly before the meal, spoon the rice salad round the edge of an oval platter and pile the chicken salad in the centre. Decorate with sprigs of watercress.

CUMBERLAND SAUCE

Keeps 1 week under refrigeration
Do not freeze

To serve with cold roast chicken joints, sliced deep-fried chicken breasts or cold roast lamb. The flavour of the sauce will benefit by maturing in the refrigerator for several hours.

1 × 8 oz (225 g) jar redcurrant jelly
2 teasp cornflour
2 fl oz (50 ml/¼ cup) sweet red kosher or port-type wine
juice of 1 orange and 1 lemon (5 fl oz/150 ml/⅔ cup in all)

1   Take the lid off the redcurrant jelly and heat it in the jar on 100% power for 3 minutes until liquid.
2   Put the cornflour into a bowl and mix to a thin cream with the wine then stir in the fruit juices.
3   Finally (take care, the jar will be too hot to handle without a cloth), whisk in the hot jelly. Cover with a plate and cook on 100% power for 3 minutes, stirring halfway until thickened and bubbly. Allow to go cold.

VEGETABLES

INTRODUCTION

Vegetables thrive in the microwave – it cooks them to just the right degree of 'doneness', while keeping their colour and nutrients intact. If necessary, it can also reheat them in their serving dish without any loss of colour or flavour. For this reason, it is sensible to cook vegetables before other dishes which have a longer cooking period.

In the Lexicon (see page 186), you will find the times and techniques for cooking vegetables plain and simple. But, in this chapter, I have gathered together a collection of the rather more sophisticated dishes that are variously dressed with sauces, nuts, toppings or glazes. There are also some very delicious purées. In every case they can be cooked in their serving dishes – a big advantage to the host or hostess cook. For advice on pre-cooking green vegetables to preserve their colour and texture over several hours, see page 186.

As with other food, the more similar in size the pieces of vegetable, the more quickly and evenly they will cook. Do follow the instructions carefully and arrange them as suggested in each recipe. It is particularly important to stir the vegetables halfway through the cooking period so that those in the centre of the dish are repositioned near the edge and get their full share of the microwave energy. Most vegetables need to stand two or three minutes after cooking to complete the transference of heat to the centre of the dish. So resist the temptation to give them extra time. Even if they seem a little firm in texture at the end of the given cooking time, they will soften further by the time they are served. However, full instructions are given with each individual recipe. For cooking all vegetables, with the exception of high bulk ones such as cabbage, I use a shallow-lidded casserole large enough to hold the pieces in an even layer. All vegetables, even potatoes, need no more than a few tablespoons of water as a cooking medium. As this water heats up and vaporizes, the vegetables are effectively steamed with the minimum loss of water-soluble nutrients. With the exception of frozen peas, which are superior to all but the home-grown variety, all the vegetables in this chapter are fresh. I do keep a small stock of frozen vegetables for emergency use only, but an enormous range of fresh varieties, which are infinitely superior in taste and texture, is now available all the year round. ∎

Chicken and Avocado Mayonnaise on a Crunchy Rice Salad

GREEN BEANS WITH GOLDEN ALMONDS

Serves 6

This is a very colourful presentation for a dinner party.

1 lb (450 g) shoestring or Kenya beans (slim green beans), topped and tailed if necessary
1½ oz (40 g/3 tbsp) butter or margarine
2 oz (50 g/½ cup) blanched and split, or flaked almonds
3 tbsp water
½ teasp sea salt
10 grinds black pepper
squeeze of lemon juice

1   Top and tail the beans and arrange in a 10 inch (25 cm) lidded casserole.
2   Melt the fat, on 100% power for 1½ minutes, in a bowl covered lightly with a paper towel. Add the almonds, stir well to coat them with the hot fat, then cook for a further 3½ minutes, stirring once, until golden brown. Leave on one side.
3   Add 3 tbsp water to the beans, cover and cook on 100% power for 8 minutes or until just tender when pierced with a slim sharp knife. Drain well, season with a sprinkle of salt and black pepper and a squeeze of lemon juice, then pour the buttered almonds over them, stirring well. Heat uncovered for 1 minute, then serve.
NOTE: if preferred, the beans can be cooked earlier in the day, then turned into a colander, drenched with cold water to set the colour, then returned to the dish. Reheat, covered, on 100% power for 3 minutes then treat as freshly cooked.

BRAISED RED CABBAGE IN THE VIENNESE STYLE

Serves 6
Keeps 2 days under refrigeration
Leftovers freeze for 3 months

This has a delectable sweet/sour flavour that makes it especially suitable to serve hot with braised meat or cold with pickled meat and cold cuts.

1¾–2 lb (800–900 g) (medium head) red cabbage, quartered, core removed and leaves finely shredded by hand or machine
2 tbsp oil
1 medium (5 oz/150 g) onion, finely chopped
2 tbsp soft medium brown sugar
2 generous tbsp crabapple, quince or redcurrant jelly
2 tbsp wine or cider vinegar
1½ tbsp water
2 teasp salt
speck white pepper
1 medium bay leaf

1   Rinse the shredded cabbage in cold water, using a colander or sieve, and leave to drain.
2   In a 3½ pint (2 litre/9 cup) lidded casserole or bowl cook the oil, onion and sugar, uncovered on 100% power for 6 minutes. Add all the remaining ingredients except the cabbage, and whisk well. Then add the cabbage and stir to coat it with the vinegar and onion mixture. (Do not worry if it overfills the dish – just press it down well as it shrinks during cooking.)
3   Cover and cook on 100% power for 25–30 minutes, stirring twice, until the cabbage is tender but still has some bite left in it. Leave to stand, covered, for 5 minutes.
4   To reheat, cover and cook on 100% power for 4 minutes or until steaming.

Stuffed Peppers, Hungarian Style Lamb Cutlets in a Honey Glaze

ORANGE GLAZED CARROTS

Serves 4
Leftovers keep 2 days under refrigeration

Carrots never soften as completely in the microwave as they do when boiled in the conventional way but they still have a little 'bite' left in them – the preferred condition for vegetables today.

8 oz (225 g) carrots and 6 stalks celery, or 12 oz (350 g) young carrots, peeled and cut in matchsticks or sliced ⅛ inch (0.5 cm) thick
4 tbsp orange juice
2 teasp finely grated orange rind
1 oz (25 g/2 tbsp) butter or margarine
1 teasp caster sugar
10 grinds black pepper
½ teasp salt
For the garnish
1 tbsp finely chopped parsley

1   Put all the ingredients (except the salt) into a casserole, cover and cook on 100% power for 12 minutes, stirring once or twice. The carrots should be 'al dente'.
2   Remove the lid and cook for 2–3 minutes, until bathed in an orange sauce. Stir in the salt.
3   Serve scattered with the chopped parsley.

CAULIFLOWER IN THE POLISH FASHION

Serves 4

Always cook cauliflower on the day of purchase as it quickly develops a 'cabbagey' flavour even when stored in the refrigerator.

2 oz (50 g/¼ cup) butter
1 heaped tbsp dry brown or white breadcrumbs
1 tight white head of cauliflower, stalk removed and broken into even-sized florets (or 1 lb/450 g prepacked fresh florets)
squeeze of lemon juice
3 tbsp boiling water
1 hardboiled egg, coarsely chopped
1 tbsp chopped parsley

1   First make the topping: melt the butter in a small basin on 80% power for 2 minutes. Stir in the crumbs and cook uncovered for 3 minutes. Set aside.
2   To cook the cauliflower, put the florets in a casserole large enough to hold them side by side. Add 3 tbsp boiling water, cover and cook on 100% power for 10–12 minutes, stirring once, until just tender when pierced with a knife. Leave covered for 2 minutes then drain off the water.
3   Sprinkle the cauliflower with the lemon juice, scatter with the buttered crumbs and sprinkle with the chopped egg and parsley.

BRAISED COURGETTES

Serves 4

Simple but delicious when made with the first baby courgettes of the season.

1 lb (450 g) tiny courgettes
1½ oz (40 g/3 tbsp) butter or margarine
10 grinds black pepper
sea salt
1 tbsp fresh chopped marjoram, oregano or parsley

1   Top and tail the courgettes, wash and arrange side by side in a shallow lidded casserole. Dot with the butter, cover and cook on 100% power for 10 minutes, stirring once, or until just tender when

pierced with a sharp, slim knife.

2   Stand covered for 3 minutes then season lightly with the salt and pepper and sprinkle with the chopped herbs.

COURGETTES
WITH A HONEY GLAZE

Serves 4
Leftovers keep 2 days under refrigeration

The honey and herbs combine to perfume this delicious dish that can be served hot with fish or chicken or at room temperature as a starter.

8 small and tender courgettes (approx 1–1¼ lb (450–575 g) total weight)
1 tbsp sunflower oil
1 medium onion, peeled and finely chopped
1 clove of garlic, peeled and finely chopped
1 tbsp fresh chopped herbs – parsley, thyme, tarragon, basil – as available
3 tbsp lemon juice (juice of a medium lemon)
1 tbsp liquid honey
½ teasp salt
pinch of white pepper
1 oz (25 g/2 tbsp) butter or margarine

1   Wash the courgettes and trim off both ends, then cut into ½ inch (1.25 cm) thick slices.

2   Brush the oil over the base of a 10–11 inch (25–28 cm) lidded casserole and then arrange the chopped onion and garlic, mixed with the herbs and 1 tbsp lemon juice, in an even layer on top. Cover and cook on 100% power for 3 minutes.

3   Uncover, stir well, then arrange the slices of courgettes in an even layer on top. Spoon over the honey and remaining 2 tbsp of lemon juice, sprinkle with the seasoning and dot with tiny pieces of the fat. Cover and cook on 100% power for 10–11 minutes, or until barely tender when

pierced with a slim sharp knife. Leave covered for 5 minutes then serve.

4   May be served cold as a starter or reheated (covered, on 100% power for 3 minutes) with fish or plainly roasted chicken.

COURGETTES NIÇOISE

Serves 4

A hearty mixture, to serve hot or cold with chicken and roasts.

1 lb (450 g) tiny courgettes, or same quantity of medium courgettes sliced ¼ inch (0.5 cm) thick
For the sauce
3 large canned tomatoes, well drained and coarsely chopped
½ teasp brown sugar or granular sweetener
1 teasp garlic granules
2 tbsp olive or sunflower oil
8 stoned and halved fat black olives
1 tbsp fresh or 1 teasp dried oregano

1   Arrange the whole courgettes side by side (or the slices, in an even layer) in a shallow lidded casserole.

2   Mix all the sauce ingredients in a jug, then pour over the courgettes, cover and cook on 100% power for 11–12 minutes, stirring once, or until the vegetables feel tender when pierced with a slim, sharp knife.

3   Stand, covered, for 3 minutes, then uncover and stir well. The sauce should be thick and juicy. If watery, cook uncovered on 100% power for a further 2–3 minutes.

CUCUMBER AND MINTED PETIT POIS

Serves 6
Keeps 1 day under refrigeration

This is a delicately flavoured dish to serve with baked, poached or grilled fish, especially salmon.

1 medium cucumber (or ½ large one), peeled
1 oz (25 g/2 tbsp) butter or margarine
12 oz (350 g/2¼ cups) petit pois
leaves from a large sprig of fresh mint, shredded, or 1 teasp dried mint
1 teasp caster sugar
1 teasp salt
pinch of white pepper

1   About an hour before you wish to serve the dish, peel the cucumber, cut it in 1 inch (2.5 cm) lengths and then in thin strips ¼ inch (0.5 cm) thick (julienne). Put in the inner basket of a salad spinner or in a colander, sprinkle lightly with salt and leave for 20 minutes (though overnight in the refrigerator will do no harm). Rinse off the salt then spin or dab dry.
2   In a shallow round 10 inch (25 cm) lidded casserole, melt the fat on 100% power for 1 minute. Add the strips of cucumber, cover and cook on 100% power for 2 minutes. Add the peas and mint, cover and cook on 100% power for a further 6 minutes, stirring once.
3   Uncover and, if there is a lot of free liquid, cook uncovered for a further 2 minutes until the vegetables are bathed in a shiny glaze, then season and stir before serving.
4   The dish can be reheated, covered, on 100% power for 3 minutes or until steaming.

MINTED PETIT POIS WITH SPRING ONIONS – *VARIATION*

Serves 6

1 oz (25 g/2 tbsp) butter or margarine
1 lb (450 g/3 cups) frozen petit pois
1 bunch spring onions, trimmed at both ends and cut into 1 inch (2.5 cm) lengths
leaves from a sprig of fresh mint, shredded, or 1 teasp dried mint
1 teasp caster sugar
sea salt
black pepper

1   In a shallow round 10 inch (25 cm) lidded casserole, heat the fat on 100% power for 1 minute, uncover and add the peas, spring onions, mint and sugar. Stir well, cover and cook for 6–8 minutes, stirring halfway, until the peas are tender.
2   Uncover, sprinkle lightly with the sea salt and black pepper and serve.
3   May be reheated, covered, on 100% power for 3 minutes or until steaming.

FRICASSÉE OF FOREST MUSHROOMS

Serves 4–6
Keeps 1 day under refrigeration
Do not freeze

This is a dish to savour for the glorious blend of flavours. It can be served in individual gratin dishes as a starter for 4 or as an exotic side dish, with plainly grilled or baked fish, such as lemon sole or halibut.

12 oz (350 g/3¾ cups) button mushrooms

4 oz (125 g/1¾ cups) shii-take mushrooms ('forest' or 'black' mushrooms)

4 oz (125 g/1¼ cups) oyster mushrooms

1 small bunch spring onions, including 1 inch (2 cm) of the green

1 oz (25 g/2 tbsp) butter

1 tbsp olive oil

1 medium clove of garlic, unpeeled, bruised with the flat of a cook's knife

1 tbsp lemon juice

2 tbsp rice wine or Amontillado (medium dry) sherry

½ teasp sea salt

10 grinds black or Sichuan pepper

5 fl oz (150 ml/⅔ cup) soured cream or creamed smetana (optional)

1   Cut off the last ¼ inch (0.5 cm) of stalk from the button mushrooms and discard. Remove any tough stalks from the other two varieties. Wipe the mushrooms with a damp cloth but do not peel them. Cut in half any very large ones. Slice the spring onions lengthwise.

2   In a 10 inch (25 cm) shallow round lidded casserole, heat the butter and oil on 100% power for 1 minute. Add the spring onions, the prepared mushrooms, the garlic and the lemon juice. Cover and cook on 100% power for 7 minutes, stirring once.

3   Uncover, stir well, add the wine or sherry and cook, uncovered, on 100% power for a further 2 minutes until the liquid has almost all evaporated. Discard the garlic.

4   Season and serve, or stir in the soured cream and cook a further 40 seconds until steaming. Serve at once.

5   The mushrooms can be reheated, covered, on 100% power for 3 minutes or until steaming.

PEPERONATA

Serves 4
Keeps 3 days under refrigeration

This luscious Italian vegetable dish is delicious served at room temperature with coarse brown bread. Warm (but never hot), it is good company for grilled steak or chicken. The peppers should still have a little 'bite' in them. The flavour improves as time goes by.

2 tbsp olive oil

1 medium (5 oz/150 g) onion, sliced paper thin

1 teasp medium brown sugar

4 large peppers, 2 red and 2 green, core and pith removed, deseeded and cut in ¾ inch (1.25 cm) wide strips

tomatoes drained from a 14 oz (400 g) can and roughly chopped

10 grinds black pepper

1 teasp sea salt

1 teasp garlic granules

½ teasp dried Italian herb mixture

1 tbsp chopped parsley

1   In a 3½ pint (2 litre/9 cup) lidded casserole or bowl put the olive oil, sliced onions and brown sugar. Mix well, cover and cook on 100% power for 4 minutes.

2   Uncover, add the pepper strips and stir well. Then, cover and cook for 8 minutes, stirring once, until the vegetables are still firm but tender.

3   In a small bowl mix the chopped tomatoes and all the remaining ingredients, except for the parsley. Add to the peppers and cook uncovered on 100% power for 5 minutes, until thick and juicy, then stir in the parsley. Re-season and serve hot or cold.

GREEN BEANS AND MUSHROOMS, CHINESE STYLE

Serves 6
A decorative dish with a delicious blend of textures and flavours.

12 oz (350 g/2½ cups) green beans (shoe string, Kenya or bobo)
3 tbsp hot water
1 tbsp sunflower oil
1 unpeeled clove of garlic, bruised with the flat of a cook's knife
1 inch (2.5 cm) piece fresh ginger, peeled and cut in tiny slivers
8 oz (225 g/2½ cups) button mushrooms, thinly sliced
2 teasp light soy sauce
10 grinds black pepper

1   Early in the day, top and tail the beans and remove any strings. Arrange in a 10 inch (25 cm) shallow lidded dish with 3 tbsp hot water, cover and cook on 100% power for 6–7 minutes or until barely tender.
2   Turn into a sieve, drench with cold water, drain, and leave until almost ready to serve.
3   In the same dish, put the oil, bruised garlic and ginger and cook on 100% power for 3 minutes, then add the mushrooms. Stir well and cook uncovered for 4 minutes, stirring once. Leave in the dish.
4   Just before serving, discard the garlic, add the beans, soy sauce and the black pepper to the mushrooms, stir well and cook, uncovered, for a further 4–5 minutes, until steaming. Serve at once.

STIR FRIED YOUNG CABBAGE

Serves 4–6

A method that preserves all the fugitive flavours of this very tender variety of cabbage.

1 young, hearted green cabbage
2 tbsp sunflower oil
½ inch (1.25 cm) fresh ginger root, peeled and cut in fine slivers
1 teasp salt
½ teasp sugar
2 teasp light soy sauce
1 teasp sesame seed oil

1   Use only the (usually) oval green cabbages available in late summer. White cabbage is too strong in flavour and tough in texture.
2   Remove any discoloured leaves, halve the cabbage and remove the core, then shred by hand or machine to resemble coleslaw. Put in a colander, drench with cold water then allow to drain.
3   In a 10–11 inch (25–28 cm) shallow casserole, heat the oil and the ginger on 100% power for 2 minutes. Add the shreds of cabbage, toss well with two spoons, then cook on 100% power for 5 minutes, tossing 2 or 3 times. The cabbage should still have some bite.
4   Add the salt, sugar and soy sauce and heat through for a further 2 minutes, then sprinkle with the sesame seed oil, toss again and serve.

CHINESE STIR FRIED VEGETABLES

Serves 4

My friend, the eminent Chinese food writer
Deh Ta Hsiung, taught me the technique of 'stir
frying' in the microwave. It uses only a minimal
amount of oil and is particularly useful if you
normally cook on a ceramic hob, which is not very
convenient for stir frying.

1 oz (25 g/2 tbsp) Wooden Ears (dried black
    mushrooms)
4 oz (125 g/½ cup) broccoli florets
4 oz (125 g/¼ cup) straw mushrooms or oyster
    mushrooms
4 oz (125 g) baby sweetcorn, fresh or canned
4 oz (125 g) courgettes
1 small green or red pepper, cored and seeded
2 tbsp vegetable oil
1 inch (2.5 cm) peeled ginger root, cut in fine
    slivers
1 teasp salt
1 teasp sugar
pinch of 5 spice powder
1 tbsp light soy sauce
a few drops of sesame seed oil (optional)

1   Soak the Wooden Ears in warm water for
about 20–25 minutes.
2   Prepare the other vegetables by cutting them
into roughly uniform slices, about ¾ inch (2 cm)
thick. The mushrooms can be left whole but, if
exceptionally large, halve or quarter them. Leave
the baby sweetcorn whole if tiny, otherwise cut
each one into 3 or 4 diamond shaped pieces.
3   Rinse the Wooden Ears and discard the hard
parts.
4   In a shallow 10 inch (25 cm) round casserole,
heat the oil with the ginger on 100% power for 1
minute, then add the broccoli, baby sweetcorn
and courgettes, mix well and cook on 100% power
for 3–4 minutes, stirring frequently.

5   Add the Wooden Ears, mushrooms and
peppers, followed by the salt, sugar, 5 spice and
soy sauce. Toss and turn until well mixed, then
cook on 100% power for 2 minutes.
6   Add the sesame seed oil, if used, and serve hot
or cold.

VARIATION

Use these vegetables with the same seasonings as
above:

½ onion, peeled, thinly sliced then cut in 4
2 large red peppers, deseeded, cut in thin julienne
    strips ½ inch (1 cm) wide
4 oz (125 g/1¼ cups) each shii-take mushrooms
    and button mushrooms, each sliced in quarters
4 oz (125 g/¾ cup) small mangetout, any strings
    removed

1   Prepare the vegetables.
2   Heat the oil with the ginger on 100% power
for 1 minute, add the onion and cook for 4
minutes, stirring once.
3   Add the peppers, mushrooms and mangetout,
together with the seasonings, and cook on 100%
power for 4 minutes or until bite tender, stirring
once.

STIR FRIED MANGETOUT (OR GREEN BEANS) WITH GARLIC AND GINGER

Serves 4
Serve hot or cold
Leftovers keep 2 days under refrigeration

These beans are crisp and flavourful. Served hot or
cold they make a delicious 'relish' to serve with
cold meat and chicken. Test for 'doneness' by
biting one after 10 minutes – the cooking time
depends so much on the freshness of the beans.

1 very thin slice of ginger, peeled and chopped

1 fat clove garlic, peeled and chopped finely

3 spring onions, coarse green discarded, split
   lengthwise and cut in 2 inch (5 cm) lengths

1 tbsp sunflower oil

pinch of dried chillies (hot peppers)

1 tbsp light soy sauce

1 tbsp wine vinegar

12 oz (350 g/2½ cups) mangetout or slim green
   beans (bobo, Kenya, shoe string), topped and
   tailed, and halved if very long

1   In a wide shallow casserole, mix the ginger,
garlic, spring onions, oil and chillies. Cook
uncovered on 100% power for 3 minutes.

2   Stir in the soy sauce, wine vinegar and
mangetout or beans, mixing well, then cook
uncovered on 100% power for 10–11 minutes,
stirring 2 or 3 times.

3   The mangetout or beans should be just bite
tender. If not, cook a minute or two longer. Stir
well and serve hot or cold.

GINGERED PARSNIP PURÉE

Serves 4
Keeps 2 days under refrigeration
Do not freeze

The spicy flavour of the parsnips goes well with
the ground ginger. The baked potato adds extra
body to make this a satisfying accompaniment to
roast or grilled meat or fish.

1 medium (6 oz/175 g) potato

1 lb (450 g) parsnips, trimmed, peeled and cut
   into 1 inch (2.5 cm) chunks

4 tbsp hot water

2 oz (50 g/¼ cup) margarine or butter, cut in
   small chunks

1 slightly rounded tbsp honey

speck white pepper

½ teasp ground ginger

½ teasp salt

1   Prick the washed and dried potato all over,
then bake on 100% power for 5 minutes.

2   Meanwhile, prepare the parsnips and lay the
pieces in an even layer in a lidded dish with the
water. Cover and cook on 100% power for 9
minutes, stirring once or twice, or until absolutely
tender when pierced with a slim, sharp knife.

3   Drain off the water and stand, covered with a
paper towel to dry them off, for 3 minutes. Then
purée in the food processor with the peeled and
cubed potato, the fat, honey and seasonings.
Process only until smooth – overprocessing may
cause them to go 'gluey'.

4   Pile into a small serving dish. Reheat, covered,
on 100% power for 3 minutes or until steaming.

COURGETTES PURÉE

Serves 4
Keeps 1 day under refrigeration
Do not freeze

A beautiful pale green, delicately flavoured purée.

1 lb (450 g) shiny-skinned courgettes, washed,
   topped, tailed and sliced ⅜ inch (1 cm) thick

2 oz (50 g/¼ cup) butter or margarine

½ teasp salt

8 grinds black pepper

good pinch ground nutmeg

1   Place the unpeeled courgette slices in a fairly
shallow lidded dish. No added water is necessary.
Cover and cook on 100% power for approximately
10 minutes or until absolutely tender when
pierced with a slim, sharp knife.

2 Stand for 3 minutes then drain off any liquid in the dish and purée in the food processor with the remaining ingredients. Pile into a serving dish.
3 To reheat, cover the dish and cook on 100% power for 3 minutes or until steaming.

BROCCOLI IN A CHEESE SAUCE

Serves 4

This is a delicious dish provided the broccoli is really fresh with tight green or purple florets. Reject any bunch that shows signs of yellowing, as any stale flavours are heightened in the microwave.

8–10 oz (225–275 g) very fresh broccoli (weight without leaves)
3 tbsp hot water
pinch of salt
5 grinds black pepper
For the sauce
1½ tbsp cornflour
10 fl oz (175 ml/1¼ cups) milk
½ teasp salt
8 grinds black pepper
pinch each of nutmeg and cayenne pepper
½ teasp Dijon mustard
1 oz (25 g/2 tbsp) butter
3 oz (75 g/¾ cup) finely grated mature Cheddar or crumbled Lancashire cheese
sprinkle of paprika (optional)

1 Cut off any thick tough stalks and discard. Then divide the broccoli into florets. Cut off the slimmer stalks and slice them thinly. Wash, then put both the stalks and the florets – stalks to the outside, florets in the middle – in a serving casserole with the hot water. Cover and cook on 100% power for 5–6 minutes or until the stalks are just tender when pierced with a sharp knife. If not, cook a little longer. Drain and leave covered.

2 Meanwhile, put the cornflour in a 2 pint (1.5 litre/5 cup) jug or bowl and mix to a cream with 4 tbsp of the milk. Gradually stir in the rest of the milk followed by all the remaining ingredients, except the butter and cheese. Cook uncovered on 100% power for 2 minutes, whisk well, then cook for a further 2–3 minutes until thick and bubbly.
3 Stir well to make sure the sauce is evenly thickened, then whisk in the butter and two thirds of the cheese (all of it, if you have no grill available). Coat the broccoli with the sauce, scatter with the remaining cheese and brown under a hot grill, or dust with paprika.

BROCCOLI WITH A SOUR CREAM SAUCE

Serves 4

A simple but delicious dish.

8–10 oz (225–275 g) broccoli (weight without leaves)
3 tbsp hot water
pinch of salt
5 grinds of black pepper
For the sauce
1 × 5–8 fl oz (150–225 ml/⅔–1 cup) carton soured cream, Greek-style yoghurt or creamed smetana
¼ teasp nutmeg
½ teasp salt
10 grinds black pepper
good pinch cayenne
For the garnish
sprinkle of paprika

1 Prepare and cook the broccoli as described in step 1 of Broccoli in a Cheese Sauce, above
2 While the broccoli is standing, prepare the sauce. Stir the seasonings into the carton of cream, yoghurt or smetana and heat on 80% power for 1

minute or until steaming. Coat the broccoli with the sauce and sprinkle lightly with the paprika.

BROCCOLI WITH SESAME SEEDS – *VARIATION*

Omit the sauce and sprinkle with 1 tbsp toasted sesame seeds instead.

FAGIOLINI VERDI CON PEPERONI E POMODORO (Green beans in a Pepper and Tomato Sauce)

Serves 6
Leftovers keep 2 days under refrigeration

A luscious dish of green beans in a pepper and tomato sauce that Tuscan cooks like to serve with their *bistecca alla Fiorentina*. It is also good with roast beef or veal.

1 lb (450 g) fresh green beans (bobo, shoe string or Kenya), topped and tailed and any strings removed

4 tbsp boiling water

For the sauce

3 tbsp olive oil

1½ tbsp minced dried onion

1 teasp dried minced garlic

1 fat red pepper, seeds removed and cut into long strips to match the beans

⅔ of a 14 oz (400 g) can tomatoes in juice

1 teasp salt

5 grinds black pepper

1 teasp brown sugar

½ teasp dried Italian herbs

1   Put all the sauce ingredients into a jug and cook, uncovered, on 80% power for 6 minutes

until as thick as a ketchup. Add 4 tbsp boiling water then pour over the beans, arranged in a shallow 10 inch (25 cm) lidded casserole and stir well. Cover and cook on 100% power for 8–10 minutes, stirring once, or until just bite tender. Stir again. Serve hot or cold.

2   To reheat, cook, covered, on 100% power for 4 minutes or until steaming.

KISHUIM REHOVOT (Courgettes in a Chilli Sauce)

A spicy sauce for the later, more mature courgettes of the season.

1 lb (450 g) courgettes, unpeeled but topped and tailed and cut in ½ inch (1.25 cm) slices

1 medium red pepper, seeds removed and cut in ½ inch (1.25 cm) cubes

For the sauce

1½ tbsp minced dried onion

1 teasp garlic granules

1 tbsp olive oil

1 teasp salt

8 grinds black pepper

1 teasp medium brown sugar

pinch of cayenne pepper or 1 teasp mild chilli powder

1 rounded tbsp tomato purée

4 tbsp hot water

2 teasp chopped parsley

1   Arrange the vegetables in a lidded casserole.

2   Whisk all the sauce ingredients together in a jug or bowl, then pour over the vegetables, cover and cook for 11–12 minutes, stirring once.

3   Stand covered for 3 minutes – the sauce should be thick and juicy. If it appears watery, cook the dish, uncovered, for a further 3 minutes or until the consistency is right.

INDIVIDUAL MUSHROOM AND HERB EGGAH

Serves 4
Freeze, uncooked, 1 month

This traditional Middle-Eastern dish, which makes an elegant starter or light vegetarian main dish, is especially creamy in texture when made with herb cream cheese instead of the more usual milk. The oven-ready mixture can be frozen uncooked but should be thawed and baked on the day it is to be served, either warm or cold.

butter for greasing dishes
1 oz (25 g/2 tbsp) butter
the bulbs and 3 inches (7.5 cm) of the green of a small bunch of spring onions, finely sliced
4 oz (125 g/1¼ cups) button mushrooms, finely sliced
3 eggs, beaten to blend
1 × 3½ oz (100 g) pack herb cream cheese or 4 oz (125 g/½ cup) loose
4 oz (125 g/1 cup) grated mature Cheddar or crumbled tasty Lancashire cheese
½ teasp salt
10 grinds black pepper
1 tbsp chopped parsley
For the garnish
tiny sprigs of parsley or other herbs

1   Grease 4 × 5–6 fl oz (150–175 ml/¾ cup) soufflé dishes or cocottes.
2   In a medium basin, melt the butter, covered by a paper towel, on 100% power for 1 minute. Add the spring onions and mushrooms, stir well to coat with the fat and cook uncovered for a further 4 minutes.
3   Meanwhile whisk the eggs in a small bowl until evenly blended.
4   Put the cream cheese in a larger bowl and stir in the grated cheese followed by the eggs, the buttered vegetables and the seasonings. Divide between the prepared dishes.
5   Arrange in a circle on the turntable or base of the oven, then cook uncovered on 30% power for 13 minutes.
6   Stand for 1 minute, then serve garnished with the sprigs of herbs.
7   The eggahs can be prepared in advance and reheated on 80% power for 1–2 minutes or until warm to the touch.

GRATIN OF PENNE, AUBERGINE AND TOMATO

Serves 4–6
Keeps 2 days under refrigeration
Do not freeze

Pasta quills that are about 1½ inches (4 cm) long and ½ inch (1.25 cm) wide are just the right size to soak up the glorious sauce. It may be more convenient to assemble the gratin in advance, omitting the top layer of cheese. Then cook it shortly before serving, when it will take about 10 minutes, covered, on 100% power and a further 5 minutes, uncovered, with the cheese topping.

1 lb (450 g) unpeeled aubergines, cut in 1 inch (2.5 cm) cubes
2 tbsp sunflower oil
For the sauce
2 tbsp olive oil
1 teasp minced dried garlic
2 × 14 oz (400 g) cans chopped tomatoes
1 tbsp tomato purée
1½ teasp salt
20 grinds black pepper
2 teasp light brown sugar
small bunch basil (12–15 leaves), finely chopped
12 oz (350 g/3 cups) penne (pasta quills)
7–8 oz (200–225 g/1 cup) mozzarella cheese, thinly sliced

1 Trim, wash and dry the aubergines and cut into small cubes. Put in a lidded casserole or bowl with the sunflower oil and mix together gently until the cubes are coated with the oil. Cover and cook on 100% power for 8 minutes, stirring once, until they are tender. Drain on paper towelling.

2 To prepare the tomato sauce: heat the olive oil in a 2 pint (1.25 litre/5 cup) bowl or jug on 100% power for 1 minute, then add all the remaining ingredients, except the basil and the cheese. Cook uncovered on 100% power for 12 minutes, stirring halfway, then add the chopped basil.

3 Cook the pasta in boiling water on top of the stove until it is tender but still very firm (about 10 minutes), drain well and add it to the aubergines. Then add the tomato sauce, stirring well.

4 Pour half the mixture into a lightly oiled ovenproof lasagne or gratin type dish about 11 × 8 × 2 inches (27.5 × 20 × 4 cm) or a round one 10 inches (25 cm) in diameter, cover with a layer of the sliced mozzarella and add the rest of the pasta mixture. Finish with a layer of mozzarella.

5 Cook uncovered at 100% power for 5 minutes or until cheese has melted.

MOUSSAKA VEGEVINA

Serves 4–5
Serve the same day
Do not freeze

This is a delicious dairy moussaka that makes a really tasty and nourishing meatless main course.

1¼ lb (600 g) (2 average) glossy aubergines, unpeeled and cut in ½ inch (1.25 cm) thick slices
1 tbsp salt
2 tbsp olive or sunflower oil
For the filling
7 oz (200 g/1¾ cups) mature Cheddar, grated
7 oz (200 g/¾ cup) herb-flavoured cream cheese or curd cheese

3 eggs beaten to blend (half reserved for topping)
½ teasp salt
10 grinds black pepper
1 tbsp chopped mixed chives and parsley
For the topping
reserved eggs
6 oz (175 g/1½ cups) mature Cheddar, grated

1 To minimize the amount of oil required, the aubergines should be pre-salted as follows: put the slices into the inner basket of a salad spinner or a colander, sprinkle lightly with salt, mixing gently to coat the slices, then leave for 30 minutes. Rinse off the salt and spin or dab dry.

2 Put the oil in a 3½–4 pint (2 litre/9–10 cup) lidded casserole or bowl and mix gently with the aubergine slices. Cover and cook on 100% power for 8 minutes (stirring once) until tender.

3 Beat the filling ingredients together and taste to make sure the mixture is highly seasoned. If not soft enough to spread, stir in a little milk.

4 In a rectangular or oval gratin dish, approx 10 × 8 × 2 inches (25 × 20 × 5 cm), layer the ingredients as follows: ⅓ of aubergine slices, half the cheese mix, ⅓ more aubergine slices, then the remainder of the cheese mix. Top with the remaining aubergines and cook uncovered on 100% power for 5 minutes.

5 Pour on the remaining eggs and scatter with the cheese. Cook uncovered on 50% power for a further 5 minutes until set, then brown briefly under a hot grill.

TOMATOES STUFFED WITH A HERB DRESSING

Serves 4

These can be served as a starter or as part of a vegetable platter with baked potatoes and Green Beans with Golden Almonds (see page 103)

4 large 'beef' tomatoes
sprinkling of sea salt
For the stuffing
4 heaped tbsp dry breadcrumbs
6 anchovies, drained and finely chopped or 2 teasp anchovy purée (may be omitted for a vegetarian meal)
½ teasp garlic granules
3 tbsp chopped parsley
6 large fresh leaves of basil, finely chopped
½ teasp dried herbes de Provence
2 tbsp finely sliced spring onion bulbs (4 bulbs plus 2 inches/5 cm of the green)
good pinch salt
10 grinds black pepper
2 tbsp olive oil
For greasing the dish
1 tbsp olive oil

1 If you have no dried breadcrumbs available, spread fresh crumbs in a thin layer on a plate covered with a paper towel. Cook on 100% power for 2½ minutes until dry to the touch.
2 Wash and dry the tomatoes. Slice off the tops then remove all the seeds, any hard core and liquid, season both the top and the cavity of each tomato with salt, then turn upside down to drain on a double piece of paper towel.
3 Prepare the stuffing by mixing all the ingredients together, then use to fill the cavity of each tomato.
4 Grease the base of a shallow dish (large enough to hold the tomatoes without touching) with the 1 tbsp of oil and arrange the tomatoes well apart in a circle round the edge.
5 Cook uncovered on 100% power for 5 minutes, then cover with the tops and cook for a further 1 minute. Leave for 5 minutes then serve at once.

POTATOES, RICE AND GRAINS

INTRODUCTION

The alchemy that can produce a 'baked' potato in five minutes was one of the first selling points used in the marketing of the microwave oven. In fact, the potato is actually steamed in its skin – an admirable method to be sure, but definitely not the same as true baking – when the skin becomes crisp and crunchy. But it is still the quickest and most convenient way to cook this starchy vegetable.

Timings for these microwave 'baked' potatoes are to be found in the Lexicon (see page 183) but, in this chapter, I have also used the method to make the traditional kind of mashed potato. If you prefer a creamier texture then you will want to cook peeled chunks of the vegetable in a little water instead. Baking is also an admirable way to cook sweet potatoes, which can go mushy when boiled on top of the stove. This initial 'baking' is used as a prelude to two delicious sweet potato purées. There are also several variations on plainly boiled new potatoes – scented with garlic, or mint, or tossed in toasted nuts. Potatoes sliced and cooked in a flavoured liquid, or even cider, make a superb dish for a dinner party. They cook extremely well in the microwave, taking half the conventional time. However, they do need a final browning to produce that delicious crustiness. For parboiling potatoes before roasting see page 122.

There is no saving of time when you cook rice in the microwave, but the convenience factor makes it well worthwhile. By adding a measured amount of stock or water and a little minced dried onion to the well-rinsed rice, you have a perfect dish or fluffy pilaff-style rice in fifteen minutes. Elaborating on this basic method, one can add all manner of spices and nuts or, in the case of the delicious Sesame Spiced Rice, a little minced meat to make a superb side dish to serve with cold meat or poultry or as a light supper dish in its own right.

As a change from rice, may I suggest a dish of bulgur, which is a form of cracked wheat that expands in the oven into tender little grains that are equally delicious served hot or cold. All rice and grain dishes reheat to perfection in the microwave – a few drops of cold water trickled onto the surface are transformed into steam which lightens and reheats the grains at the same time. For instructions on reheating rice, see page 184. ∎

CREAMY MASHED POTATOES

Serves 4
Keeps 2 days under refrigeration

Perhaps the most comforting food of all – smooth, satisfying and full of flavour.

1½ lb (675 g) mashing potatoes such as King Edward, Desirée or Maris Piper
4 tbsp hot water
1½ teasp salt
¼ teasp white pepper
1½ oz (40 g/3 tbsp) butter or margarine
4 fl oz (125 ml/½ cup) milk or chicken stock

1   Peel the potatoes and cut into 1 inch (2.5 cm) chunks. Arrange in a circle round the rim of a 10 inch (25 cm) shallow lidded casserole. Add the water, cover and cook on 100% power for 12 minutes or until there is no resistance when the potatoes are pierced with a slim, sharp knife.
2   Leave covered for 2 minutes, then drain and cover lightly with a paper towel, or tea towel, to absorb excess moisture.
3   While the potatoes are standing, put all the remaining ingredients into a 3½ pint (2 litre/9 cup) bowl and heat uncovered on 100% power for 3 minutes or until bubbling. Add the potatoes then whisk with a hand-held electric whisk, or a balloon whisk, until they lighten in colour and are creamy in texture.
4   Pile into a 7–8 inch (18–20 cm) shallow casserole and reheat for 1½ minutes until steaming, then serve.
NOTE: if desired, the mashed potatoes can be prepared up to an hour in advance then reheated, covered, for 4 minutes or until hot to the touch.

POTATOES PURÉED IN THE FRENCH STYLE – *VARIATION*

Prepare in exactly the same way but drop a whole egg into the potatoes before mashing them and add a further seasoning of ¼ teasp nutmeg. Either reheat uncovered on 100% power for 1½ minutes or put under a hot grill until golden brown. Alternatively, the potatoes can be covered with a thick layer of grated Cheddar before grilling until golden brown.

TRADITIONAL MASHED POTATOES

Serves 2 or 3
Keeps 2 days under refrigeration

If peeling potatoes seems a bore and you prefer a firmer textured mashed potato, the potatoes can be baked, when it is easier to strip off the skins, rather than boiled. The mashed texture is similar to that when you drop a nut of butter into a baked potato and mash it down at table.

If you use three potatoes (to serve 4 or 5), they will bake in 16 minutes and you will need to increase the other ingredients by half.

2 × 8 oz (225 g) baking potatoes, well scrubbed, nicked twice with the point of a sharp knife
1 oz (25 g/2 tbsp) butter or margarine
3 fl oz (75 ml/⅓ cup) hot milk or chicken stock
1 teasp salt
good pinch white pepper

1   Cook the potatoes on 100% power for 11 minutes. Leave for a few minutes until cool enough to handle.
2   Meanwhile, heat all the remaining ingredients in a large bowl on 100% power for 2½ minutes.
3   Strip the peel off the potatoes and cut in

roughly 1 inch (2.5 cm) chunks. Add to the hot milk mixture then beat with a balloon whisk until creamy.

4   Pile into a dish and reheat uncovered on 100% power for 1 minute, then enjoy.

A PURÉE OF SWEET POTATOES

Serves 4–6
Keeps 2 days under refrigeration
Do not freeze

A lovely dish to serve with baked or grilled fish.

1¾ lb (800 g) sweet potatoes
8 oz (225 g) Maris Piper or other mashing potatoes
2 oz (50 g/¼ cup) butter or margarine
1½ teasp salt
good pinch white pepper
2 egg yolks

1   Wash the potatoes well, prick all over with a fork (to prevent bursting), then cook uncovered on 100% power for 21 minutes.

2   Leave to rest for 5 minutes then, when cool enough to handle, skin and put into a warm bowl. Beat in all the remaining ingredients (most easily with a hand-held electric mixer or balloon whisk).

3   Turn into a microwave-safe dish and decorate with a fork. Reheat covered on 100% power for 4 minutes, or brown under a hot grill until crispy.

SWEET POTATO & APPLE PURÉE

Serves 4–5

This goes well with either a fish or a meat meal. The apples add an unusual dimension of flavour.

2 lb (900 g) sweet potatoes
nut of butter or margarine
1 large (8 oz/225 g) baking apple, peeled, cored and cut into roughly ½ inch (1.25 cm) cubes
1 teasp salt
8 grinds black pepper
additional 1 oz (25 g/2 tbsp) butter or margarine

1   Wash and dry the potatoes, prick all over with a fork and bake uncovered on 100% power for 20 minutes. Allow to stand until cool enough to handle.

2   In a shallow lidded casserole, melt the fat on 100% power for 40 seconds. Add the apple cubes, stir well, then cover and cook for 5 minutes, stirring once, until soft and collapsed.

3   Strip the skin from the potatoes and put in a warm bowl with the apples. Using a hand-held electric whisk, or a balloon whisk, cream the mixture until it is fluffy, beating in the seasonings and the ounce of fat. Pile into a dish and serve.

4   To reheat, cover and cook on 100% power for 4 minutes or until steaming.

NEW POTATOES

Serves 4
Always cook for the minimum period then add extra time by the minute. Overcooked new potatoes can become spongy in texture.

1 lb (450 g) small, even-sized new potatoes, scrubbed or scraped
2 tbsp water
coarsely ground sea salt
5 grinds black pepper
nut of butter or margarine

1   Put the potatoes in a lidded casserole with the water. Cover and cook for 9–11 minutes, stirring once. Test with a slim, sharp knife and cook an extra minute if necessary.

2   Drain and season with ½ teasp sea salt and 5 grinds black pepper.

3   Serve plain or with a nut of butter or margarine gently spooned round to coat them.

MINTED NEW POTATOES WITH BEURRE NOISETTE – *VARIATION*

Serves 6
This is rather more of a party dish.

1½ lb (675 g) small, even-sized new potatoes, scrubbed or scraped

2 tbsp water

3 small sprigs of mint

coarsely ground sea salt

8 grinds black pepper

For the beurre noisette

2 oz (50g g/¼ cup) unsalted butter

For the garnish

2 teasp chopped fresh mint

1   Put the potatoes in a lidded casserole with the water. Cover and cook on 100% power for 12–15 minutes or until cooked through when pierced with a sharp knife. Drain and leave covered.

2   Put the butter in a medium sized bowl and cook on 80% power until a pale fawn in colour (about 2 minutes).

3   Sprinkle the potatoes lightly with the salt and pepper then gently toss with the butter and garnish with the chopped mint.

NEW POTATOES AMANDINE – *VARIATION*

Serves 6

Cook exactly as for Minted New Potatoes, with these exceptions: omit the mint. Add 2 oz (50 g/½ cup) flaked almonds to the butter and cook as directed.

GARLIC SCENTED NEW POTATOES

Serves 6

These are excellent with roast lamb or grilled chops.

1½ lb (675 g) small new potatoes, scrubbed and dried

2 cloves of garlic, peeled and crushed

3 tbsp extra virgin olive oil

½ teasp sea salt

8 grinds black pepper

1   Put the potatoes in a 3 pint (1.75 litre/8 cup) lidded casserole.

2   Mix all the remaining ingredients in a small bowl, then pour over the potatoes and stir gently until they are coated with the seasoned oil.

3   Cover and cook on 100% power for 12–15 minutes or until the potatoes feel tender when pierced with a slim, sharp knife.

POTATOES BAKED IN CIDER

Serves 6
Leftovers keep 2 days under refrigeration
Do not freeze

This is a very good-tempered dish to serve at a dinner party. Complete the microwaving of the potatoes before the meal, then reheat briefly until steaming at the start and brown under the grill for 2–3 minutes just before serving.

2 lb (900 g) small, even potatoes (Wilja, or Maris Piper or other waxy varieties) sliced ⅛ inch (0.25 cm) thick
½ teasp garlic granules
4 tbsp sunflower oil
margarine for greasing the dish
sea salt
white pepper
10 fl oz (275 ml/1¼ cups) dry cider

1   Use a food processor, if possible, to slice the potatoes so they are of an even thickness.
2   Mix the garlic with the oil.
3   Lightly grease an entrée dish about 9 inches (23 cm) long and 2 inches (5 cm) deep and arrange a third of the potatoes in an even layer on the bottom. Drizzle a third of the oil over them, then lightly season with the salt and pepper. Arrange the remaining potatoes to make two further layers, sprinkling with the oil and seasoning as before.
4   Gently pour the cider down the side of the dish, cover and cook on 100% power for 30 minutes or until the potatoes feel tender when pierced with a slim, sharp knife.
5   Leave to stand for 5 minutes, then uncover and grill until golden brown and crispy.

POTATOES BAKED IN BEEF STOCK – *VARIATION*

Substitute 10 fl oz (275 ml/1¼ cups) hot beef stock for the cider and sprinkle each layer with a pinch of nutmeg.

POMMES CHÂTEAU – *VARIATION*

Serves 6
Leftovers keep 2 days under refrigeration
Do not freeze

Substitute melted butter or margarine for the oil and grate 8 oz (225 g/2 cups) Edam cheese. Sprinkle ⅓ of this cheese on each layer of potatoes. Grill as before.

POTATOES AND CELERIAC EN CASSEROLE – *VARIATION*

Substitute 1½ lb (675 g) potatoes and 12 oz (350 g) celeriac for the 2 lb (200 g) potatoes in any of the other three recipes.

TO PARBOIL POTATOES FOR ROASTING

Parboiling before roasting ensures that the potatoes are tender and fluffy inside with a really crunchy brown crust. Use a good roasting potato such as Desirée, King Edward or Pentland Dell.

1 lb potatoes (450 g) (to serve 2–3)

1   Peel the potatoes and cut into 1–1½ inch (2.5–3.5 cm) thick wedges.

2   Put in a shallow casserole with 2 tbsp water and cook covered on 100% power for 5 minutes, drain, stand covered with a paper towel for 5 minutes to dry off.

---

2 lb potatoes (900 g) (to serve 4–5)

---

1   Add 3 tbsp water and cook covered on 100% power for 8 minutes, then stand, covered, as described above.

SAVOURY RICE

Serves 6
Keeps 2 days under refrigeration
Freeze 3 months

This is the basic recipe to use whenever you want plainly cooked rice. Cooked in this way, every grain stays separate and the flavour is delicious.

---

10 oz (275 g/1⅔ cups) Patna or Basmati rice
2 tbsp oil
1½ tbsp minced dried onion
1 pint (575 ml/2½ cups) hot chicken or vegetable stock
1½ level teasp salt
10 grinds black pepper

---

1   Turn the rice into a sieve and hold under the cold tap until the water runs clear (this will remove excess starch).
2   Put the drained rice into a 3 pint (1.5 litre/8 cup) lidded casserole or bowl.
3   Mix all the ingredients, except the rice, in a large jug then add to the rice and stir well. Cover and cook on 100% power for 5 minutes or until bubbling, then cook on 80% power for a further 10 minutes.
4   Allow to stand covered for 5 minutes, then

fluff up with a fork.
5   To reheat, sprinkle the surface with a little cold water, cover and cook on 100% power for 3–4 minutes or until steaming. Fluff up with a fork and serve as freshly cooked.

SAVOURY RICE WITH PINE KERNELS – *VARIATION*

Just before serving, stir in 1½ oz (40 g/⅓ cup) of pine kernels, which have been cooked on 100% power for 3 minutes, stirring once, until golden.

A PISTACHIO AND SWEET SPICE PILAFF

Serves 6
Keeps 2 days under refrigeration
Freeze 1 month

This is no more time-saving than conventional cooking but the rice will not catch and it cooks to perfection every time without being watched. This is a delicious pilaff by any standards, with an interesting blend of flavours and textures.

---

10 oz (275 g/1⅔ cups) white Basmati rice
2 oz (50 g/½ cup) shelled pistachios, coarsely chopped (or 2 oz/50 g/½ cup toasted cashews)
1½ oz (40 g/3 tbsp) butter or margarine
1 medium onion, finely chopped
1 pint (575 ml/2½ cups) hot vegetable or chicken stock (water plus cube)
¼ teasp ground turmeric
½ teasp salt
½ teasp mixed sweet spice

---

1   Turn the rice into a sieve and hold under the

cold tap until the water runs out clear (this removes excess starch).

2   Cook the nuts on 100% power for 3 minutes, stirring once, until golden.

3   Melt the fat in a 3 pint (1.75 litre/8 cup) lidded casserole or bowl on 80% power for 1½ minutes.

4   Stir in the onion, cover and cook for 4 minutes.

5   Put the hot stock in a large jug or bowl and stir in all the remaining ingredients, except the rice and nuts.

6   Uncover the dish and add the drained rice and the hot liquid mixture. Cover and cook on 100% power for 5 minutes until bubbling, then reduce to 80% power and cook for a further 10 minutes.

7   Leave to stand, covered, for 5 minutes, then stir in the nuts with a fork.

GOLDEN RICE – *VARIATION*

Serves 6
Keeps 2 days under refrigeration
Freeze 1 month

Make in exactly the same way as the Pistachio and Sweet Spice Pilaff but without the nuts and with these ingredients:

10 oz (275 g/1⅔ cups) white Basmati rice, soaked in cold water for 15 minutes then rinsed and drained in a sieve
1½ oz (40 g/3 tbsp) butter or margarine
1 medium onion, finely chopped
1 pint (575 ml/2½ cups) hot vegetable or chicken stock (boiling water plus cubes)
½ teasp salt
¼ teasp powdered saffron or ground turmeric
½ teasp ground cumin
1 cinnamon stick
¼ teasp ground cardamom (or the seeds from 2 cardamom pods)
1 bay leaf

Discard the bay leaf and cinnamon stick before serving.

SESAME SPICED RICE

Serves 4–5
Keeps 2 days under refrigeration
Freeze 3 months

A delicious side dish to serve with cold meat or chicken.

8 oz (225 g/1⅓ cups) Basmati rice
1 tbsp oil
8 oz (225 g) raw minced beef
5 fl oz (150 ml/⅔ cup) full red wine (such as Côte du Rhône)
1½ tbsp dried minced onion
1 tbsp soy sauce
2 teasp paprika
1 teasp salt
15 fl oz (425 ml/2 cups) strong hot beef stock
For the garnish
4 tbsp brown sesame seeds

1   Turn the rice into a sieve and leave under the cold tap until the water runs out clear (this removes excess surface starch). Leave to drain.

2   Put the oil and the raw meat into a 3½–4 pint (2 litre/9–10 cup) deep lidded casserole or bowl, stir well with a fork to break up any lumps, then cook uncovered for 5 minutes, stirring once. The meat will be brown.

3   Add the wine, stir well and cook uncovered for 3 minutes to concentrate the flavour. Add the drained rice and all the remaining ingredients, stir well, cover and cook on 100% power for 5 minutes until bubbling, then cook on 80% power for a further 10 minutes.

4   Allow to stand for 3 minutes, then fluff up with a fork, scatter with the sesame seeds and serve.

5   To reheat from cold, sprinkle the surface with a little cold water, cover and cook on 100% power for 4 minutes or until steaming, then fluff up with a fork.

BULGUR AND PINE KERNEL PILAFF

Serves 4–5 people
Keeps 2 days under refrigeration
Freeze 3 months

This is a marvellous dish that is equally good served hot with a main dish or cold as a salad.

6 oz (175 g/1 cup) medium bulgur (cracked wheat)

2 teasp freshly grated orange rind

3 tbsp raisins

15 fl oz (425 ml/2 cups) boiling chicken stock (cubes plus boiling water)

2 teasp minced dried onion

1 tbsp oil

1½ oz (40 g/⅓ cup) pine kernels, toasted (see page 182)

1 oz (25 g/1 rounded tbsp) chopped parsley (enough to 'green' the pilaff)

1 small bunch spring onions, trimmed and finely sliced

1   Put the bulgur, orange rind and raisins in a 2½ pint (1.5 litre/6 cup) deep lidded casserole. Mix the stock, onion and oil in a jug or bowl, then pour onto the bulgur. Cover tightly and cook on 100% power for 4 minutes until bubbling, then turn down to 50% power for a further 4 minutes.
2   Take out of the microwave and leave to stand, covered, for 5 minutes.
3   To serve hot, fluff the pilaff with a fork and stir in the pine kernels, parsley and spring onions. Reheat, covered, on 100% power for 2 minutes.
4   To serve cold, allow the pilaff to cool for 15 minutes before stirring in the remaining ingredients.

DESSERTS

INTRODUCTION

With the exception of several sauces and a baked custard, every dish in this chapter contains fruit in one form or another, so each can be used as an alternative to fresh fruit.

There are homely dishes, such as baked and stewed apples, albeit with some sophisticated additions, and a variety of fresh fruit compotes and salads, some of which are flavoured with a little caramel. (I have gone in some depth into the preparation of this useful ingredient in the microwave because the technique is little short of miraculous in its simplicity and effect.) There are also several dishes – based on poached fruit, such as pears and bananas – that are cooked in cider or red wine.

Many of the dishes can be sweetened with a granular sweetener instead of sugar which makes them a useful addition to a sugar-free regime. I have, however, used a variety of brown sugars for such dishes as the luscious Gingered Peach Crumble and the Pecan and Pineapple Upside-Down Cake. I worked long and hard to produce a creamy-textured microwave 'baked' custard. There is a choice between a simple milk-based crème caramel and the richer crème brûlée. Despite its name my version doesn't require a grill to crispen the mirror-like caramel on the top. At the end of this chapter, I have included three preserves – an exquisite lemon curd, a tangy mint jelly and a luscious conserve of dried apricots. Despite my earlier reservations, I have to admit that for producing a small amount of any jam or fruit butter, the microwave way is sure and speedy and requires no special equipment. I am particularly impressed with the method of sterilizing jam jars in it that avoids the need to add the heat of a conventional oven to that of a summer's day. ■

CHOCOLATE SAUCE 1

Serves 6
Keeps 2 weeks under refrigeration
Freeze 2 months

This is ideal for serving with icecream or pouring over little choux buns.

6 oz (175 g) dessert chocolate
1 oz (25 g/2 tbsp) butter or margarine
2 tbsp double, whipping or non-dairy cream or strained Greek-style yoghurt
1 tbsp Tia Maria or Sabra liqueur

1   Break the chocolate into small pieces and put into a small bowl with the fat. Cover with a plate and cook on 100% power for 1½ minutes.
2   Uncover and whisk in the cream or yoghurt until the mixture is smooth.
3   Finally, whisk in the liqueur. Serve warm or cold.
4   To reheat, cook on 100% power for 1½ minutes. Do not boil.

CHOCOLATE SAUCE 2

This is ideal to serve with poached pears or peaches and is lighter in texture.
   Omit the fat and the liqueur and replace them with 3 tbsp of poaching syrup from the fruit.

RASPBERRY CRÈME BRÛLÉE

Serves 4–5
The rich little custards are set on a bed of raspberries and topped with a shiny glaze of crisp caramel. Serve the same day or the glaze may begin to 'weep'.

8 oz (225 g/1½ cups) fresh or part-defrosted frozen raspberries
1 oz (25 g/2 tbsp) sugar
For the crème
15 fl oz (425 ml/2 cups) whipping cream
1 teasp vanilla essence or 1 vanilla pod
3 level tbsp caster sugar
5 egg yolks
1 recipe dark brown caramel (see page 140, Basic Caramel)

1   Have ready 4–6 × 4 fl oz (125 ml/½ cup) ramekins, *petit pots* or soufflé dishes.
2   Divide the hulled raspberries between the little dishes and sprinkle lightly with the sugar.
3   Put the cream (and the vanilla pod if used) in a 2 pint (1.5 litre/5 cup) jug and heat covered on 100% power for 2½ minutes or until steaming (do not let it boil). Remove the pod and dry for further use.
4   Meanwhile, put the sugar in a bowl and gradually whisk in the egg yolks until creamy and light in colour. Slowly pour the hot cream (and the essence if used) on to the egg mixture, whisking only until the mixture is evenly blended, no longer, or the custard may be full of holes. Pour into the ramekins.
5   Cook uncovered on 30% power for 13 minutes until the custards are barely set when gently shaken – they will set further as they cool. Allow to stand on a cooling tray, then chill thoroughly.
6   Make the caramel (see recipe on page 140), plunge the base of the dish into a bowl containing one inch (2.5 cm) of cold water, then gently spoon the caramel over the chilled crèmes. Allow to set (about 10 minutes). Refrigerate until required.

MOCHA MOUSSE LAYERED WITH WHITE PEACHES, PEARS OR MORELLO CHERRIES

Serves 6
Will keep 4 days under refrigeration
Freeze 3 months (without fruit)

The fruit makes a refreshing contrast to the richness of the mousse. However, you may prefer to replace the fruit layer with one of nuts, and serve an assortment of exotic fruits – fresh figs, berries, pineapple, mango – at the side of the mousse.

1 medium can white peaches, choice pears or stoned morello or black cherries
4 oz (125 g) plain dessert chocolate, broken into small pieces
1½ teasp dark coffee granules dissolved in 3 teasp boiling water
4 eggs, separated
1½ tbsp orange or chocolate-flavoured liqueur
3 teasp caster sugar
For the garnish
1 oz (25 g/¼ cup) toasted almond nibs or chopped hazelnuts (see page 182)

1   Drain the fruit (reserve the syrup for other use) and lay on paper towels to dry as much as possible, then slice or cut in small dice (leave the cherries whole).
2   In a large bowl, melt the broken-up chocolate with the hot coffee at 100% power for 1 minute. Stir well, then drop in the egg yolks one at a time, stirring vigorously between each addition so that the mixture thickens evenly. Stir in the liqueur, then allow the mixture to go cold.
3   Whisk the whites until they hold soft peaks, then whisk in the caster sugar a teaspoonful at a time. Stir a quarter of this meringue into the chocolate mixture to lighten it, then gently fold in

the remainder.
4   Spoon half the mixture into 6 wine glasses, scatter with fruit, then cover with the remaining mousse. Chill overnight then decorate with the nuts shortly before serving.

A KISSEL OF SUMMER FRUIT

Serves 7–8
Kissel may be made 2 days in advance
Leftovers freeze 3 months

The sliced fruit adds a most pleasing texture contrast to the smooth fruit 'jelly'.

1 lb (450 g/4 cups) fresh or frozen blackcurrants
8 oz (225 g/2 cups) fresh or frozen redcurrants
3 tbsp water
6–8 oz (175–225 g/¾–1 cup) caster sugar
9 fl oz (250 ml/1 cup plus 2 tbsp) boiling water
blackcurrant cordial, if necessary
2 level tbsp arrowroot, or cornflour, for each pint (575 ml/2½ cups) of fruit liquid (arrowroot is the preferred thickener as it gives a lighter gel)
2 tbsp Crème de Cassis (blackcurrant liqueur) or lemon juice
To fold into the kissel
8 oz (225 g/1½ cups) strawberries
2 large ripe bananas, sliced

1   To defrost frozen fruit, put in a wide shallow dish, cover and cook on 30% power for 10 minutes stirring once. Leave covered for 2 minutes then treat as fresh.
2   To cook the fruit, put it into a wide, shallow dish, 10–11 inches (25–27.5 cm) in diameter and 2 inches (5 cm) deep, or a large bowl, add 3 tbsp of the measured water, cover and cook on 100% power for 7½ minutes, or until a blackcurrant can easily be squashed between the fingers.
3   Purée through a fine food mill into a 3½ pint

(2 litre/9 cup) jug or bowl and stir in sugar to taste until it dissolves, then stir in the boiling water. There should be 1 pint (575 ml/2½ cups) of liquid. If not, make up to the pint (575 ml/2½ cups) with a little blackcurrant cordial.

4   In a small basin, mix the arrowroot or cornflour with the liqueur (or lemon juice if preferred) then stir into the purée. Cover and cook on 100% power for 4 minutes, stir and cook a further 1 minute until bubbly and clear.

5   Allow to cool for 20 minutes, then stir in the fresh fruit. Turn into a glass bowl, or individual glasses, and chill for several hours or overnight.

GINGERED FRESH PEACH, OR NECTARINE, AND HAZELNUT CRUMBLE

Serves 4–5
Keeps 2 days under refrigeration
Do not freeze

A party version of a family favourite, the combination of juicy fruit and nutty crumble is irresistible. If you prefer them to hazelnuts, grind whole unskinned almonds in the food processor until like coarse sand.

For the fruit
1½ lb (675 g) ripe peaches or nectarines, stoned and sliced ½ inch (1.25 cm) thick

2 oz (50 g/¼ cup) soft light brown sugar

2 teasp cornflour

¼ teasp ground nutmeg

2 oz (50 g/¼ cup) crystallized ginger, finely chopped (optional but nice) or ½ teasp ground ginger

1 tbsp fresh lemon juice

For the topping
3 oz (75 g/¾ cup) white or 85% extraction (wheat meal) plain flour

pinch salt

3 oz (75 g/⅓ cup) light brown sugar

3 oz (75 g/¾ cup) coarsely ground hazelnuts

3 oz (75 g/⅓ cup) butter or margarine, cut in roughly 1 inch (2.5 cm) cubes

For the accompaniment (optional)
Greek yoghurt, smetana or 8% fromage frais

1   Put the peaches or nectarines in a large bowl, toss with the mixed sugar, cornflour, nutmeg and ginger, then sprinkle with the lemon juice. Turn into a lightly greased oven-to-table dish measuring approx 11 inches × 8 inches (28 cm × 20 cm) (e.g., gratin or lasagne-type), and arrange in an even layer.

2   To make the topping, put all the ingredients into a bowl and rub lightly to a moist crumble. Sprinkle evenly over the fruit, and cook uncovered on 100% power for 11 minutes, or until bubbling round the edges and when the fruit feels tender when pierced with a sharp knife. If not ready, cook for a further 30 seconds–1 minute.

3   If you like a really crunchy topping, grill gently for 3 minutes. In either case, leave to stand for 10 minutes before serving.

PINEAPPLE AND PECAN UPSIDE-DOWN CAKE WITH FRUIT SAUCE

Serves 4–5
Keeps 2 days under refrigeration
Freeze 1 month

This is a very light sponge under a delectable butterscotch glaze. It is nicest served warm.

For the glaze
2 oz (50 g/¼ cup) butter or margarine

1 rounded tbsp golden syrup

2 oz (50 g/¼ cup) dark brown (dark muscovado) sugar

For the fruit sauce
1 small (8 oz/225 g) can pineapple (6 rings)

1 oz (25 g/¼ cup) shelled pecans

For the cake

4 oz (125 g/½ cup) soft margarine

4 oz (125 g/1 ½ cup) caster sugar

4 oz (125 g/1 cup) self raising flour or special
   sponge flour or 4 oz cake flour plus 1 teasp
   baking powder

2 eggs

1 teasp vanilla essence

For the sauce

3 teasp cornflour

2 tbsp caster sugar

1 tbsp lemon juice

2 tbsp orange juice

reserved syrup from the fruit (8 fl oz/225 ml/1 cup
   liquid in all)

1 teasp each grated orange and lemon rind

1   Select a soufflé dish or round microwave-safe plastic or glass container about 7–8 inches (18–20 cm) across and 2 inches (5 cm) deep.

2   Melt the fat in a small bowl lightly covered with a paper towel on 100% power for 1 minute. Use a little butter or margarine to grease the chosen container. To the remainder of the butter or margarine add the golden syrup and sugar, stir, then cook uncovered on 100% power for 1 minute, stir and cook a further 1 minute. Pour this butterscotch into the chosen dish.

3   Drain the pineapple, reserving the juice, and arrange on the glaze, placing the pecans in the gaps between the rings of fruit.

4   Beat all the cake ingredients together by hand or machine until smooth and glossy – 2 minutes by hand – 15 seconds in a food processor. Spoon over the fruit and cook on 100% power for 5½ minutes or until a cocktail stick comes out clean from the centre. If still moist, give it another minute (there may still be areas of dampness on the surface that will disappear during the resting time).

5   Allow to rest for 5 minutes, then turn out onto a serving dish.

6   To make the sauce: in the serving jug, mix the cornflour and sugar thoroughly, then stir in the

liquids and the rinds. Microwave on 100% power for 1½ minutes, stir and cook for a further 2½ minutes until bubbling and clear. Serve hot. May be reheated on 80% power for 2 minutes.

CARAMEL FRUIT SALAD WITH TOASTED PECANS

Serves 6–8
Leftovers keep 1 day under refrigeration

The jewel-like colours of the fruits are shown off to their best advantage when the salad is piled into champagne flutes or sundae glasses. Serve with a crisp not-too-sweet biscuit, such as a finger of shortbread.

For the syrup marinade

juice squeezed from the remaining orange pith

2 tbsp lemon juice

1 recipe dark caramel (see page 140, Basic
   Caramel)

2 tbsp Grand Marnier (or other orange-flavoured
   liqueur)

3 large navel oranges, peeled and segmented

1 large ripe mango, peeled and sliced

8 oz (225 g/1½ cups) seedless green or black
   grapes

3 ripe bananas, peeled and sliced

2–3 oz (50–75 g/½–¾ cups) shelled toasted
   pecans

1   For the syrup marinade, squeeze any remaining juice from the 'skeletons' of the oranges into a small bowl and add the lemon juice.

2   Prepare the dark caramel and then check further cooking by standing the base in a bowl containing 1 inch (2.5 cm) of cold water.

3   Heat the fruit juices on 100% power for 1½ minutes then, covering your hand to avoid any spattering liquid, add to the hot caramel and stir.

4   Return to the microwave and reheat on 100% power for 1 minute, or until the sauce is smooth and homogenous when stirred. Add the Grand Marnier, mixing well.

5   Prepare the fruit and put into a bowl, then pour over the caramel syrup. Leave for 2 hours at room temperature, during which time juice will be drawn out from the fruit to make a glorious sauce. Chill until required.

6   Meanwhile, cut the shelled pecans lengthwise, arrange on a flat dish in a single layer. Cook in 100% power for 3 minutes or until crunchy.

7   Sprinkle on the fruit salad just before serving.

CARAMELIZED CLEMENTINES

Serves 6–8
Keeps 3 days under refrigeration
Do not freeze

The slightly bitter taste of the caramel contrasts well with the rather bland sweetness of the juice. This dish looks stunning decorated with sprigs of clementine leaves.

12–16 clementines (according to size)

5 tbsp orange juice

1 tbsp lemon juice

1 recipe dark caramel syrup (see page 140, Basic Caramel)

1 tbsp orange-flavoured liqueur (Curaçao, Grand Marnier, Cointreau, Aurum)

1   Several hours before serving, peel the clementines, removing as much of the pith as possible but leaving them whole, then place them side by side in a lidded container.

2   Put the orange and lemon juice in a small microwave-safe bowl.

3   Prepare the caramel and, as soon as it is ready, check any further cooking by standing the dish in a bowl of cold water.

4   Heat the juices uncovered on 100% power for 1 minute, or until steaming, then, covering your hand with a towel to protect it from spattering liquid, add to the caramel, stirring well. If some of the caramel has set return it to the microwave and heat on 100% power for 1–2 minutes until smooth and homogenous.

5   Stir in the liqueur, then pour over the clementines. Leave for 2 hours at room temperature, basting several times with the syrup, then cover and chill until required.

FRESH ORANGE AND PINEAPPLE COMPOTE

Serves 6
Keeps 1 day under refrigeration
Do not freeze

The slight thickening of the juices gives this kind of fruit compote a little more body. It is delicious served with a vanilla or caramel-flavoured icecream or with thick yoghurt lightly sweetened with honey.

4–6 slices, each ¾ inch (2 cm) thick, cut from one fine ripe pineapple (number of slices depends on the size of the fruit)

2 navel oranges

For the syrup

3 oz (75 g/⅓ cup) granulated sugar (2 oz/50 g/¼ cup if fruit syrup is used, see below) or granular sweetener added after cooking

4 fl oz (125 ml/½ cup) hot water or leftover syrup (from poached or canned fruit)

3 fl oz (75 ml/⅓ cup) orange juice (from 1 medium orange)

2 teasp cornflour

2 tbsp lemon juice

2 tbsp Cointreau or Grand Marnier (optional)

A Quartet of Vegetables – (clockwise) – Braised Red Cabbage in the Viennese Style, Broccoli (see Lexicon), here topped with toasted Sesame Seeds, Orange Glazed Carrots, Courgettes with a Honey Glaze

1 With a serrated knife (a bread knife is excellent), remove the skin from the pineapple, slice and cut out the core with a 1 inch (2.5 cm) cutter, or cut each slice in half and then remove the core section.

2 Remove the skin and pith from the oranges, using a knife with a serrated blade, then cut in between the sections to release the flesh from the pith. Put all the fruit in a serving dish.

3 Put the sugar, water (or fruit syrup) and orange juice into a jug or bowl, cover and heat on 100% power for 2 minutes.

4 Add the cornflour, mixed to a cream with the lemon juice, then heat for 3 minutes until thickened and bubbly, stirring once. Add the liqueur, if used, then pour over the fruit and mix gently.

5 Chill for several hours, stirring once.

PINEAPPLE, MANGO AND KIWI FRUIT COMPOTE – *VARIATION*

Serves 6

This is a delightful presentation when served in halves of small pineapples.

3 small pineapples
1 can (14 oz/400 g) lychees
1 large ripe mango
syrup from the same ingredients above, but using juice strained from the lychees and Amaretto liqueur (if available)
For the garnish
2 kiwi fruit

1 Cut the pineapples lengthwise through the flesh and the leaves, then scoop out the flesh with a grapefruit knife, discarding the hard core. Cut in pieces about 1 inch (2.5 cm) × ¾ inch (2 cm) and put in a bowl with the drained lychees.

2 Peel the mango either with a potato peeler (if firm), or a serrated knife (if fairly soft), then cut away from the stone in slices as though it were a peach. Cut these slices in two or three according to the size and add to the other fruit.

3 Pour on the hot syrup, stir well and refrigerate when cold. Shortly before serving, spoon into the pineapple shells and garnish with slices of the peeled kiwi fruit.

CRESCENTS OF GALIA OR OGEN MELON IN A CHERRY WINE SAUCE

Serves 6
Keeps 4 days under refrigeration

Buy the melon several days beforehand to ensure it is fully ripe – it should then have a musky perfume and the skin of the Galia will have turned an even yellow.

1 large ripe melon (any canteloupe type but preferably Galia or Ogen)
For the sauce
1 tbsp soft light brown sugar
1 tbsp cornflour
1 can (15 oz/425 g/2 cups) stoned black or morello cherries in syrup
2 tbsp lemon juice
4 tbsp fruity red wine, orange juice or mango juice
2 tbsp cherry brandy

1 In a large microwave-safe jug or bowl mix the sugar and cornflour, then gradually add the juice strained from the cherries, the lemon juice and the wine (or fruit juice).

2 Cook on 100% power for 2 minutes, then stir well and cook for a further 2–3 minutes until slightly thickened and glossy. Stir in the cherry

Tomatoes Stuffed with a Herb Dressing, Gratin of Penne, Aubergine and Tomato

brandy and cherries and allow to go cold.

3   An hour before serving, halve and quarter the melon, remove the seeds then cut into crescents 1·inch (2.5 cm) thick. Carefully remove the peel with a sharp knife, then arrange the crescents in a circle on a large flat plate, with the bowl of cherry sauce in the centre.

NOTE ON BAKING APPLES

The cooking time will vary according to the maturity of the apples, so it is a good idea to check progress from time to time. The cooked apples should look slightly wrinkled but not completely collapsed as cooking will continue during the standing time.

If you find that the apples burst during cooking, it may be that the sugar in the filling is attracting the microwaves and causing uneven cooking. Try putting only half the filling in the core cavity and the remainder in the dish around the apples. This can then be spooned into the cavity just before serving.

To allow plenty of room for filling, enlarge the cavity slightly once the core has been removed.

NOTE: 2 apples filled with half the stuffing and surrounded by 2 tbsp of the liquid will take 6–7 minutes.

The flavour of a baked apple is at its peak when served warm rather than cold.

POMMES BONNE FEMME

Serves 4
Keeps 2 days under refrigeration

Fruity and spicy.

1 tbsp rum or lemon juice
4 rounded tbsp sultanas or raisins
4 × 7–8 oz (225 g) Bramley baking apples

For the filling

4 tbsp medium brown sugar
1 tbsp toasted ground hazelnuts
⅛ teasp each of ground nutmeg, cinnamon and cardamom (or mixed sweet spice)
1 oz (25 g/2 tbsp) butter or margarine
4 tbsp orange or mango juice

1   Pour the rum or lemon juice over the sultanas in a small bowl, cover tightly and heat on 100% power for 1½ minutes. Leave to stand while you mix together the sugar, nuts and spices.

2   Core the apples and nick the skin round the centre of each apple with a slim, sharp knife to prevent it from bursting.

3   Arrange the apples slightly apart in a baking dish and put a tbsp of the sultanas at the bottom of each core cavity. Then fill up with the spiced sugar mixture, strewing any that will not fit in around the apples in the dish. Dot with the butter or margarine, pour the fruit juice over the apples and cook uncovered on 100% power for 10–11 minutes.

4   Allow to stand 10–15 minutes before serving.

TUTTI FRUTTI BAKED APPLES

Serves 4
Keeps 2 days under refrigeration

A simple but refreshing dessert to serve plain or with custard or yoghurt.

4 × 8 oz (225 g) Bramley baking apples
For the filling
4 tbsp chopped walnuts
4 tbsp raisins
2 tbsp lemon juice
4 teasp soft brown sugar
2 tbsp golden syrup
4 tbsp orange or apple juice

1 Core the apples and nick the skin round the centre with a slim, sharp knife to prevent them from bursting. Arrange slightly apart in a round dish.

2 Mix the filling ingredients together and use to stuff the core cavity of each apple loosely.

3 Mix the juice with the golden syrup and spoon over the apples. Cook uncovered on 100% power for 10–11 minutes. Stand for 10–15 minutes before serving.

BAKED APPLES STUFFED WITH NUTS AND RAISINS IN SPICED WINE

Serves 4
Keeps 2 days under refrigeration

A rather more sophisticated version.

4 × 8 oz (225 g) Bramley baking apples
For the filling
4 tbsp raisins
4 tbsp kosher or other port-type sweet red wine
4 tbsp light brown sugar
1 teasp ground cinnamon
4 tbsp water or apple juice

1 Put the raisins in a small bowl, add the wine, cover and cook on 100% power for 1½ minutes. Stir in the remaining filling ingredients.

2 Core the apples and nick the skin round the centre to prevent them from bursting. Arrange the apples well apart in a round dish and stuff the core cavity of each one loosely with the filling. Add the liquid to the dish and cook uncovered on 100% power for 10–11 minutes. Stand for 10–15 minutes before serving.

NOTE: 2 apples, filled with half the stuffing and surrounded by 2 tbsp of the liquid, will take 6–7 minutes.

CARAMEL

This is a particularly delicious and versatile preparation but many feel fearful of making it on top of the stove as the process can be beset with pitfalls: the sugar sometimes crystallizes into tiny lumps that are impossible to melt down and it takes experience to judge the exact moment to remove it from the heat.

After very careful experimentation, I have now worked out a completely foolproof method in the microwave. The dish is covered during the entire cooking period so that the condensing steam washes any undissolved sugar from the sides and so prevents it crystallizing.

Boiling sugar is hot stuff so it is important to choose the right cooking dish and to follow the instructions for handling it carefully. At first it is a wise precaution to have a large bowl of cold water standing in the sink to arrest cooking when the sugar has reached the right degree of caramelization. But when you are more experienced you may find that the particular dish you use for caramel does not retain heat out of the oven so you can dispense with this safeguard.

The easiest and most foolproof container is a shallow lidded casserole of opaque glass-ceramic with a clear glass lid, which makes it easy to see the progress of caramelization. I use one 7½ inches (18 cm) in diameter and 2½ inches (6 cm) deep, made of Corning Microwave Ware.

USES FOR CARAMEL

Before you start to make the caramel it is vital to decide how you intend to use it, as it sets very quickly.

1 Immediately it has been made it can be used without further additions to line a mould for a conventional crème caramel or to run on top of Raspberry Crème Brûlèe (see page 130).

2   It can be diluted immediately with hot water or fruit juice to make a sauce to serve with Individual Crème Caramel (see page 141), or a syrup for fruit (Caramelized Clementines or Caramel Fruit Salad with Toasted Pecans see pages 133–134).

3   It can be combined with cream to make a Blond Caramel Sauce (see page 140).

If it *should* set before you can use it, simply reheat, uncovered, on 100% power for 2 minutes until it liquefies again.

THE BASIC CARAMEL

Serves 6–8
Keeps for months in the refrigerator

6 oz (175 g/¾ cup) granulated sugar
3 tbsp cold water

1   Have ready a large bowl of cold water (standing in the sink).

2   In a round lidded glass-ceramic casserole measuring approx 7½ inches × 2½ inches (18.75 cm × 6 cm) mix the sugar and water to a smooth mush, cover and cook on 100% power for 2 minutes. Uncover, stir well to ensure that the sugar has melted and the liquid is clear, then re-cover and cook for a further 6½ minutes.

3   Uncover and stir well. At this stage, the caramel should be a light golden brown or 'caramel blond' – ideal for a creamy sauce.

4   To reach a rich brown 'burnt sugar' caramel it needs a further 30 seconds–1 minute, making 9 minutes in all. Add extra time in 30-second bursts if necessary.

5   Remove with care from the oven using a cloth or towel, and immediately plunge the base of the container into the bowl of cold water to arrest the caramelization process.

6   It is now ready to be used.

BLOND CARAMEL SAUCE

Keeps 2 weeks under refrigeration
Freeze 2 months

Served on icecream or with poached pears or peaches, this is a sauce with an unforgettable flavour.

1 recipe caramel blond (see above, Basic Caramel)
10 fl oz (275 ml/1¼ cups) whipping cream
3 tbsp soured cream, strained Greek-style yoghurt or 8% fromage frais

1   Have the cream ready in a jug. As soon as the caramel is ready (after 8½ minutes' cooking), put the cream in the microwave and heat on 100% power for 3 minutes or until steaming.

2   Protecting your arm with a cloth (for fear of spitting caramel), slowly add the cream to the caramel, stirring constantly.

3   Finally, stir in the soured cream, yoghurt or fromage frais. If part of the caramel has already set on the bottom of the dish, reheat it on 100% power for 1 minute or until it is liquid again. Refrigerate until required.

A RICH CARAMEL SAUCE

Keeps for months in the refrigerator

This is the delectable sauce to serve with Individual Crème Caramel (see page 141) or over icecream. It should flow lazily – like golden syrup – off a spoon. If too thick, simply stir in a little extra hot water.

1 recipe Basic Caramel (see page 140)
4–5 tbsp hot water

1   Boil the water and keep it ready to use.
2   As soon as the caramel has reached the right colour – chestnut brown – cover your arm and hand, holding the dish with a tea towel (to avoid splashes of the boiling mixture), and add the hot water to the dish.
3   Stir until it dissolves in the caramel.
4   If part of the caramel sets, reheat on 100% power for 1–2 minutes until it can be combined into a homogeneous mixture.

INDIVIDUAL CRÈME CARAMEL

Serves 5–6
Keeps 1 day under refrigeration
Do not freeze

These luscious custards are cooked on a very low setting that ensures a perfect texture without the need for a bain-marie (waterbath). To simplify even further, do not turn them out, simply run a layer of Caramel Sauce on top of each custard.

1½ oz (40 g/3 tbsp) caster sugar
2 eggs
2 additional egg yolks
½ teasp vanilla essence
15 fl oz (425 ml/2 cups) full-cream milk
1 recipe Rich Caramel Sauce (see page 140)
strained Greek-style yoghurt or fromage frais

1   Put the sugar in a bowl and gradually whisk in the whole eggs, the egg yolks and the vanilla, until evenly blended, using a balloon whisk.
2   Heat the milk in a 2 pint (1 litre/5 cup) jug covered by a plate on 100% power until steaming, then very slowly add to the eggs, whisking only until homogenous. Do not over whisk or the custard will be full of holes.
3   Pour into 6 × 5 fl oz (150 ml/⅔ cup) capacity ramekins or soufflé dishes (avoid metallized ones

or ones with a gold or silver decoration), arrange in a circle on the turntable and cook on 30% power for 11 minutes. The custards will tremble slightly when shaken and will finish setting as they cool. Do *not* be tempted to overcook.
4   Allow to go cold on a rack then chill. Just before serving, pour a thin layer of caramel sauce over the surface of each custard and serve with the yoghurt or fromage frais.

SPICED PEARS IN CIDER

Serves 6
Keeps 3 days under refrigeration

The pears become translucent and golden after they have been marinated in the syrup for several hours.

6 small Conference pears
bowl of cold water plus 2 tbsp lemon juice
15 fl oz (425 ml/2 cups) dry cider
3 oz (75 g/⅔ cup) caster sugar
1 level tbsp soft medium brown sugar
1 cinnamon stick or ¼ teasp ground cinnamon
2 tbsp lemon juice
Optional
5 fl oz (150 ml/⅔ cup) fromage frais, thick yoghurt or creamed smetana
2 teasp honey or caster sugar
½ teasp ground cinnamon

1   Select a casserole large enough to hold the pears side by side. Add all the ingredients except the pears and acidulated water, stir well, then cover and cook on 100% power for 5 minutes or until the liquid is bubbling. Meanwhile, peel the pears, but leave whole, and place immediately in the acidulated water.
2   Add the drained pears to the syrup, baste them with the liquid then cover and cook on 100%

power for a further 8–10 minutes, turning once, until just tender when pierced with a slim, sharp knife. Exact time will depend on the maturity of the pears.

3   Lift out the fruit with a slotted spoon and boil the syrup, uncovered, for 5 minutes until reduced in volume and intensified in flavour. This can be judged by taste.

4   Return the pears to the dish, baste well, cover and leave until tepid, then refrigerate for several hours, turning occasionally. Remove the cinnamon stick.

5   Serve plain or with the fromage frais, yoghurt or creamed smetana flavoured with 2 teasp honey or caster sugar and ½ teasp ground cinnamon.

PEARS IN RED WINE WITH RASPBERRY LIQUEUR

Serves 6
Keeps 3 days under refrigeration
Do not freeze

An elegant, refreshing dish of gently spiced pears in a beautiful pink sauce. I cannot be more specific about the cooking time – it depends so much on the ripeness of the fruit.

6 small medium-ripe Conference pears, peeled, halved and cored
1 pint (575 ml/2½ cups) cold water
2 tbsp lemon juice
10 fl oz (275 ml/1¼ cups) any fruity red wine, e.g. Côte du Rhône
1 tbsp dark brown sugar
1 tbsp fresh lemon juice
3 oz (75 g/⅓ cup) granulated sugar
2 strips orange rind
2 strips lemon rind
1 cinnamon stick
few whole cloves

To thicken and flavour the sauce

2 teasp cornflour
2 tbsp raspberry liqueur (Crème de Framboises)

1   As soon as they have been prepared, put the pear halves into the water mixed with the lemon juice, to prevent them discolouring.

2   Put the wine, the sugars, rinds, spices and the 1 tbsp fresh lemon juice into a measuring jug, cover with a plate and cook on 100% power for 3 minutes, until bubbling. Uncover and boil 2 minutes to intensify the flavour.

3   Meanwhile, arrange the drained pears, cut side down, side by side and alternating wide and narrow ends, in a 2 inch (5 cm) deep round baking dish. Pour over the liquid, cover and cook on 100% power for 8–10 minutes, turning once, until tender when pierced with a slim, sharp knife. Lift out the pears with a slotted spoon and arrange in a serving dish.

4   In the jug, mix the cornflour to a cream with the liqueur, then pour on the wine syrup. Cook on 100% power until bubbling – about 2 minutes.

5   Pour over the pears and chill for several hours. Remove the rinds and spices just before serving.

POACHED PEARS WITH CARAMEL OR CHOCOLATE SAUCE

Serves 5–6
Pears keep 2 days under refrigeration
Do not freeze

You may need to adjust the cooking time according to the ripeness of the pears – fully ripe ones should be avoided as they will go mushy when cooked.

5–6 ripe dessert pears (e.g. William) (2 lb/1 kg total weight)
a bowl of cold water plus 2 tbsp lemon juice

For the syrup

3½ oz (90 g/½ cup) caster sugar

6 fl oz (175 ml/¾ cup) cold water

2 tbsp fresh lemon juice

1   Peel and halve the pears then scoop out the core with a teaspoon. Place in the water and lemon juice as soon as they have been prepared to avoid discoloration.

2   In a dish large enough to hold the pears side by side, mix the sugar, water and lemon juice. Cover and cook on 100% power for 3½ minutes or until boiling.

3   Uncover and add the pears, laying them side by side but alternating the thick and thin ends. Baste well, cover and cook on 100% power for 4 minutes, turning once.

4   Turn the pears over, baste well then leave covered for 5 minutes. If still not tender when pierced with a sharp knife, cook for a further 1–2 minutes. Refrigerate when cold.

5   Serve with Chocolate Sauce 2 (see page 130) or with a sauce made by mixing the Basic Caramel (see page 140) with 4 tbsp of the poaching liquid as soon as it comes out of the oven, protecting your arm with a cloth in case of spattering.

RHUBARB
AND ORANGE COMPOTE

Serves 4

Keeps 3 days under refrigeration

The rhubarb can be cooked from frozen and will then take 9 minutes instead of 5. The oranges add a pleasing sweetness.

1 lb (450 g) forced (pink) rhubarb

5 oz (150 g/⅔ cup) caster sugar

2 large navel oranges, peeled, pith removed and
     sectioned

1   Cut the rhubarb into 1 inch (2.5 cm) lengths, discarding discoloured ends of sticks.

2   Put half the fruit into a bowl or casserole dish and sprinkle with half the sugar. Add the remaining rhubarb and sugar. Then cover and cook on 100% power for 5 minutes, stirring gently but thoroughly halfway, so that the centre pieces of fruit are on the outer edge of the dish.

3   Leave covered until cool then gently add the oranges and refrigerate until required.

BANANAS IN SPICED WINE

Serves 6

Keeps 2 days under refrigeration

Do not freeze

Simple and delicious.

6 medium bananas

6 fl oz (175 ml/¾ cup) fruity red wine

4 oz (125 g/½ cup) soft dark brown sugar

1½ tbsp fresh lemon juice

zest of ½ lemon cut into thin julienne strips

nut of butter

1 cinnamon stick

For the garnish

toasted coconut or chopped almonds (see page 174)

1   Put all the ingredients except the bananas into a 10 inch (25 cm) approx round dish, stir well, cover and cook on 100% power for 3 minutes.

2   Meanwhile, peel the bananas and trim ½ inch (1.25 cm) from either end.

3   Take the syrup from the oven, uncover and stir well, then add the bananas in a pinwheel shape, baste well, cover and cook for 5 minutes or until they feel tender when pierced with a knife.

4   Taste and if the flavour of the sauce needs intensifying, simmer uncovered for a further 2–3 minutes. Allow to go cold.

LUSCIOUS LEMON CURD

Makes approx 1¼ lbs (575 g/3 cups)
Keeps 3 months under refrigeration

The flavour of this curd is superb, the tang of the lemon being juxtaposed with the gentler flavour of the eggs and butter. The use of the food processor ensures that the curd will thicken evenly without any fear of curdling.

rind of 3 lemons, finely grated
6 fl oz (175 ml/¾ cup) lemon juice, from about 3 large lemons
3 oz (75 g/⅓ cup) unsalted or lightly salted butter
8 oz (225 g/1 cup) caster sugar
3 whole eggs

1   Have ready 2 washed and rinsed 8 oz (225 g) jars plus a small soufflé or jam dish.

2   Two hours in advance, leave the rind to soak in the lemon juice in a large microwave-safe jug to extract the flavouring oils. Pour this mixture through a sieve then discard the rind.

3   In the same jug, melt the butter at 100% power for 1 minute (cover lightly with a paper towel to prevent spattering). Stir in the lemon juice and sugar and cook uncovered on 100% power for 2 minutes. Then stir again to ensure that the sugar is dissolved in the liquid.

4   In a food processor or blender, process the eggs to blend for 10 seconds then slowly add the hot buttery liquid through the feed tube, processing all the time.

5   Return the mixture to the jug and microwave on 100% power for 2½ minutes, stirring halfway.

6   Take out and stir vigorously to ensure the curd is even in texture – it should be the consistency of a thick coating custard. If not, cook for a further 30 seconds.

7   Sterilize the jars as follows: fill them a quarter full with cold water and heat uncovered on 100% power for about 2 minutes – until the water is boiling. Remove carefully from the oven as they will be very hot. Pour away the water and stand them upside down to drain on a paper towel. Turn them over immediately and fill to the brim with the curd, then cover with a lid with an inset rubber ring. The small amount left can be put in the smaller dish as a 'taster'. Store in the refrigerator.

SOMERSET APPLE COMPOTE

Serves 4–6
Keeps 4 days under refrigeration
Freeze 4 months

This treatment transforms plain 'stewed apple' into a far more elegant and flavoursome dish.

1½ lb (675 g) well-flavoured eating apples, peeled, cored and cut into ¾ inch (2 cm) slices
For the syrup
3 level tbsp caster sugar
3 level tbsp soft brown sugar
4 fl oz (125 ml/½ cup) dry cider
1 tbsp smooth apricot jam
½ cinnamon stick
1 teasp each finely grated orange and lemon rind
2 teasp lemon juice
4 tbsp orange juice
To serve (optional)
5 fl oz (150 ml/⅔ cup) Greek-style yoghurt or fromage frais
3 teasp liquid honey

1   Arrange the apples in one layer in a 9–10 inch (23–25 cm) diameter lidded casserole.

2   Whisk all the syrup ingredients in a 3½ pint (2 litre/9 cup) jug and cook uncovered on 100%

Crescents of Ogen Melon in a Cherry Wine Sauce, Caramelized Clementines, Date Bars (overleaf)
Gingered Fresh Peach and Hazelnut Crumble, Poached Pears with Chocolate Sauce, A Kissel of Summer Fruit

power for 3 minutes. Whisk again then pour over the apple slices, cover and cook on 100% power for 7 minutes, stirring once, or until barely tender when pierced with a fork.

3   Leave covered until cool, then remove the cinnamon stick and refrigerate until required.

4   Serve plain or with the yoghurt or fromage frais sweetened with honey.

MINT JELLY

Makes about 1½ lb (675 g/3 cups)

A beautiful clear jelly with a delectable flavour, but only worth making with garden crabapples and home-grown mint.

For the crab apple juice

2 lb (1 kg) crab apples

1 pint (575 ml/2½ cups) cold water, or just
   enough to cover the fruit

For the mint jelly

1 pint crab apple juice (see above)

juice and grated rind of half a large lemon

2 tbsp white wine vinegar

1 lb (450 g/2 cups) preserving or granulated sugar

3 tbsp finely chopped fresh mint

1   To make the crab apple juice: remove the stalks from the crab apples but leave the fruit whole. Wash them in cold water and drain in a colander then place in a large bowl, cover with a plate and cook on 100% power for 30 minutes, stirring every 10 minutes, until absolutely tender.

2   Dampen a jelly bag, then suspend it over a large bowl: an easy way to do this is to fix the loops over the legs of an upturned stool. Turn the fruit pulp into the bag and leave it to drip through overnight – do *not* press the juice through the bag or the jelly will be cloudy.

3   Next day measure the juice – there should be about 1 pint (575 ml/2½ cups). If it is only short of the amount by a tablespoon or two, make up the quantity with water. Otherwise, use proportionally less sugar.

4   Wash four small glass jars (each approximately 6 fl oz/175 ml/¾ cup), rinse them in hot water then sterilize as described for Luscious Lemon Curd (see page 144).

5   Put the crab apple juice, lemon rind and juice, and vinegar into a bowl with the sugar and cook on 100% power for 5 minutes or until the sugar has dissolved see page 180 for testing for setting. Stir well, then continue to cook for a further 15 minutes, stirring occasionally, until the jelly reaches setting point. Stir in the chopped mint and leave the jelly in the bowl until it is beginning to thicken – about 10 minutes. Stir well to distribute the mint evenly and turn into the pots. Cover with wax discs and allow to go cold, then cover with cellophane or lids with rubber seals.

Luscious Lemon Curd, Apricot and Amaretto Conserve, Mint Jelly
Lime Cheesecake with a Fresh Strawberry Sauce (previous page)

APRICOT AND AMARETTO CONSERVE

Makes 2 lb (900 g/6 cups)
Keeps for months in a cool ventilated cupboard

A golden orange conserve of translucent apricots in a lemon and liqueur-flavoured syrup. Perfect to serve with warm croissants, homemade scones or buttered matzo. Any of the orange-flavoured liqueurs, such as Cointreau or Grand Marnier, or an Apricot Brandy, also go well with this fruit.

This is the easiest way I know to make a small quantity of the conserve – it all happens in one big bowl.

1 × 9 oz (250 g) packet dried apricots
1 pint (575 ml/2½ cups) cold water
1 lb 2 oz (550 g/2½ cups) preserving or granulated sugar
2 tbsp plus 2 teasp lemon juice
1½ oz (40 g/⅓ cup) blanched split almonds
2 tbsp Amaretto or Passover liqueur

1   Put the apricots into a lidded casserole, pour on the cold water (it should cover them – if not, add a little more), cover and cook on 100% power for 10 minutes then leave covered for 20 minutes.
2   Meanwhile, if the almonds need blanching put them in a small bowl, add 3 tbsp water, cover and cook on 100% power for 1½ minutes. Uncover, pour off the hot water and replace with cold, then slip off the skins and split along the grain.
3   Lift the apricots out of the liquid and put in a 4 pint (2 litre/9 cup) bowl. Add 5 fl oz (150 ml/⅔ cup) of the liquid, the lemon juice, sugar and almonds and cook on 100% power for 3 minutes then stir well to ensure the sugar is dissolved. Cook uncovered for a further 15 minutes until syrup will just coat the back of a wooden spoon. The mixture should have been bubbling fiercely for 10 minutes. Take out and stir in the chosen liqueur.
4   Put 4 tbsp cold water in 2 clean 1 lb (450 g) jam jars and bring to the boil, uncovered, on 100% power – about 1½ minutes – then turn upside down to drain on paper towelling.
5   Turn right side up, fill with the conserve and seal with the lid.

SPECIALITY BAKING

INTRODUCTION

Baking in a combination microwave oven brings no problems – standard recipes can be used and the only difference will be in the shorter cooking time.

However, without this facility the range of confectionery that can be produced to a worthwhile standard is very limited, mainly because the lack of browning makes most cakes look anaemic and unappetizing, their texture is more like that of a steamed pudding than a cake, and the magic dextrinization that produces the tender, flavourful crust on a normal cake cannot take place.

However, all the recipes in this chapter make very good eating and are without exception ready for the table in a fraction of the normal time. It is a great comfort to know that you can produce a moist and 'moreish' tea loaf in 11 short minutes, or a batch of superb chocolate walnut squares in 6 minutes. The Gâteau Reine de Saba is particularly interesting because it illustrates the point that a pure starch (in this case potato flour) cooks more efficiently in the microwave than ordinary flour. The two glorious cheesecakes are treated more like custards than cake but they too are thickened with another pure starch – cornflour. (See flour in the microwave page 178.)

I have included a microwave method of producing the egg-based filling for that most popular confection, the Schaum Torte, as it is so quick and easy. However, do not attempt to cook the meringue layers themselves in the microwave or you will be doomed to disappointment. If time is short one can always buy ready-to-fill meringues though they do not compare with home-made.

I have included a recipe for the crunchy date bars because they make the perfect after-school or mid-morning snack – nourishing, tasty and not too sweet to cloy the appetite for the meal ahead.

I have been very explicit as to the size and the surface area of the baking dishes, as that does affect the final result. A heatproof glass sandwich dish measuring 8 inches (20 cm) in diameter and 2 inches (5 cm) deep is ideal for the cheesecakes. As the dish does not have a loose bottom, the cake cannot of course be unmoulded easily but once it has been chilled it is easy to cut neat slices from it and arrange them either on one large dish or individual ones. Microwave-safe pliable plastic dishes of different dimensions, which are easily and cheaply available are also recommended. ∎

DATE BARS

Makes 12
Keep 4 days in an airtight container
Freeze 4 months

A juicy date filling is sandwiched between layers of a delicious crumble.

For the filling

6 oz (175 g/1 cup plus 2 tbsp) chopped stoned
    dates

2½ fl oz (65 ml/¼ cup plus 1 tbsp) hot water

2 tbsp lemon juice

1 teasp cinnamon

½ oz (15 g/1 tbsp) butter or margarine

2 oz (50 g/½ cup) walnuts (optional)

For the topping

3½ oz (90 g/⅓ cup plus 1 tbsp) butter or
    margarine

4 oz (125 g/1 cup) fine-milled plain wholemeal
    flour

3 oz (75 g/⅓ cup) soft medium brown sugar

2 oz (50 g/⅔ cup) porridge oats

1   Put dates, hot water and lemon juice in a small lidded casserole or bowl, cover and cook on 100% power for 2 minutes. Allow to stand covered for 5 minutes, then stir until a paste is formed. Stir in the cinnamon, butter or margarine and nuts.
2   To make the topping, put the butter or margarine in a small bowl and cook on 80% power for 2 minutes. Add to the topping ingredients and mix thoroughly with a fork or your fingers.
3   Put half the topping mixture into a 8 × 6 × 1 inch (20 × 15 × 2.5 cm) shallow microwave-safe dish and press down with a wetted spoon, then spread the filling evenly on top. Cover with the remainder of the topping, pressing it into an even layer. Cook uncovered on 100% power for 6 minutes.
4   Leave to cool and firm up for 30 minutes then cut into slices.

NUTTY STREUSEL KUCHEN

Makes 1 cake measuring 11 × 6 × 3 inches
(28 × 15 × 8 cm)
Keeps 2 days under refrigeration
Freeze 3 months

This is a light and tender cake but the topping is not caramelized as in a conventional oven. It also makes a wonderful pudding to serve with custard or stewed fruit.

For the topping

2 oz (50 g/½ cup) chopped walnuts or toasted
    nibbed almonds

1 oz (25 g/2 tbsp) butter or soft margarine

3 oz (75 g/⅓ cup) soft medium brown sugar

1 oz (25 g/¼ cup) flour

1 teasp cinnamon

For the cake

flavourless oil for greasing the dish

8 oz (225 g/2 cups) sponge self-raising flour plus
    ½ teasp baking powder or 8 oz (225 g/2 cups)
    plain flour plus 2½ teasp baking powder

3 oz (75 g/⅓ cup) soft margarine

5 oz (150 g/⅔ cup) caster sugar

1 egg

5 fl oz (150 ml/⅔ cup) milk

1   Choose a dish approximately 11 × 6 × 3 inches deep (28 × 15 × 8 cm) – I use a microwave-safe plastic one. The exact dimensions do not matter as long as the area of the top surface is between 66 square inches (420 sq cm) and 72 square inches (450 sq cm) and it is the right depth. Do check that it will fit on the turntable.
2   Grease the dish lightly, then line with a strip of silicone paper cut to fit the base and two narrower sides.
3   Chop the walnuts, if used, coarsely by pulsing in the food processor, then remove.

4   Toast the almond nibs, if used, by arranging in one layer on a plate and cooking on 100% power for 2 ½–3 minutes, stirring once, until golden brown.

5   Gently rub all the topping ingredients together with your fingers until the mixture forms a crumble.

6   Put all the cake ingredients into a bowl and beat by hand or machine until a smooth soft batter is formed (3 minutes by hand, 2 minutes by mixer, 15 seconds in a food processor).

7   Spoon into the dish, and smooth level. Then cover the batter at each end with a 2 inch wide (5 cm) strip of foil – this stops the short ends drying out before the centre is cooked. Cook on 80% power for 6 minutes until the top is just set. If not, give it another 30 seconds.

8   Remove the foil strips then sprinkle the streusel topping evenly on top and cook for a further 2½ minutes.

9   Leave on a cooling rack for 10 minutes then turn out onto a plate. Finally, turn right side up on to a serving dish.

LEMON FILLING FOR A SCHAUM TORTE

Serves 8–10
Leftovers keep 3 days under refrigeration
Freeze 1 month

This is a quick foolproof way of making this favourite filling with its sharp and refreshing lemon flavour.

This is sufficient to fill a torte made with the following ingredients:

4 egg whites
¼ teasp cream of tartar
8 oz (225 g/1 cup) caster sugar, mixed with 2 teasp cornflour

The meringue mixture can be shaped in 2 rectangles measuring 11 inches (28 cm) by 5 inches (12 cm) or 2 × 9 inch (23 cm) diameter rounds. Both shapes are baked at Gas No. 1 (275°F, 140°C) for 1 hour, until the meringue is crisp to the touch and can be lifted, with a spatula, off the silicone paper with which the baking tin has been lined.

For the lemon filling
4 egg yolks
4 oz (125 g/½ cup) caster sugar
5 tbsp fresh lemon juice
finely grated rind of 1 lemon
10 fl oz (275 ml/1¼ cups) double cream or 8 fl oz (225 ml/1 cup) non-dairy cream

1   Process the yolks, sugar, juice and rind for 30 seconds in the food processor or blender. Pour into a 2 pint (1·25 litre/5 cup) jug or bowl and cook on 100% power for 2 minutes, stirring well halfway. Cook for a further 30 seconds and stir well again – the mixture should resemble a thick custard. If not, cook for a further 30 seconds. Take out and stir for 30 seconds – it will then continue to thicken even more.

2   Chill in the freezer or refrigerator until completely cold – 30–40 minutes.

3   Whip the cream until it holds firm peaks then gently whisk in the lemon custard a tablespoon at a time. Use to fill the layers.

4   Freeze until 20 minutes before serving, then leave at room temperature – the filling will be the consistency of soft icecream when it is served.

LIME CHEESECAKE WITH A FRESH STRAWBERRY SAUCE

Serves 8 as a dessert, 10 with coffee or tea
Cheesecake freezes 4 months, sauce for a year

This magnificent cake must be chilled for at least twelve hours, during which time its texture changes dramatically, becoming richer and creamier to eat. The combination of colours makes this as decorative as it is delicious.

For the crust

4 oz (125 g) ginger biscuits (12 × 2½ inch/6 cm biscuits)

2 level tbsp caster sugar

1 oz (generous)(25 g/2 tbsp) butter, melted (100% power for 1 minute)

OR

enough sponge slices cut ⅜ inch (1 cm) thick to cover the base of the cooking container (about 4 trifle sponges)

For the filling

1 lb (450 g/2 cups) curd (medium fat) cheese

2 oz (50 g/¼ cup) caster sugar

1 oz (25 g/2 tbsp) very soft butter

2 level tbsp cornflour

3 × no. 3 eggs

grated rind of 1 fresh lime

1 tbsp fresh lime juice (½ lime)

2 tbsp proprietary brand lime cordial

For the topping

1 × 5 fl oz (150 ml/⅔ cup) carton soured cream or strained Greek-style yoghurt

2 teasp caster sugar

For the sauce

8 oz (225 g/1½ cups) strawberries

2 oz (50 g/¼ cup) caster sugar

2 teasp fresh lime juice

1   Have ready a microwave-safe cake dish, 8 inches (20 cm) in diameter and 2 inches (5 cm) deep. An ovenproof glass one is ideal.

2   Crush the biscuits to fine crumbs either in the food processor or with a rolling pin, then mix thoroughly with the butter and sugar. Press evenly on the bottom and part-way up the sides of the dish. Or arrange the slices of sponge cake in an even layer on the bottom of the dish.

3   Put the cheese in a bowl. If it is rather firm, soften on 30% power for 2 or 3 minutes, then add

the sugar, butter, cornflour, eggs and beat by hand or machine until smooth and creamy, then beat in the juice and rind.

4   Turn into the tin, smooth level, and cook on 50% power for 10 minutes then turn down to 30% power for a further 10 minutes – the cheesecake will be firm 1 inch (2.5 cm) round the edge but still a little wobbly in the centre (add an extra minute if necessary). Immediately spread with the soured cream, mixed with the sugar, and chill.

5   To make the strawberry sauce, purée all the ingredients for 1 minute in the food processor or blender until smooth. Turn into a bowl or jug and refrigerate – it will thicken on standing.

6   Serve wedges of the chilled cheesecake plain or coated with the sauce.

7   If you wish to serve the cake whole, chill well, loosen from the edges, cover with a plate of similar diameter, turn over, then shake gently to ease it out. Then turn right side up on to a plate.

CHEESECAKE, AMERICAN STYLE

Cake keeps 4 days under refrigeration
Cheesecake freezes 2 months, sauce for 1 year

An old favourite, the archetypal, transatlantic rich and creamy version of this classic cake.

For the crust

1½ oz (40 g/3 tbsp) butter, melted on 80% power for 45 seconds

2 oz (50 g/1 cup) digestive biscuits, crushed

1 tbsp caster sugar

1 oz (25 g/¼ cup) crushed hazelnuts, toasted for preference

For the filling

2 eggs, separated

1 lb (450 g/2 cups) curd cheese

½ teasp vanilla essence

juice of ½ lemon (1½ tbsp)

rind of ½ lemon

2 oz (50 g/¼ cup) butter, melted as above

2 oz (50 g/¼ cup) caster sugar

2 level tbsp cornflour

2 teasp caster sugar

5 fl oz (150 ml/⅔ cup) sour cream

For the glazed fruit

3 level teasp cornflour

2 tbsp caster sugar

1 tbsp lemon juice

8 fl oz (225 ml/1 cup) syrup or juice from canned fruit or 8 fl oz (225 ml/1 cup) bottled mango or exotic fruit juice

1 medium can choice fruit (sliced peaches, pears, bilberries, blackcurrants), drained, or 1 lb (450 g/3 cups) fresh fruit (sliced mangoes, strawberries, whole raspberries, loganberries, redcurrants, or a mixture)

1   Mix melted butter with crushed biscuits, sugar and nuts. Use the mixture to line a microwave-safe round dish 8 inches (20 cm) in diameter and 2 inches (5 cm) deep (I use one of ovenproof glass). Chill.

2   For the filling, put èg yolks in a large bowl with other remaining ingredients in the order given, except for the caster sugar. Beat until smooth.

3   Whisk egg whites until stiff and glossy, then whisk in the 2 teasp caster sugar. Fold this into the cheese mixture.

4   Spoon on to the crumb base, smooth level, then microwave, uncovered, on 50% power for 10 minutes, then on 30% power for a further 10 minutes until just firm round the edge. The centre may still be a little wobbly but will set as it cools. Leave to cool completely, then either refrigerate or cover with the fruit topping.

5   To make the fruit topping, mix the cornflour and sugar with the lemon juice in a 1½ pint (1 litre/4 cup) jug or bowl. When creamy stir in the remaining juice. Cook uncovered on 100% power for 1 minute, stir, then cook a further 2½ minutes until thick and glossy. Take out, stir, then leave until it has stopped steaming and is beginning to set.

6   Meanwhile, arrange the fruit on top of the cake then gently spoon over the glaze.

CHOCOLATE WALNUT SQUARES

Makes 15 × 2 inch (5 cm) squares
Keep 1 week in an airtight container
Freeze 6 months

These cook to perfection in the microwave, staying tender and moist. They seem to cook more evenly if the dish is placed on a trivet or rack.

2 oz (50 g/½ cup) walnuts

3 oz (75 g/¾ cup) sponge self-raising flour (or ¾ cup cake flour plus 1 teasp baking powder)

4 tbsp cocoa

2 eggs

8 oz (225 g/1 cup) soft dark brown sugar

5 oz (150 g/⅔ cup) soft margarine

1 teasp vanilla essence

3 tbsp boiling water

For sprinkling on the cooked squares

2 tbsp caster sugar

1   Choose a dish approximately 11 × 6 × 3 inches deep (28 × 15 × 8 cm). I use a microwave-safe plastic one. The exact dimensions do not matter as long as the area of the top surface is between 66 square inches (420 sq cm) and 75 square inches (460 sq cm) and it is the right depth. Do check that it will fit on the turntable. Grease lightly, then cut a strip of silicone paper to fit the base and two narrower sides.

2   Chop the walnuts coarsely by pulsing in the food processor, then remove.

3   Sift the cocoa and flour. Put the eggs and sugar in the food processor and process for 1 minute. Divide the margarine into 4 or 5 lumps and drop on top, then pulse 2 or 3 times until it disappears.

Add the vanilla and the water, then process until smooth – about 2 seconds. Add the flour and pulse in until it also disappears. Clean down the sides of the bowl with a rubber spatula. Then briefly pulse in the nuts.

4   Turn into the prepared container and cover tightly with clingfilm – there is no need to pierce it. Cook on 100% power for 6 minutes, then remove the top clingfilm carefully. Cool for 5 minutes, then turn out on to a cooling tray. After 10 minutes, carefully turn over and sprinkle thickly with caster sugar.

5   Divide into squares. Store in an airtight tin when quite cold.

BANANA TEA BREAD

Makes 1 loaf – approximately 16 slices
Keeps 4 days foil-wrapped in the refrigerator
Freeze 3 months

This moist and 'moreish' tea bread may lack the brown top of a similar recipe baked in a conventional oven but it is still most delicious cut and buttered or spread with cream cheese or honey. I have also simplified the mixing (pre-cooking the bananas in the microwave means they can be mashed quickly with a fork) and have refined the baking time to a fifth of normal. I suggest using an 80% extraction wheatmeal self-raising flour, but you can also use fine milled 100% extraction wholemeal flour or half and half ordinary wholemeal and white flour. If the flour is plain, add a teasp of baking powder.

12 oz (350 g) (2 large) bananas
5½ oz (165 g/1⅓ cups) 80% extraction wheatmeal self-raising flour
the finely grated rind of 1 orange
5 oz (150 g/⅔ cup) soft medium brown sugar
5 fl oz (150 ml/⅔ cup) sunflower oil
2 eggs, whisked until fluffy

2 teasp vanilla essence
2 oz (50 g/½ cup) coarsely chopped walnuts

1   Oil, then line the bottom and two short sides of a plastic loaf dish approx 6 × 8 × 3 inches (15 × 20 × 7.5 cm) with silicone paper.

2   With a slim pointed knife, pierce each unpeeled banana all over to prevent it bursting then cook on 100% power for 3 minutes. Leave to stand for 5 minutes then scoop out the soft pulp and mash to a purée with a fork. Set aside.

3   Put all the remaining ingredients into a large bowl in the order given and stir thoroughly (but not too vigorously) until smooth and evenly-moistened. Finally, stir in the bananas.

4   Spoon the mixture into the prepared dish and smooth level. Cut two strips of foil, each about 2 inches (5 cm) wide and long enough to overlap the edges of the shorter sides. Lay these in place at each end of the dish and place it in a roasting rack or trivet. Cook on 50% power for 9 minutes, then on 100% power for 2 minutes. Remove the foil and leave to stand for 3 or 4 minutes, then turn out onto a cooling tray.

5   When cold, slice and butter as required.

GÂTEAU REINE DE SABA WITH BRANDIED CHOCOLATE ICING

Keeps 3–4 days in an airtight container
Freeze 3 months

This is a superb cake – tender and moist – far and away the best result I have had from a microwave cake. The reason lies in the use of pure starch – either potato or cornflour – instead of ordinary flour, which tends to produce a 'puddingy' texture.

6 oz (175 g) plain chocolate, broken in small pieces

4 oz (125 g/½ cup) butter (unsalted if available)

4 oz (125 g/½ cup) caster sugar

4 eggs, separated

1 teasp vanilla essence

2 oz (50 g/⅓ cup) potato flour or cornflour

1 level teasp baking powder

For the icing

2 oz (50 g/¼ cup) butter

4 oz (125 g) plain chocolate

1 tbsp brandy, or chocolate or coffee-flavoured liqueur

For decorating the cake

1 oz (25 g/2 tbsp) chopped walnuts or grated chocolate

1   Grease then bottom-line with silicone paper the base of a round dish 8 inches (20 cm) × 2–3 inches (5–7.5 cm) deep (e.g. a Pyrex sandwich dish or a soufflé dish). Fix a 3 inch (7.5 cm) wide strip of foil round the outside of the dish, folding the top 1 inch (2.5 cm) over the dish to secure it.

2   In a bowl, melt the broken-up chocolate and butter at 100% power for 1½ minutes. Stir to blend then add the sugar and cook at 100% power for a further minute.

3   Stir in the egg yolks, followed by the vanilla and the potato flour mixed with the baking powder. Whisk the whites until they hold stiff, glossy peaks then fold into the chocolate mixture.

4   Turn into the prepared dish and cook at 100% power for 3 minutes, then remove the foil and cook for a further 2½ minutes.

5   Leave to stand until the top surface has completely dried out. Turn on to a cooling tray.

6   To make the icing, put all the ingredients into a bowl and cook on 100% power for 1½ minutes or until the chocolate has melted. Stir to blend, then pour over the cooled cake and decorate with nuts and grated chocolate.

THE MICROWAVE LEKACH

Keeps 1 month in an airtight container
Freeze 3 months

For the busy baker, here is a speedy way to make traditional, moist and spicy honey cake for Rosh Hashanah. Even though it is baked in the microwave, the dark sugar and the honey give this cake a rich, warm colour. However, do leave it (wrapped in foil) to mature for at least 4 days.

8 oz (225 g/¾ cup) warm honey

3 oz (75 g/⅓ cup) dark brown sugar

6 oz (175 g/1½ cups) plain flour

½ teasp bicarbonate of soda

½ teasp ground cinnamon

½ teasp ground ginger

1 teasp mixed sweet spice

4 tbsp any flavourless oil

1 egg

3 fl oz (75 g/⅓ cup) warm coffee

1   Select a rectangular microwave-safe baking dish measuring 10 × 6 × 2½ inches (25 × 15 × 6.5 cm). Lightly grease it with oil, then line the bottom with a strip of silicone paper.

2   Measure the honey into a large bowl, add the sugar, then heat on 100% power for 2 minutes and then stir well.

3   Allow to cool a little while you sift together the flour, bicarbonate of soda, cinnamon, ginger and sweet spice. Add this to the honey mixture with the oil, egg and coffee, mixing until smooth after each addition – the mixture will be very thin.

4   Turn into the dish and cover each short end of the dish with a 2 inch (5 cm) strip of foil. Cook on 50% power for 7 minutes – the top of the cake will be slightly tacky on top and will set as it cools. Remove the foil and leave on a cooling tray. When cold, turn out of the dish and wrap in foil. Leave 4 days before cutting.

TRADITIONAL AND FESTIVAL MEALS

INTRODUCTION

As the many-stranded tapestry of the Festivals slowly unrolls through the year it brings much colour and warmth into the Jewish home.

But it also can be the cause of a great deal of worry mingled, it must be said, with apprehension, as we try to make up our minds how, what and when to cook for the various ceremonial meals. Earlier generations had it much harder of course - not for our grandmothers a freezer or even a refrigerator in which they could stockpile the Festival food and so spread the work over weeks, rather than having to condense all the hard labour into a short forty-eight hours. And the nearest thing to a food processor was a hand mincer, screwed on to the edge of the kitchen table, a boon indeed compared with chopping 12 or 14 pounds of fish with a hand-held *hackmesser* to feed a host of family and friends.

But, today, with all our electronic kitchen assistance, we are still left with the age-old problem: what shall we make for that special meal? Certain parts of the menu are of course enshrined in tradition: there must be potato latkes at Hanukkah and cheesecake at Shavuot. Rosh Hashanah is not the same without a carrot tsimmes and a honey cake and there must be a platter of stuffed vegetables and a plate of strudel for Sukkot. And however good the baker's offerings may be, Pesach is not the same unless we exhaust our purses and our energy producing vast trays of coconut pyramids, cinnamon balls and nine-egg sponge cakes.

And so it has been for hundreds of years, for each of the dishes I have mentioned is there because one or more of its ingredients is symbolic of a particular Festival.

But symbolic food, however delicious, is not the sum total of preparing for a Festival. There are many other dishes, perhaps less traditional but certainly suitable or even convenient for a particular occasion.

So in this chapter I have trawled through all the recipes in the book and picked out those particular ones that, whether through their ingredients or their timing, will I hope be of help in deciding menus and making the whole business of preparing for a Festival more of a pleasure than the penance it can sometimes seem.

In addition, I have listed other recipes which, because they can be prepared in advance, are particularly suitable for serving on Shabbat.

In these preparations, the microwave comes into its own in preparing food in advance more quickly and easily than any other method. Of course, for large family meals it will probably be more practicable to use a conventional oven but there are still a host of jobs the microwave can do, such as toasting nuts and softening butter before a baking session, par-cooking potatoes before roasting, softening dried fruit without an overnight soak, and making both sweet and savoury sauces, that will more than help it to pay its way. I suggest you flip through the 'Guide for the Perplexed' for more helpful ideas. Even with many faces round the table, the microwave can still be pressed into service – providing the festival does not fall on Shabbat – for reheating vegetables, puddings, casseroles and sauces in their serving dishes.

There are two Festivals for which there are no microwave recipes. All the traditional and symbolic dishes that we cook at Hanukkah and Purim are based either on deep frying or baking and, for these, the microwave has little specialized help to offer. That is why I have not listed any particular recipes in this chapter. However, I am sure that once you have read the book, you will devise your own ways of bringing our age-old traditions into the twenty-first century. ■

SHABBAT

To ensure that Shabbat is truly a day of rest from the normal humdrum household tasks, sufficient food must be prepared before the Eve of the Sabbath (Erev Shabbat) to last from Friday evening to Saturday night.

Over the years, Jewish households have built up a wide repertoire of suitable dishes, many of which actually improve in flavour when refrigerated overnight. In addition, there are casseroles like tsimmes and cholent that can be left to cook in a low oven from Friday afternoon to Saturday lunchtime. With these slow-cooking dishes, the microwave can be of little help. However, it can be used to prepare excellent soups for the eve-of-the-Sabbath meal as well as a large variety of cold fish dishes and some meat. There are also chicken dishes that are equally delicious when served cold.

RECIPES FOR SHABBAT AND YOM TOVIM

PESACH

Passover (15th Nissan) March/April

Each spring, during the Passover week which commemorates the liberation of the Jews from generations of slavery in Ancient Egypt more than three and a half thousand years ago, the Jewish household takes on an appearance quite different from that it presents during the rest of the year, or indeed during any other festival. In the kitchen unfamiliar pots and pans that only get an airing during these brief eight days stand on the cooker top and counters. In the food cupboards, matzot, matzo meal and other Passover foods are stacked on the newly covered shelves and there is no trace of either bread or flour.

I have written elsewhere (*The Complete International Jewish Cookbook* and in the *New Jewish Cuisine*, Robson Books) about the detailed preparations for this delightful festival but until recently there has been no religious guidance on the use of the microwave at this time.

Now, however, Dayan O. Y. Westheim of the Manchester Beth Din has drawn up the following comprehensive guidelines. For further guidance, consult your local rabbi.

'It is preferable to try to manage without the use of the microwave oven for Pesach. If, however, it is vital to use the microwave, the following procedure should be followed, after the oven has been left unused for 25 hours, and before the end of time for eating Chometz (leaven).

1   The inside of the oven should be thoroughly cleaned, paying special attention to the area under the turntable where applicable. Where browning elements or grills are present, these must also be thoroughly cleaned, paying special attention to the part where it is joined to the inner casing. Where the lining is made of two different materials, the point where they join must be carefully cleaned. Also give special attention to the ventilation holes that these are free of any particles or condensation.

2   Place a glass of warm water inside the oven and boil for about 10 minutes.

3   Where a conventional heating element is present, turn this to the highest setting for at least a quarter of an hour.

4   Where a turntable is used, this should preferably be replaced. Alternatively, the existing turntable can be covered with at least two layers of clingfilm that will be left on throughout Pesach. All Pesach dishes that will be placed in the oven should be completely wrapped around with clingfilm or other suitable material. If the instruction booklet advises holes to be perforated in the food covering this may be done, as a few holes do not really matter. However, this should be avoided whenever possible.

NB For general use all year, it is advisable to treat a microwave oven (with or without a browning element) as a conventional oven with regard to milk and meat dishes. Therefore one should ensure that either all meat or all milk dishes are always covered in the oven (with domes or clingfilm with a few small perforations) and that the base of the oven or the turntable has a separate cover for milk and meat dishes.'

PESACH RECIPES

NOTE instead of cornflour, substitute an equal quantity of potato flour in any of the following recipes. Use Passover packs, when available, and substitute Passover vegetable oil for any of the other oils specified.

SHAVUOT

Feast of Weeks or Pentecost (6th Sivan) May/June

One of the most delightful of the 'pilgrim festivals', in earlier days, Shavuot was celebrated in Palestine as a great harvest festival. Every man would gather the choicest of the harvest fruit, and his wife would bake bread and cakes sweetened with honey, using flour she had milled from the first of the new season's wheat. And these would be taken as offerings to the Temple in Jerusalem. Today, we relive those early days by decorating our homes and synagogues with plants and flowers of the season.

As Shavuot commemorates the time of the giving of the Law to Moses on Mount Sinai, the delightful custom has arisen of using white ingredients, such as, milk, cheese and cream, to symbolize not only the purity and inviolability of the Torah that Moses received that day, but also to recall that with the dietary laws that are enshrined in that Law, and in particular the division between meat and dairy food, a new importance was given to milk and all its products in the Jewish kitchen.

That is why cheesecakes, cheese blintzes, cheese knishes and a host of other delicious dairy dishes appear on all our Shavuot tables.

RECIPES FOR SHAVUOT

ROSH HASHANAH

New Year (1st and 2nd Tishri) September/October

We are told that as the exiled Jews sat down by the Waters of Babylon, they wept for the country from which they had been taken as slaves. Yet when they returned to their beloved Zion, they quickly adopted the Babylonian custom which has endured to this day, of preparing all kinds of sweet food to mark a special celebration.

Honey might be called the leitmotif of this Festival: with apples it is eaten in all kinds of sweet and savoury dishes as an expression of hope for a good and sweet New Year. Besides being used in pies, cakes and strudels, slices of apple are spread with honey and eaten on the Eve of the Festival after the blessing has been made over the wine and the bread (which is baked in the shape of a spiral only at this season).

RECIPES FOR ROSH HASHANAH

YOM KIPPUR

**The Day of Atonement (10th Tishri)
September/October**

Although Yom Kippur is a Fast Day, a great deal of activity is involved in making two meals, each of which demands very careful menu-planning. With twenty-five hours of complete abstention from food ahead, it is essential that the meal before the Fast should be sustaining while not provoking thirst, while the one that follows it should be light and composed of easily digested food.

That is why many families have a pre-Fast meal of chicken soup with kreplach, followed by a lightly seasoned casserole of chicken with potatoes or rice and a fruity dessert. After the Fast and that first welcome cup of tea and buttered kuchen, it is the custom to serve some kind of *forschpeisse* – a savoury starter to stimulate the taste buds. This is often followed by a comforting cream soup, some kind of cold fish and a dessert that is not over-laden with cream.

YOM KIPPUR RECIPES

SUKKOT

Tabernacles (15th Tishri) September/October

This autumn harvest festival, which commemorates the forty years of wandering in the wilderness before the Jewish people finally reached their promised land, is an especially happy occasion in the Jewish household. Many families make their own Sukkah – a tabernacle to remind their children of the makeshift huts their ancestors had to live in for four long decades. The house and the Sukkah are filled with the perfume of autumn flowers and fruit, such as chrysanthemums and melons, and tables are laden with all manner of stuffed food – *holishkes* (stuffed cabbage leaves), *sarmali in foie de vitza* (stuffed vine leaves) and *pilpel mimulad* (stuffed peppers). Aubergines, tomatoes, avocados and courgettes figure large in the menus, and there are strudels to be stuffed and cakes to be baked in large trays to serve at the communal Kiddush after the service in the synagogue.

RECIPES FOR SUKKOT

LEXICON

A Guide for the Perplexed

LEXICON – A GUIDE
FOR THE PERPLEXED

AL DENTE: a culinary expression used to describe the texture of a cooked food – usually pasta – which is soft or tender enough to be edible but still has a little 'bite' left in it. It is also used to describe the texture of a vegetable and is particularly easy to achieve in the microwave.

APPLES baked: the flesh of a cooking apple, such as a Bramley, is particularly fluffy when cooked in the microwave but the skin is tougher than usual. Standing time is particularly important as it is then that the final 'steaming' takes place. Too long in the oven and the build-up of steam will cause the apple to burst (see page 138 for recipes).

APPLES stewed: to stew apples for 4: peel core and slice, then cut into ½ inch (1.5 cm) slices 1½ lb (675 g) baking or eating apples and arrange in a 9–10 inch (23–25 cm) lidded casserole or large bowl. Pour over 2 fl oz (50 ml/4 tbsp) orange juice or water and 1 tbsp lemon juice then sprinkle with 4 oz (125 g/½ cup) white or golden granulated sugar. Cover and cook on 100% power for 7 minutes, then leave to stand for 5 minutes. Serve warm or cold.

APPLE SAUCE sweet: peel, core and very thinly slice 1 lb (450 g) cooking apples and arrange in a dish as for stewed apples, but add only 1 tbsp each lemon juice and water and no sugar at this stage. Cover and cook on 100% power for 3 minutes, stir well and cook for a further 3 minutes. Stand covered for 2 minutes then beat to a purée with 3–4 oz (75–125 g/⅓–½ cup) granulated or caster sugar.

APPLE SAUCE savoury: cook as for sweet apple sauce but beat in a nut of margarine and only a rounded tbsp of sugar. Serve with duck or cold meat.

ASPARAGUS fresh: unless you have an asparagus pan – a tall double boiler – in which the fibrous stalks are cooked in water while the tender heads are steamed, the microwave is undoubtedly the preferred method of cooking this delectable vegetable to the correct 'al dente' stage. Choose a green-stemmed variety (avoid those with a large portion of woody stalk) with tight heads. Bundles of asparagus contain stalks of even thickness but if you are buying it loose, you will have to do this selection for yourself to ensure all the spears cook to an even tenderness. To prepare, trim off any woody part of the stalk, wash thoroughly in a bowl of cold water then shake dry gently.

To cook 1 lb (450 g) asparagus: arrange the stalks side by side in a lasagne-type oblong dish, with the tender tips to the centre. Sprinkle with 4 tbsp water, cover and cook on 100% power for 4 minutes then rearrange by bringing the outer stalks to the middle and vice versa (keep the tips always to the centre of the dish). Re-cover and cook a further 4–6 minutes, or until a stalk is just tender when pierced with a sharp knife. Drain and serve with melted butter or Hollandaise Sauce (see page 179).

ASPARAGUS frozen: this will already have been trimmed and blanched so the cooking time will be much shorter than for fresh. However, arrange and rearrange the stalks in the dish as for the fresh vegetable but for the time recommended on the pack.

AUBERGINE baked: this is a quick and easy way to cook this vegetable if it is to be puréed. Use medium (½ lb/225 g) aubergines to ensure even cooking. Cut off the prickly calyx, prick all over with a fork then arrange on a double thickness of paper towelling. When the minimum cooking time is up, test for 'doneness' by piercing with a skewer. If not completely tender (the vegetable will also look slightly collapsed), cook for a further 2 minutes. See Aubergine and Tahina Mezze, page 46.

½ lb (225 g)	takes 6 minutes
1 lb (450 g)	takes 10 minutes
1½ lb (675 g)	takes 15 minutes

Allow to cool before halving and removing the pulp.

AUBERGINE slices for a casserole: this is an excellent way to cook aubergines for dishes such as Moussaka, using very little oil. However, do not expect them to be as golden brown as when sautéed. Peel the aubergines (the skin toughens in the microwave), then cut in ½ inch (1.25 cm) slices and arrange in layers in a colander or salad spinner, sprinkling each layer lightly with cooking salt. Leave for 30 minutes, rinse and dry, then in a 3½–4 pint (2 litre/9–10 cup) casserole or bowl, toss to coat on all sides with 2–3 tbsp oil. Cook covered on 100% power (stirring gently halfway to rearrange the slices) until tender when pierced with a sharp knife, then treat as sautéed. See Moussaka Vegevina, page 114.

1–1¼ lb (450 g-600 g)	takes 8 minutes
1½ lb (675 g)	takes 10 minutes
2 lbs (900 g)	takes 14 minutes

BAIN-MARIE: this hot water bath is used in conventional cookery to prevent particularly heat-sensitive foods, such as custards, from over-cooking and curdling. Some authorities recommend using this technique in the microwave but I have found that the same protection as a bain-marie can be given more simply by cooking the food on 30% power (defrost) until barely set. See Raspberry Crème Brûlée, page 130.

BAY LEAVES to dry: when you prune the bush, lay the leaves in one layer on a double thickness of paper towelling and cook uncovered on 100% power, stirring once, until dry to the touch. A loosely packed cupful will take approximately 2 minutes on 100% power. Store in a tightly closed jar. If fresh bay leaves are left to dry in the atmosphere, I find they become

bleached and most unattractive.

BAY LEAVES powdered: this is a useful option, particularly for soup as you do not need to remember to fish out the whole leaf before liquidizing the mixture. However, use the powdered herb by the pinch as it is quite pungent – you can always add more, but there is no way you can subtract it.

BEANS, DRIED AND PULSES to soak: this process reduces the time from a minimum of 12 hours to under an hour and a half and can be used for cannellini, haricot, kidney and butter beans, as well as legumes such as chick peas and split peas. Put up to 1 lb (450 g/2½ cups) beans or pulses in a lidded casserole and add enough cold water to cover them generously (approx 15 fl oz/425 ml/2 cups), cover and cook on 100% power for 15 minutes. Leave covered for 5 minutes then add a further 15 fl oz (425 ml/2 cups) boiling water, and leave covered for a further 1 hour. Drain and cook as desired.

BEANS, DRIED AND PULSES cooked in the microwave: because they need a long standing time, it is just as speedy to cook beans on top of the stove.

BEANS, WHOLE GREEN to prepare and cook: including string, Kenya and bobo beans. Remove strings if necessary, top and tail, then arrange in one layer in a shallow lidded casserole. Add 4 tbsp water, cover and cook on 100% power. Cooking times are based on very fresh beans, older or more mature ones will take a little longer. Drain well, and season with sea salt and black pepper.

4 oz (125 g)	takes 4 minutes
½ lb (225 g)	takes 4½ minutes
1 lb (450 g)	takes 6–9 minutes

BISCUITS: 'baking' biscuits by microwave power alone is a tedious business as you can only cook the equivalent of one normal trayful at a time. You are also restricted to those varieties that do not need to be browned or crispened in the oven. If you have a combination oven, you can use a regular recipe but time according to manufacturer's instructions.

BLACKCURRANTS to prepare and cook: remove the stalks from 1 lb (450 g) blackcurrants, top and tail (most easily with kitchen scissors) and arrange in a lidded casserole or bowl. Sprinkle with 2 tbsp water and scatter with 4 oz (125 g/½ cup) sugar. Cover and cook on 100% power for 7½ minutes, stirring once. Stand covered for 3 minutes then check for sweetness and stir in extra sugar, if necessary. *On a sugar-free diet*, add 4 rounded tbsp granular sweetener *after* cooking.

BLOCK FILLET: a fish fillet removed in one piece from the entire side of a small flat fish, such as plaice or lemon sole. The fishmonger thus cuts 2 fillets instead of the usual four from each fish.

BRAISING STEAK: do not attempt to casserole stewing steak in the microwave. Although the flavour is good, the tough sinews and connective tissues need the long slow simmer of conventional cookery to break them down and tenderize the meat. Instead use true braising cuts such as chuck steak (also known as 'alki' steak or round bola), blade steak (which can be sliced rather than cubed), top rib and first-cut shoulder steak. Your butcher is probably your best guide.

BREAD: I have read many recipes for cooking yeast-raised bread in the microwave but I have never been in such dire circumstances that I needed to use one. The bread will certainly rise and set, but the colour remains pale and insipid, the loaf lacks a crunchy crust and the texture is poor due to the way in which the wheatflour attracts moisture in the microwave. (In a combination oven there is, of course, no problem.) On the other hand, tea breads raised with baking powder work well (see Banana Tea Bread, page

157). However, you can speed the rising and proving of the dough (see *Proving dough*) before baking it in a combination or conventional oven.

BREADCRUMBS to dry for coating: Challah and French bread make the finest crumbs for coating fried foods, e.g. gefilte fish balls, fish steaks or fillets, or salmon cutlets. I usually allow leftover slices of bread to dry out in the bread drawer or container over several days or weeks and then crumb the dried-out pieces in the food processor. However, if you need crumbs in a hurry, use this microwave method: remove the crusts from a small loaf (approximate weight 14 oz/400 g) or leave them on as you prefer. Tear into roughly 1 inch (2.5 cm) chunks and reduce to crumbs in the food processor. Arrange in an even layer in the largest gratin or lasagne-type dish that will fit in the microwave. Cook on 100% power for 8–9 minutes (stirring twice) until the crumbs feel dry to the touch. Allow to cool, then store in an air-tight container – they keep almost indefinetely.

BROCCOLI to prepare and cook: the brilliant green that fades so quickly in a pan of boiling water is miraculously retained in the microwave, providing the vegetable is prepared so that the florets and stalks can become tender at the same time. However, the vegetable must be completely fresh with no sign of yellowing. Cut off any thick tough stalks and discard, then divide the broccoli into florets. Cut off the slimmer stalks and slice them thinly. Put both in a microwave-safe serving dish, arranging the stalks to the outside with the heads in the centre. Add 3 tbsp water, cover and cook on 100% power until the stalks are just tender when pierced with a slim, sharp knife. For immediate use, drain, salt lightly and serve or coat with a sauce. For later use, put in a colander and drench with cold water to set the colour. Season and reheat as required.

8–10 oz (225–275 g)	take 5–6 minutes
1 lb (450 g)	takes 7–9 minutes

BROWNING cubes or slices of meat: on top of the stove – this helps to seal cut surfaces to prevent excess leakage of tasty juices into the cooking liquid and also to promote a good colour in the finished sauce. This browning cannot be achieved by microwave power alone. However, putting the meat into a richly coloured sauce that is already simmering achieves very much the same effect. Joints of meat will brown to a certain extent because of their surface fat which colours if the cooking time is longer than 30 minutes.

BROWNING of sugar: works miraculously well and is easier to control than top of stove. See Caramel, page 140.

BROWNING of cheese and savoury crumb toppings: can only be achieved by grilling or finishing off in a conventional oven. However, a sweet crumble top made with brown ingredients such as flour, sugar, oats and ground hazelnuts does appear to have an acceptable colour, but it will only crispen if exposed to direct radiant heat.

BRUSSELS SPROUTS: to prepare and cook: choose very green, very tight sprouts as even in size as possible (to ensure even cooking). Trim the stalks and then arrange in a single layer in a shallow lidded casserole. Add 4 tbsp water, cover and cook on 100% power until just tender when pierced with a slim, sharp knife – time will vary according to size and maturity. Drain, season and serve.

8 oz (225 g)	take 4–5 minutes
12 oz (350 g)	take 6–6½ minutes
1 lb (450 g)	takes 7–8 minutes

BULGUR (also known as cracked wheat, pourgoul or bourghoul) is the 'alien corn' mentioned in the Book of Ruth. As it is generally sold par-cooked (also called 'parched'), it cooks very quickly to a delicious nutty texture that is much lighter than rice. It is equally delicious served hot as an accompaniment to a main dish or cold as the basis for a salad. See Bulgur and Pine Kernel Pilaff, page 125

To cook bulgur for 4–5: put 1 cup bulgur, 2 teasp minced dried onion and 2 cups boiling chicken or vegetable stock into a 2½ pint (1.5 litre/6 cup) deep lidded casserole. Stir in 1 tbsp oil, cover and cook on 100% power or until bubbling. Turn down to 50% power for a further 4 minutes, then leave to stand, covered for 5 minutes. Fluff up with a fork and serve.

To cook bulgur for 8–10: double all the ingredients, but cook on 100% power for 7 minutes or until bubbling, then cook exactly as directed for the smaller amount.

BUTTER to soften: remove the wrapper and place on a plate or in a bowl (depending how it is to be used). Microwave on 50% power for 30 seconds, adding extra time in 10 second steps until it is the desired consistency.

BUTTER to melt: place in a bowl and if more than 4 oz (125 g/½ cup) in quantity, cut into chunks. Cover lightly with a piece of paper towelling (to prevent spattering) and cook on 100% power. (Some people prefer to use 80% power and cook a little longer without the paper cover.)

4 oz (125 g/½ cup)	melt in 2 minutes
8 oz (225 g/1 cup)	melt in 2½ minutes
1 lb (450 g/2 cups)	melts in 4 minutes

BUTTER to gloss a sauce thickened with cornflour: drop a nut of butter or margarine into the sauce *after* cooking. This will compensate for the fat normally used in a roux-based sauce.

CABBAGE to cook: there is no saving of time when cabbage is cooked in the microwave but there is one big advantage – it can be done in the serving dish. The only kind worth cooking this way is the hearted green cabbage of late summer and early autumn.

To cook 1 lb (450 g) finely-shredded cabbage: put in an oven-to-table microwave-safe dish, add 3 tbsp water, cover and cook on 100% power, stirring once, for 8–10 minutes or until bite tender. Drain thoroughly, salt and pepper lightly and serve plain or with a sprinkle of caraway seeds. See also Stir Fried Young Cabbage, page 173.

CABBAGE, RED: for the definitive recipe see Braised Red Cabbage in the Viennese Style, page 103. This method can be varied by adding 2–3 tbsp of sultanas, or a peeled, cored and finely chopped cooking apple.

CAKES testing for 'doneness': in most cases a cake completes the final cooking during standing time, so piercing the centre with a skewer or cocktail stick when the cooking time is up is not a good guide. Instead, test by piercing midway between the centre and the side. If the skewer or stick comes out clean the cake is ready to be removed from the oven. If not, add extra time in 30 second steps.

CARROTS to cook: avoid fibrous old carrots as they never get really tender. Peel, or scrape, if young, then slice in thin rings or in thin julienne strips. Put in an even layer in a shallow lidded casserole, add 3 tbsp water, cover and cook on 100% power, stirring once, until 'al dente'. See page 169.

½ lb (225 g) carrots	cooks in 6½–7 minutes
1 lb (450 g) carrots	cooks in 10–12 minutes

CAULIFLOWER to cook: use only a very fresh, very white cauliflower and cook it if possible on the day of purchase – even slightly stale cauliflower develops an 'off' flavour in the microwave. Do not attempt to cook a whole head – it is too big a mass to cook evenly. However, florets can be cooked to perfection. Cut them away from their stalk – each floret should be about 2 inches (5 cm) in diameter (or use a prepack of florets). 1 lb (450 g) is the equivalent of a medium head of cauliflower. Arrange in a single layer in a shallow lidded round casserole or serving dish. Add 3 tbsp water, cover and cook on 100% power, stirring once to reposition the florets. Test by piercing with a slim, sharp knife, or nibble a piece – it should be tender but still crisp. Drain, then season with salt, pepper and a pinch of nutmeg.

½ lb (225 g)	takes 6–7 minutes
1 lb (450 g)	takes 10–12 minutes

CHESTNUTS to shell: this simplifies one of the most tedious of all kitchen jobs. Using a small knife with a serrated blade, cut through the tough outer skin right around the middle of each nut. There is no need, however, to cut through the tough scar. Arange on a plate and cook uncovered on 100% power. The shells and skins willl then slip off as if by magic.

12 chestnuts	take 1½ minutes
½ lb (225 g)	takes 4 minutes
1 lb (450 g)	takes 6 minutes

They can now be cooked until tender as required.

CHICKEN to poach chicken or turkey breast meat for salads and savoury dishes: The chicken or turkey can be cooked covered without liquid but the flavour is improved by the addition of a little chicken stock. A sprig of tarragon can also be added. When two or more breasts are to be cooked, arrange like spokes of a wheel with the thicker part to the outside.

Always test by cutting through a portion of chicken to ensure all pinkness has disappeared and the flesh is an even white. If not, cook for an extra 30 seconds at a time then retest. Season if necessary *after* cooking.

The chicken is cooked on 100% power unless different instructions are given.

To cook chicken breast meat off the bone:

4 oz (125 g) (one serving)	2½ minutes covered and steamed in 4 tbsp chicken stock

8 oz (225 g)	3½ minutes	covered and steamed in 4 tbsp chicken stock
12 oz (350g)	4 minutes	covered and steamed in 4 tbsp chicken stock
1 lb (450 g)	6 minutes	covered and steamed in 4 tbsp chicken stock
1½ lb (675g)	7 minutes	covered and steamed in 4 tbsp chicken stock
2 lb (900 g)	8 minutes	covered and steamed in 4 tbsp chicken stock

To cook chicken breasts on the bone:

1 breast portion	3 minutes	covered and steamed in 4 tbsp chicken stock
2 breast portions	4 minutes	covered and steamed in 4 tbsp chicken stock
3 breast portions	6 minutes	covered and steamed in 4 tbsp chicken stock
4 breast portions	7½ minutes	covered and steamed in 4 tbsp chicken stock

To cook chicken legs:

1 whole leg (or thigh and drumstick)	5 minutes	covered and steamed in 4 tbsp chicken stock
2 whole legs (or thighs and drumsticks)	7½ minutes	covered and steamed in 4 tbsp chicken stock
4 whole legs (or thighs and drumsticks)	12 minutes	covered and steamed in 4 tbsp chicken stock

To poach or casserole whole birds, cut into 4 or 6 portions. This works better than trying to poach the bird whole. It is also more economical than buying ready-cut portions (most butchers will portion the bird for you). The liquid can be chicken stock or the flavoured sauce of a casserole.

3½ lb bird cut into 4 or 6 portions	10 minutes at 100%, 10 minutes at 50%	covered and cooked with 15 fl oz (425 ml/2 cups) liquid, alone or with vegetables
4 lb bird	12 minutes at 100%, 10 minutes at 50%	covered and cooked with 15 fl oz (425 ml/2 cups) liquid alone or with vegetables

Approximate yield of chicken meat by cupfuls:

1 × 4 lb bird (1.75 kg) gives 1½ lb (675 g) chicken meat, 4½ cups of cubed meat

2 breast portions (on or off the bone) give approx 1½ cups cooked meat in cubes or slivers

3 breast portions (on or off the bone) give approx 2¼ cups cooked meat in cubes or slivers

4 breast portions (on or off the bone) give approx 3 cups cooked meat in cubes or slivers

NOTE I have assumed the weight of one chicken breast portion, skinned and boned, as 4–5 oz (125–150 g). It will naturally weigh more on the bone but will yield a similar amount of meat.

CHOCOLATE to melt: this is a joy compared to the hassle of heating over hot water or risking the chocolate 'seizing up' over direct heat. You will notice that when chocolate is melted together with a liquid such as water or coffee, it will take 25% less time than when melted alone. Always break up the chocolate before putting it in the oven – it will appear to retain its shape after melting but when it is stirred it will liquefy immediately. Cook uncovered on a plate or in a bowl on 100% power.

2 oz (50 g)	take 1 minute
4 oz (125 g)	take 1½ minutes
6 oz (175 g)	take 2½ minutes

CLINGFILM the safety element: doubts have been raised as to the advisability of using clingfilm in the microwave. To clarify the position, the Ministry of Agriculture, Fisheries and Food has issued its proposal for the form of wording to be incorporated in packaging used on *all* types of clingfilm, whatever their constituents may be. This reads:

> Suitable for general food use. In a microwave oven: use for defrosting or reheating food; when cooking, use for covering containers but not for wrapping food or lining dishes. Do not use for cooking in conventional ovens.

COCONUT, DESSICATED to toast to a pale gold colour: spread in an even layer on a 9–10 inch (22.5–25 cm) plate or shallow casserole and microwave on 100% power, stirring 2 or 3 times to ensure even browning.

2 oz (50 g)	take 4–5 minutes
4 oz (125 g)	take 6–7 minutes

CORNFLOUR *to thicken sauces:* this is used in place of flour as it does not need to be incorporated into a roux. Simply mix the cornflour with approximately twice its volume of cold liquid (i.e. 1 tbsp cornflour is mixed with 2 tbsp cold liquid). This creamy mixture can either be stirred into a sauce that is already bubbling in the microwave, or have the remainder of the liquid added to it and then cooked until bubbling and clear. Cornflour has twice the thickening power of flour, so use half the quantity of flour specified in a conventional recipe. When cooking a liquid containing cornflour, it is important to stir it thoroughly several times during the cooking period to ensure even thickening. The starch may otherwise set in insoluble little lumps that cannot be removed even with a whisk.

COURGETTES *to cook:* these retain their colour and texture superbly well and cook in their own juices without added liquid. Choose firm ones with shiny unblemished skins. Tiny ones the size of a finger can be cooked whole; slice or halve lengthwise then quarter when more mature. Rinse the courgettes and arrange in an even layer in the dish. Cover and cook on 100% power then stand covered for 3 minutes before seasoning and serving with a sprinkle of fresh herbs such as sliced fresh basil leaves or chopped parsley. See also Braised Courgettes, Courgettes with a Honey Glaze, Courgettes Niçoise, pages 104–6.

| 8 oz (225 g) | take 8–9 minutes |
| 1 lb (450 g) | takes 10–12 minutes |

CREAM CHEESE *to soften:* for spreading or mixing in a cheesecake, place in a bowl and cook on 30% power for 30–60 seconds – timing will depend on the temperature of the cheese.

COVERINGS: for techniques and suitable materials see 'Getting it right', page 17.

CUSTARD *made with custard powder:* cooking and serving and even reheating in the same jug is a wonderful convenience and there is no sticky saucepan to wash up afterwards. Measure 1 tbsp each custard powder and sugar into a 1½ pint (725 ml/4 cup) serving jug. (If you use a smaller one you will need to watch that it does not boil over as it cooks.) Mix to a smooth cream with 4 tbsp of the measured milk then stir in the rest. Cook on 100% power for 1½ minutes, stir thoroughly to ensure even thickening, then cook for a further 1½ minutes and stir again. Finally, cook for a further minute until smoothly thickened and bubbling.

To reheat, cook on 80% power for 2 minutes or until bubbling again.

For a sugar-free custard, stir in a tbsp of granular sweetener after the custard is cooked.

CUSTARD SAUCE *made with eggs:* a little cornflour added to the traditional eggs and milk removes any fear of curdling and gives the sauce a wonderfully unctuous texture.

In a medium bowl mix 2 egg yolks and 1 oz (25 g/2 tbsp) castor sugar until creamy. Meanwhile, in another bowl mix until creamy 2 teasp cornflour or potato flour and 4 tbsp from ½ pint (10 fl oz/1¼ cups) cold milk. Add the remainder of the milk, then cook on 100% power for 3 minutes stirring twice. Add this liquid to the egg mixture together with ½ teasp vanilla essence. Cook on 50% power for 4 minutes, stirring twice until smoothly thickened.

DEFROSTING: for most people, the days of large-scale 'cook-ins' are over. If, however, you do still stockpile *home-cooked* food in the freezer on a regular basis, you will probably have the foresight to remove them to the refrigerator in good time for them to defrost slowly – overnight – undoubtedly the most efficient and satisfactory way. They can then be reheated in the microwave like any freshly cooked dish that has been allowed to go cold. However, *for impulse use* – to serve to the unexpected guest or for a 'snack' meal – one- or two-person portions of home-cooked food such as soups, casseroles and beefburgers, as well as small amounts of staples, such as meat and fish stock, fruit and vegetable purées, sauces and gravies, can be lifesavers. They are quickly defrosted and reheated in the microwave without any loss of flavour or texture – larger quantities take too long to defrost to be practicable. My experience is that it is quicker and more convenient to experiment a little with defrosting cooked food than to look up a chart which, in any case, may not cover the exact size and density of a particular food. As with other aspects of microwave usage, let experience be your guide, keeping in mind the principle that you can always add on extra time if necessary.

If you keep a stock of *raw joints of meat* and *whole birds* in the freezer I would only advise microwave defrosting as an emergency measure; even if the machine is equipped with an auto-defrost cycle, it is very difficult to avoid cooking part of the surface before the centre is defrosted thoroughly enough to avoid the risk of food poisoning from bacteria such as salmonella. If you do need to thaw them, follow meticulously the directions in your instruction book, being particularly careful to shield thinner parts with foil (to avoid them drying out), and allow the full standing time recommended. Smaller items like *chicken portions*, *chops and beefburgers* are much easier to defrost because their bulk is so much less, and the microwaves can penetrate to the centre as in the cooking process. If they have become frozen together, separate as soon as sufficient thawing has taken place to make this possible. Treat *raw minced meat* in a similar manner, removing any thawed meat from the surface of the block to allow the microwaves to penetrate the remainder. *Fish fillets* once thawed sufficiently to be separated from each other are best cooked from frozen, allowing extra time to that given in the normal recipe. (Again consult your instruction book for guidance.) *Baked food* – scones, cakes and bread – defrost well, provided you avoid the temptation to speed up the process by using 100% power instead of 30% (defrost). More than any other food they quickly become dry and inedible with too much microwave energy. With all defrosting, you cannot go wrong if you use a low setting and add extra time if necessary.

FRUIT to thaw home-frozen: if there is no time to allow *fruit* that is to be served *raw* to defrost slowly in the refrigerator, only partially defrost it in the microwave, then let it stand at room temperature to complete the thawing process. Too much microwave energy will cause the cell walls to collapse, particularly in the case of soft fruit. If the fruit is to be *cooked* after thawing, the two processes can be combined by following the times recommended for thawing below, but using 100% rather than 30% power. (See entries under individual fruit for details.) Stir the fruit once or twice during thawing, then allow to stand covered for 5 minutes. Defrost and cook in a fairly shallow lidded casserole with the fruit arranged in an even layer.

NOTE: Defrost all fruit, covered, at 30% power.

Blackberries	
½ lb (225 g)	takes 4–5 minutes
1 lb (450 g)	takes 5–7 minutes

Blackcurrants, raspberries, loganberries or strawberries	
8 oz (225 g)	take 3–4 minutes
1 lb (450 g)	takes 5–6 minutes

Gooseberries	
8 oz (225 g)	take 2½–3½ minutes
1 lb (450 g)	takes 5–6 minutes

DRIED FRUIT: to avoid overnight soaking of *regular dried fruit* such as prunes, apricots and pears, proceed as follows:

Cover ½ lb (225 g) dried fruit with 1 pint (600 ml/2½ cups) cold water (use tea for prunes). Cover and cook on 100% power for 10 minutes, stirring once. Leave to stand for a further 30 minutes then cook on 100% power for a further 15 minutes, stirring once. Stir in sugar to taste – 2 rounded tbsp should be sufficient – then leave covered for at least 5 minutes before serving. *For tenderized fruit,* the first cooking period and the standing time can both be omitted. Use only half as much water as with regular fruit (10 fl oz/275 ml/1¼ cups) and cook on 100% power for 15 minutes then sweeten as before.

DRIED FRUIT to plump currants, raisins and sultanas: put in a small bowl and add water or a spirit such as brandy, rum or whisky, cover and cook on 100% power.

4 oz (125 g/¾ cup) fruit plus 1½ tbsp liquid plump up in 1½ minutes	
8 oz (225 g/1½ cups) fruit plus 2½ tbsp liquid plump up in 2½ minutes	

EGGS to cook: never try to cook an egg in its shell – it will explode, covering the interior of the oven with a myriad tiny pieces of shell and egg. Even when poaching or baking, it is necessary to pierce the membrane covering the yolk with a slim sharp knife to avoid a similar if less dramatic eruption. There is a great vogue for *scrambling eggs* and *frying omelettes* in the microwave that I do not care for. I do not like the texture of the cooked eggs and I find the need for constant stirring tedious. If you use a non-stick saucepan (for the scrambled eggs) or a solid-base frying pan (for the omelette) and cook in the normal manner on top of the stove, the process will be almost as quick and the result far more delicious to eat.

EGGS, in sauces and custards: if the cooking temperature is too high the protein in an egg can over-coagulate causing the phenomenon we know as 'curdling'. To avoid this, sauces and custards containing egg that are cooked for longer than 2 minutes should always be cooked at a lower power setting – 50% or 30%. You will find that the mixture will continue to thicken during the standing time, as for example the lemon sauce for Gefilte Fish, page 65.

FAT: you will notice that very little fat is used in the majority of microwave recipes. This is because

it is not needed (as in conventional cookery) to avoid food sticking to the base of the cooking dish, so its main use (apart from cakes and puddings) is as a flavouring agent (e.g. the olive oil in the Israeli Vegetable Ragout (page 48), to gloss a sauce (as in Chicken Breasts in a Honeyed and Raisin Sauce, page 94) or as a binding agent (Tomatoes Stuffed with a Herb Dressing, page 115). Butter and olive oil both add a distinctive flavour to a dish, but for most purposes a flavourless oil that is high in polyunsaturates (such as sunflower or safflower) is to be preferred for dietary reasons. Walnut, almond and hazelnut oil are not only too expensive for general use but deteriorate in flavour when reheated so they are best reserved for salad dressings. To prevent them going rancid, any flavoured oils should be stored away from the light; olive oil at room temperature, the nut oils in the refrigerator.

FISH, cooking times: the following cooking times are useful if you want to cook fish in quantities different from those given in the recipes. They should also be helpful in converting conventional fish recipes for the microwave.

NOTE: if stock or wine is added for flavour, allow 30 seconds extra cooking time for each 4 fl oz (125 ml/½ cup) liquid.

Thin fillets e.g. small plaice or sole ½ inch (1.5 cm) thick, covered and cooked flat on a plate on 100% power:

4 oz (125 g)	1 minute
6–8 oz (175 g-225 g)	2 minutes
12 oz-1 lb (350 g-450 g)	2½ minutes
1½–2 lbs (675 g-900 g)	5 minutes

Allow to stand, covered, for 3 minutes.

Thick fillets e.g. haddock, cod, salmon, hake 1 inch (2.5 cm) thick, covered and cooked flat on a plate on 100% power:

8 oz (225 g)	3 minutes
12 oz-1 lb (350 g-450 g)	4½ minutes
1½ lb–2 lbs (675 g-900 g)	6 minutes

Allow to stand, covered, for 3 minutes.

Steaks of fish e.g. halibut, salmon, cod, haddock ¾ inch (2 cm) thick, weight 6–7 oz (175–200 g), arranged in a circle with thinner part to centre of the dish, covered and cooked on 100% power:

1 fish steak	3 minutes
2 fish steaks	4½ minutes
4 steaks	6 minutes
6 steaks	8 minutes

Allow to stand, covered, for 3 minutes.

Small whole fish e.g. trout, weight 8–10 oz (225–275 g), cleaned and head removed, laid side by side, tail to head, covered, steamed plain or with enough melted butter to moisten the skin:

1 fish	3 minutes
2 fish	5 minutes
3 fish	6½ minutes
4 fish	8–9 minutes

Allow to stand, covered, for 3 minutes.

FISH testing for doneness: minimum cooking times are given. The exact time will depend on the temperature of the fish and personal taste. After the fish has been allowed to stand for 3 minutes test to make sure the fish is opaque (rather than glassy) right through to the centre and will flake easily with a fork.

FISH IN SAUCE to reheat: cover and cook on 80% power for 5 minutes or until steaming.

FISH STOCK: this is a well flavoured stock that can be used as a poaching liquid or (stored in small containers) can form the basis for any fish sauce. It freezes for 2 months.

2 lb (900 g) white fish heads and bones
2 carrots

1 large onion
some mushroom stalks (if available)
1 fat stalk celery
large sprig of parsley (with the stalk)
1 bay leaf
10 peppercorns
1¾ pints (1 litre/4 ½ cups) boiling water

Finely chop all the vegetables on the food processor. Wash the fish heads and bones thoroughly (any blood will make the stock bitter) break up into 2 inch (5 cm) pieces then put in a 7 pint (4 litre/1 gallon) lidded casserole or bowl together with all the other ingredients. Cover and cook on 100% power for 10 minutes then reduce to 50% power and continue to cook for another 10 minutes. Strain through a fine sieve and use as required or freeze in portions of 5 fl oz (150 ml/⅔ cup) for future use.

FOIL IN THE MICROWAVE: unless the instruction book of your machine states specifically that foil should not be used, it can be safely and successfully used when necessary providing the following conditions are fulfilled:

1   The foil, whether in sheet form or a shallow container should never be placed within ¾ inch (2 cm) of another metal surface. This surface can be the walls, another aluminium foil container or the base of the oven (when there is no glass/ceramic tray or turntable).
2   Food must never be completely enclosed in foil. For example, if an aluminium foil container has a lid laminated with foil, this should be removed and clingfilm or another suitable covering used instead.

FLOUR: cakes made with ordinary flour tend to taste more like steamed puddings as the gluten in the flour seems to absorb and hold moisture in a way that does not occur in a conventional oven. However, if a pure starch – such as potato flour – is used, the cake has an excellent texture, almost indistinguishable from one cooked in a conventional oven. See Gâteau Reine de Saba, page 157.

FRUIT WITH STONES toughness of skin: the action of the microwave seems to toughen the skins of greengages, plums and apricots and I prefer to cook them by poaching top of stove.

GARLIC for the optimum flavour: there is nothing to compare with a clove of garlic, either crushed or chopped according to the recipe. However, when speed and convenience are the main considerations, dried minced garlic makes a very acceptable substitute, provided it is to be cooked in a liquid and thus has time to soften and dissolve (as in Mushrooms in the Turkish Style, page 47). I do not recommend garlic salt as this is usually made from inferior-grade garlic and quickly becomes rancid.

GARLIC smashed or bruised: if only a hint of garlic is required, for example to flavour oil for frying or a salad dressing, it is often left unpeeled but bruised by flattening with the side of a heavy knife. The whole clove can then easily be removed when required.

GELATINE to soften and dissolve: sprinkle powdered gelatine on the amount of liquid recommended in the recipe then cook on 100% power for 40 seconds. Stir well until clear then add to the other ingredients.

GINGER, FRESH to store: Keep the root loosely wrapped in foil in the refrigerator where it will keep for at least a month – it becomes soggy in the freezer. To prepare, carefully peel the amount you require – usually not more than an inch (2.5 cm) as it is very pungent – then either grate or cut in tiny slivers according to the recipe.

GOOSEBERRIES to cook: put 1 lb (450 g) gooseberries in a shallow lidded dish and add 2 tbsp water and 4 oz (125 g/½ cup) caster sugar.

Cover and cook on 100% power for 4–5 minutes according to size. For a *Gooseberry Purée* cook for a further 3 minutes or until the fruit collapses, then purée through the fine mesh of a mouli (vegetable mill).

GRANULAR SWEETENERS look and taste like sugar but contain, spoon for spoon, only one tenth of the calories. Those based on 'aspartame', contain no saccharine and therefore do not leave a bitter aftertaste. As the sweetness fades in the prolonged presence of heat, they should be added to a dish only after it has been cooked in the microwave. Granular sweeteners are approved by the British Dietetic Association, provided they are fitted into the individual diet allowance.

HERBS to dry in the microwave: up to 1 oz (25 g) of any herb can be dried quickly and successfully. Arrange the washed and drained leaves on one sheet of paper towelling and cover them with another. (Small leaved herbs that are difficult to strip can be left on the stalks and then separated from them after drying by pushing through a metal sieve.) Cook on 100% power for 2 minutes, then uncover and cook for a further 1–2 minutes until the leaves feel absolutely dry when rubbed between the fingers. To dry larger quantities, spread out on a fine-meshed metal cooling tray and leave in a conventional oven at Gas No. ¼ (200 °F/100°C) for 45 minutes-1 hour or until the leaves feel absolutely dry when tested as above.

HOLISHKES to blanch cabbage leaves: ready for stuffing for this delectable dish, remove the leaves one at a time from a firm white cabbage by cutting them free at the base. Put 6 leaves at a time into a dish, add 2 tbsp of water, cover and cook on 100% power for 2 minutes or until pliable. Turn into a colander and drench with cold water. Cut out the coarse stalk at the base of the leaf then stuff as directed in the recipe.

HOLLANDAISE SAUCE: this most elegant but tricky-to-make egg yolk based sauce can be quickly

179

and safely cooked in the microwave provided the following directions are carefully followed. Put 4½ oz (140 g/½ cup plus 1 tbsp) slightly salted butter or margarine (cut into roughly 1 inch/2.5 cm chunks), into a small bowl, lightly cover with a paper towel and cook on 100% power for 1½ minutes. Meanwhile, in a medium basin put 2 egg yolks, 3 teasp lemon juice, 2 teasp wine vinegar, ½ teasp caster sugar, a pinch of salt and a speck of white pepper. Whisk to blend with a balloon whisk, then gradually whisk in the hot melted butter and cook on 30% power for a further 2 minutes, whisking halfway. At this point the mixture will resemble a thick custard but will thicken to mayonnaise consistency on standing. Leftover sauce can be frozen for up to 3 months. It should be allowed to defrost at room temperature rather than in the microwave.

JAMS AND PRESERVES: the microwave is an ideal medium for making small quantities (up to 1½ lb/675 g) of this delectable food using the minimum amount of time and effort. Both the colour and flavour of microwave jams are excellent, and there is no fear of sticking or burning nor is there a need for special equipment – only a wooden spoon and a large (approximately 6 pint/3 litre/15 cup) heatproof bowl – remember that boiling jam needs plenty of room for expansion. As there is less surface evaporation, only one third of the quantity of liquid is needed when converting from a conventional recipe. However, the normal principles of jam making still apply – the fruit must be completely softened before the addition of the sugar and the correct balance of acid (lemon juice) and pectin (either natural in the fruit or commercial) must be present for the jam to set. Microwave jams are tested in the normal manner. My favourite method is the *flake test:* when the recommended minimum cooking time has elapsed, dip a wooden spoon into the jam, then lift it above the bowl and twirl it round two or three times to cool it. Hold the spoon steady above the bowl and let the cooled jam that is sticking to it

drip back into the pan. If the jam has reached setting-point, drops of the jam will run together along the spoon to form a large *flake* that will break off sharply from the edge of the spoon. But if the jam runs off the spoon in *separate drops,* setting point has not been reached and the jam needs further boiling. See Mint Jelly, page 149.

JAM JARS to sterilize: the microwave method is very quick and easy and avoids over-heating the kitchen on a hot summer's day. While the jam is cooking, thoroughly wash and rinse the required number of jars, quarter fill them with cold water then put in the microwave and heat uncovered on 100% power until the water boils – 1½–2½ minutes according to the number of jars. Remove the jars with an oven cloth (they will be very hot), pour off the water, then turn them upside down to drain and dry by evaporation on a double piece of kitchen paper. Turn over and fill with the hot jam – a metal jam funnel will simplify what can be a very sticky job. Cover with a screw-top lid.

JULIENNE: these are thin straw-like strips of meat, vegetable or fruit. It is a suitable way of cutting some of the slower cooking vegetables such as carrots to ensure quick and even penetration by the microwaves, see Orange-glazed Carrots, page 104. The same method is used for cutting decorative strips of citrus peel, see the decoration on the Lime Cheesecake, page 154.

LEMON: the average capacity of a lemon can vary enormously, depending not only on its size but also on the thickness of the skin. So in the recipes I have expressed the required amount of lemon juice in tablespoons. As a rough buying guide, a medium lemon contains approximately 3 tbsp juice, a larger one 4 tbsp. If the lemon feels very hard, or you do not want to dirty a squeezer, cut the lemon in half, place it in a small bowl and microwave it on 100% power for 1½ minutes. Allow to cool for 3 or 4 minutes then squeeze with your fingers and the juice will positively gush out.

MATURING: this expression is used to describe the process by which the flavour of a cooked dish is intensified by allowing it to stand for 12–24 hours and then reheating it just before serving. Food with a fairly high liquid content such as soups, stews and casseroles will all improve during this period, but if time is of the essence it can be omitted for all except the few recipes (indicated in the text) for which it is absolutely essential.

METAL TRIM: whether silver or gold – used to decorate china – will be blackened irrevocably if used in the microwave. Many companies now make elegant serving dishes without this trim that are labelled 'microwave-safe'.

MILK: boiling milk froths up in the microwave just as it does on top of the stove, so to avoid a mopping-up operation, always use a jug or bowl three times the capacity of the milk. Thus when boiling 10 fl oz (275 ml/1¼ cups) milk use a container of at least 1½ pint (750 ml/5 cup) capacity. To heat milk to *steaming point* (e.g. for custards) cover and cook on 100% power as follows:

10 fl oz (275 ml/1¼ cups)	2 minutes
15 fl oz (425 ml/2 cups)	3 minutes
20 fl oz (575 ml/2½ cups)	3½ minutes

MUSHROOMS: cook extremely well in the microwave. To cook *without fat* heat 5 fl oz (150 ml/⅔ cup) vegetable or chicken stock in a wide, lidded casserole for 1 minute. Add 8 oz (225 g/2½ cups) thickly sliced closed cup mushrooms, cover and cook on 100% power for 2 minutes, stirring once. Remove the mushrooms with a slotted spoon and serve, reserving the stock for a soup or sauce. To cook mushrooms in a *flavoured butter,* put 1 oz (25 g/2 tbsp) butter or margarine and 1 crushed clove of garlic or 1 teasp chopped fresh herbs into a wide lidded casserole and cook on 80% power for 1 minute. Add 8 oz (225 g/2½ cups)

button mushrooms, turning them in the melted fat until well coated. Cover and cook on 100% power for 2 minutes, then season with sea salt and black pepper. This makes an ideal quick snack or starter for one or a vegetable accompaniment for two. For 4, simply double the quantity of mushrooms and the cooking time.

NUTS to blanch almonds or pistachios: put in a small basin, add 3 tbsp water, cover and cook on 100% power then drain off the water, replace with cold and slip off the skins with the fingers.

| 2 oz (50 g/½ cup) nuts | 1½ minutes |
| 4 oz (125 g/1 cup) nuts | 2½ minutes |

OLIVE OIL: it is not by chance that some of the finest olive oil is sold by wine merchants. For like wine, olive oil also has its good and bad seasons. However, unless you are a connoisseur you will be quite satisfied by any oil that is labelled 'extra virgin' on an English or American label, *huile vierge fine* on a French one and *olio extra vergine* on an Italian one. This means that the oil has come from the first pressing of the olives so that its flavour has not been affected by the heat used to extract later pressings. For general *cooking purposes,* I use a supermarket own-brand virgin olive oil and only buy more expensive oil from a named area, such as Provence or Tuscany, to use in salad dressings where the flavour is of paramount importance.

ONIONS: pickling or shallots: to remove the skins using a food processor. Instead, you can do it very speedily with a sharp knife by 'cubing' it as follows.

ONIONS: pickling or shallots: to remove the skins quickly and without tears, cut off the root and top end, put in a casserole with 3 tbsp water, then cover and cook on 100% power until the skins are softened – about 3–4 minutes according to the weight of onions. The skins will then slip off easily.

ORANGE: to segment an orange, lemon or grapefruit, first equip yourself with a small vegetable knife with a razor-sharp, serrated blade. Peel the fruit completely, at the same time removing the bitter white pith that lies beneath the skin, then cut between the sections of the fruit so that the flesh can be removed in pith-free segments, leaving the inedible 'skeleton' of the fruit behind. Squeeze this 'skeleton' over a bowl then use the juice either in a salad dressing or for a fruit salad. Put the segments in a shallow dish and cover tightly with film until required.

PARSNIPS To cook in the microwave: trim 1 lb (450 g) parsnips at either end then peel and cut into 1 inch (2.5 cm) chunks. Lay the chunks in an even layer in a shallow lidded casserole, add 4 tbsp hot water then cover and cook on 100% power for 9 minutes, stirring once, until absolutely tender when pierced with a slim pointed knife. Drain, re-cover and allow to stand for 3 minutes. Mash with a little butter or margarine or purée. See Gingered Parsnip Purée, page 110.

To par-cook for roasting: leave small parsnips whole. Cut larger ones in half lengthwise, then cook as above but for only 4 minutes. Drain well and add to ¼ inch (1 cm) deep hot fat, then roast for 30–40 minutes until golden brown and tender.

PASTA: to cook to the correct 'al dente' texture, pasta of all kinds needs to be cooked in a pan of boiling water large enough to allow it to 'swim'. This is not a good scenario for cooking in the microwave. However, small amounts of egg noodles can be cooked in soup as a garnish. See Chicken and Tomato Soup with Fine Lokshen, page 39.

PEARS: for *cooking times and techniques* see Poached Pears with Caramel or Chocolate Sauce and Spiced Pears in Cider, page 141. You will notice that in both cases the pears are cooked in a sweetened syrup. However, the cooking time

varies enormously as one dish uses dessert pears while the other uses a firmer variety that needs a much longer time to become tender. The firmer pears – and therefore the longer cooking time – are needed when the recipe requires the pears to macerate in the syrup rather than use it simply as a poaching medium.

PINE KERNELS: the flavour of these slim nuts, much used in Middle-Eastern cooking, is intensified when they are toasted. As they have a very high oil content they burn all too easily on top of the stove – so it is actually easier to do the job in the microwave. *To toast in the microwave,* arrange the nuts in a single layer in a shallow dish. Cook on 100% power, stirring once or twice according to the quantity and therefore the length of the cooking time.

2 oz	4 minutes
4 oz	6½ minutes

PISTACHIOS: these nuts are most often sold in their shells as a salted cocktail snack, but once the inner papery skin has been removed the vivid green kernel, much prized for its decorative quality, is revealed. (See the cover photograph showing A Pistachio and Sweet Spice Pilaff.) To use as an ingredient or for decoration, buy the *shelled* nuts and remove the papery skins by blanching as described under *Nuts* page 181.

PITTA BREAD to reheat in the microwave: place on a piece of paper towelling and heat on 100% power for 1 minute or until puffed.

PLUM PUDDING: it is not advisable to microwave a quantity of rich plum pudding larger than will fill a 1½ pint (900 ml/4 cups) basin as it is difficult for the microwave energy to penetrate evenly to the centre of such a dense mixture. However, a large pudding that has already been cooked by steam can be successfully reheated in the microwave by cooking on 100% power for

2½–3½ minutes (according to size). If you do want to cook a raw (1½ pint/900 ml) size pudding in the microwave, proceed as follows: cover the pudding with pierced clingfilm and microwave on 50% power for 15 minutes. Immediately remove the film and replace with a fresh (unpierced) piece (preferably of freezer thickness). Microwave on 100% power for a further 15 seconds only then allow to cool completely – the film will have produced an airtight seal. When cold, cover the top of the pudding with foil and leave in a cool dry place for a minimum of 4 weeks (preferably 6–8 weeks) before using.

For myself I prefer to cook and reheat this type of pudding by steaming in the conventional manner, particularly if it is to be eaten only two or three weeks later. I have found that a long initial steaming followed by a long (3–4 hour) reheating period is as effective in maturing a pudding as a long storage time.

POTATOES to boil: (e.g. for mashing) peel and cut into 1 inch (2.5 cm) chunks. Arrange in one layer in a wide lidded casserole. Add 4 tbsp hot water cover and cook on 100% power until there is no resistance when the potatoes are pierced with a slim, sharp knife. Leave covered for 2 minutes then drain and cover lightly with a paper towel to absorb excess moisture. Use as required.

1 lb (450 g) potatoes	cooks in 8–10 minutes
1½ lb (675 g)	cook in 10–12 minutes
2 lb (900 g)	cook in 12–14 minutes

POTATOES to parboil for roasting: parboiling before roasting ensures that the potatoes are tender and fluffy inside with a really crunchy brown crust. Use a good roasting potato such as Desiree, King Edward or Pentland Dell.
Peel the potatoes and cut into 1–1½ inch (2.5–3.5 cm) thick wedges. Put in a shallow casserole with 2 tbsp water, cover and cook on 100% power for 5 minutes, then drain and stand covered with a paper towel for 5 minutes to dry off.

1 lb (450 g) potatoes takes 5 minutes (and serves 2–3)
2 lb (900 g) potatoes take 8 minutes (and serve 4–5)

POTATOES to bake: although the flesh of a potato is particularly fluffy when cooked in the microwave, the skin will not be crisp unless a combination oven is used. You can achieve a certain degree of crispness however by grilling the potatoes after they come out of the microwave. Choose a prepacked baking potato or use a good baking variety such as Maris Piper or King Edward. If not prepacked, wash and dry the potatoes and prick them all over to prevent them bursting. Arrange in a circle (if several are cooked together) on a piece of kitchen paper. Cook on 100% power, turning over once.

Cooking times for 5 oz (150 g) potatoes	
1 potato will take	5 minutes
2 potatoes	6–8 minutes
3 potatoes	9–10 minutes
4 potatoes	10–11 minutes

Cooking times for 8 oz (225 g) potatoes	
1 potato will take	6 minutes
2 potatoes	12 minutes
3 potatoes	17 minutes
4 potatoes	20 minutes

To cook new potatoes: always cook for the minimum period then add extra time by the minute. New potatoes can become unpleasantly spongy if overcooked. Put the scrubbed potatoes in a lidded casserole with 2 tbsp water. Cover and cook on 100% power, stirring half way. Test by piercing with a slim sharp knife. If there is any resistance, add another minute. Drain thoroughly and season with sea salt and black pepper.

1 lb (450 g) small, even sized potatoes	takes 9–11 minutes
1½ lb (675 g)	take 12–14 minutes
2 lb (900 g)	take 16–18 minutes

PULSE ACTION OF THE FOOD PROCESSOR:
this makes it much easier to control the degree of
fineness to which foods are processed e.g. when
chopping onions or *raw fish* or *mixing cakes*. If your
machine does not have a built-in pulse switch, you
can get the same result manually by operating the
machine in short bursts instead of using a
continuous processing action.

PROVING DOUGH: as a general rule, the slower
the rising and proving process (ideally overnight),
the finer the texture of the bread or kuchen when
it is baked. However, this is a counsel of perfection
and a one hour period for rising a bread dough and
a 1½–2 hour one for a kuchen (enriched) dough
give a very acceptable result. Rarely, however, is
the kitchen warm enough to meet this timetable,
so the microwave can be used to duplicate the
conditions in a professional baker's proving oven.
Once the dough has been kneaded, it should be
placed in an oiled bowl (large enough to allow for
it to double in size) turned over so that it is
covered with a fine film of the oil, then covered
with clingfilm to prevent the surface drying out.
Leave on 100% power for 40 seconds. Allow to
rest for a further 10 minutes then repeat. At this
stage it should feel comfortably warm to the touch
and should then be allowed to rise at normal room
temperature.

REHEATING: if you need to reheat *home-cooked*
food, there can be no better medium than the
microwave. The food is reheated so quickly that
there is no time for any health hazard to develop
and both the colour and texture are as if they'd
been freshly cooked. While much food –
vegetables in particular – are cooked ahead and
then reheated for convenience, others – such as
soups and casseroles – are actually improved in
flavour by their second 'cook'. All kinds of dishes
other than breads and rolls will reheat more
quickly and without any fear of drying out if they
are covered during the process. When *rice* or any
other *cereal* is to be reheated, lightly sprinkle the
surface with water. As the dish heats up this will
be transformed into steam, making every grain
light and fluffy again. Be warned that reheated
bread and rolls tend to become tough and dry as
they cool, so do not plan to make use of any that
are leftover from the meal. Bread double-wrapped
in paper towelling will become warm after 2
minutes on 100% power. A single roll will take 10
seconds.

If you wish to reheat a complete plate of food
for a latecomer, put denser food such as rice or
potatoes towards the outer edge of the dish and
more delicate food such as fish or chicken towards
the centre. Slices of cold meat or poultry will be
more succulent if masked with a sauce before
reheating. Try and arrange the food so that it is an
even height from one rim of the plate to the other,
cover tightly and reheat with the confidence that
the food will taste as though it had been freshly
cooked. To work out the correct timing, start by
microwaving for 2 minutes and progress by an
extra minute at a time until the food is steaming on
the plate.

RHUBARB: the peel of ordinary garden rhubarb
tends to be tough and stringy when cooked in the
microwave, so I use only the tender pink forced
variety available in spring and early summer. *To
cook:* cut 1 lb (450 g) pink rhubarb into 1 inch (2.5
cm) lengths, discarding any discoloured ends.
Layer in a casserole with 5 oz (150 g/⅔ cup) caster
sugar. Add no water but cover and cook on 100%
power for 5 minutes, stirring gently, but
thoroughly, halfway so that the centre pieces of
fruit are moved to the edge of the dish. Leave
covered until the fruit stops steaming, then
refrigerate. This compote is delicious with the
custard recipe given under *Custard Sauce* on
page 175.

RICE: there are so many varieties on sale that I will
not attempt to list them. Suffice it to say that for
cooking in the microwave, I prefer white Basmati
rice, which is grown in the foothills of the

Himalayas. It is sweet and nutty in flavour and every grain stays separate when it is cooked. This method has no time advantage over conventional cooking but it is a simple way to cook rice right in the serving dish and without any fear of sticking. See Savoury Rice, page 123 for the basic method of cooking. Allow 2 fl oz (50 ml/¼ cup) of hot liquid for each 1 oz (25 g/2 tbsp) rice to be cooked.

ROASTING: there is no such thing as true roasting in a microwave oven unless it has a separate browning facility. Given the choice, I would always use a conventional oven for roasting a joint of meat rather than the microwave. However, any meat or poultry that has some fat on the surface will appear to brown after a certain length of time – as the fat attracts the microwaves. Only small (up to 3 lb/1.25 kg) boneless joints of top quality, well hung (in the case of beef) should be 'roasted' in the microwave. For suggestions for glazes and other browning agents that promote a good colour on the surface of the food, see pages 74–75.

SALT: I prefer the clean unadulterated flavour of *sea salt* to that of ordinary cooking salt, which is mixed with an anti-caking agent to keep it running freely. But just because it contains no additives, the sea salt is actually more salty, and less of it should therefore be used than ordinary salt. In general, use less salt in the microwave than in conventional cooking as in most cases there will be less liquid than normal to dilute it.

SALT when to add it: unless salt has been dissolved in liquid, it is advisable not to sprinkle it on meat, fish or vegetables until after they have been cooked as it tends to draw liquid out of them making them appear dehydrated.

SAUCES: these are more easily thickened in the microwave by cornflour rather than the traditional roux (see *Cornflour*, page 175 for details). Other sauces, such as the Pizzaoila on page 82, are thickened by reduction. This involves cooking the sauce uncovered until some of the water content

has evaporated so that the texture thickens and the flavour becomes more intense. This process usually takes about 5 minutes on 100% power once the liquid has come to the boil.

SESAME OIL: regular sesame oil which is a pale gold in colour is often used for stir frying. However, the brown *oriental* sesame oil which is extracted from toasted seeds has a delicious but much more powerful aroma and should be used sparingly as a condiment rather than as a frying agent.

SHERRY: the medium-dry *Amontillado* sherry is a delicious addition to certain savoury sauces and soups and goes particularly well with mushrooms. It also reinforces the flavour of clear soups based on a stock or beef consommé.

SHII-TAKE MUSHROOMS: these are also called *forest mushrooms* or *black mushrooms* in oriental recipes and, until recently, were only available dried. The colour of the fresh variety may vary from creamy brown to a very dark chestnut. They are cultivated on sawdust or cut logs and have a pronounced meaty flavour. To prepare, remove and discard most of the woody stalk, then slice or leave whole according to the recipe. Do not allow them to boil or they will lose their aroma and become tough and woody in texture.

SIMMERING: as in conventional cooking, a dish that is to be simmered is first brought to the boil and then cooked at a reduced level of heat so that only occasional bubbles break on the surface of the liquid. In practice this means bringing the dish to boiling point on 100% power and then reducing to 50% or 30% (according to the recipe instructions) for the remainder of the cooking period.

SOY SAUCE: for the finest flavour, it is best to use a brand that has been prepared in the traditional way by fermentation (check the label). *Light* sauce looks most pleasing with fish or chicken, *dark* or *rich* soy sauce with beef.

STOCK CUBES: always check the label of a stock cube and do not buy any which list monosodium glutamate (MSG) high on the list. This is used as a flavour reinforcer and when it is listed as a major ingredient, it suggests that it is being used to hide the absence of genuine flavourings extracted from beef, chicken or vegetables.

SUGAR FOR JAM: warm the measured sugar on 100% power for 2 minutes and it will dissolve more readily when it is added to the fruit.

VEGETABLES FOR A PARTY: a quantity of vegetables that is too large to cook in the microwave can be blanched earlier in the day then arranged in serving dishes and covered with a lid or clingfilm. They can then be briefly reheated in the microwave in between courses. *To blanch:* earlier in the day, half fill a large pan with water and bring to the boil on top of the stove then add a teasp of salt and the chosen vegetable. Cook at a vigorous boil with the lid only partly on (to preserve the colour) until the vegetables are still slightly chewy. Immediately drain through a colander, then hold under the cold tap until steaming stops (to 'set' the colour). Allow to drain thoroughly (this can be done by spinning in a salad basket). Arrange in a serving dish and refrigerate until an hour before serving then leave at room temperature. Reheat in the microwave, season and serve.